LATE LIFE

LATE LIFE

COMMUNITIES AND

ENVIRONMENTAL POLICY

Edited by

JABER F. GUBRIUM

Marquette University

CHARLES C THOMAS · PUBLISHER

Springfield · Illinois · U.S.A.

Published and Distributed Throughout the World by
CHARLES C THOMAS • PUBLISHER
Bannerstone House
301-327 East Lawrence Avenue, Springfield, Illinois, U.S.A.

© *1974, by* CHARLES C THOMAS • PUBLISHER
ISBN 0-398-03249-1 (cloth)
ISBN 0-398-03248-3 (paper)
Library of Congress Catalog Card Number: 74 9566

With THOMAS BOOKS *careful attention is given to all details of
manufacturing and design . It is the Publisher's desire to present books
that are satisfactory as to their physical qualities and artistic possibilities
and appropriate for their particular use.* THOMAS BOOKS *will be true
to those laws of quality that assure a good name and good will.*

Library of Congress Cataloging in Publication Data

Gubrium, Jaber F
    Late life; communities and environmental policy.

    1. Aged—Addresses, essays, lectures. 2. Aged—
Dwellings—Addresses, essays, lectures. I. Title.
[DNLM: 1. Aged. 2. Social environment. WT30 G921L]
HQ1061.G82   301.43'5   74-9566
ISBN 0-398-03249-1
ISBN 0-398-03248-3 (pbk.)

Printed in the United States of America
W-2

CONTRIBUTORS

Bert N. Adams, Department of Sociology, University of Wisconsin, Madison, Wisconsin.

Gordon L. Bultena, Department of Sociology, Iowa State University, Ames, Iowa.

Albert Chevan, Department of Sociology, University of Massachusetts, Amherst, Massachusetts.

Donald O. Cowgill, Department of Sociology, University of Missouri, Columbia, Missouri.

Marshall Graney, Department of Sociology, Tulane University, New Orleans, Louisiana.

Jaber F. Gubrium, Department of Sociology and Anthropology, Marquette University, Milwaukee, Wisconsin.

Tom Hickey, Gerontology Center, College of Human Development, Pennsylvania State University, University Park, Pennsylvania.

James W. Hodgson, Gerontology Center, College of Human Development, Pennsylvania State University, University Park, Pennsylvania.

Eva Kahana, Department of Sociology, Wayne State University, Detroit, Michigan.

Christie W. Kiefer, Human Development Program, University of California, San Francisco, California.

Morton Lieberman, Department of Psychiatry, University of Wisconsin, Madison, Wisconsin.

David O. Moberg, Department of Sociology and Anthropology, Marquette University, Milwaukee, Wisconsin.

Nina Nahemow, Department of Anthropology and Sociology, University of South Carolina, Columbia, South Carolina.

John O'Rourke, Department of Sociology, University of Massachusetts, Amherst, Massachusetts.

Jennie-Keith Ross, Department of Sociology and Anthropology, Swarthmore College, Swarthmore, Pennsylvania.

INTRODUCTION

THIS COLLECTION OF papers was conceived originally as a forum for the discussion of both ideas and research on the environments of old people. There were at least three reasons for this, two practical and one scientific.

First, although there were a few available collections of articles dealing with the social behavior of elders, most had no distinct environmental focus. Rather, the available collections either were concerned with such "internal" problems of aging as perceptions, attitude systems, and age-related value structures or broadly dealt with topics of concern to gerontologists ranging from psychobiological to environmental issues. This collection focuses exclusively on the environments of the aged.

Second, the papers in this book are new ones. They are being published here for the first time. The intent of this is to bring some recent, but generally unavailable thinking and research on elder environments to the gerontological audience. Bringing together already available papers might be convenient both for reference and classroom use, but it offers "nothing new."

Third, in recent years, gerontologists have come to realize that the behavior of elders is not mostly an individual affair. For example, such personal problems as morale, life satisfaction, and "senility" are being seen as having important environmental contingencies. Morale and life satisfaction may be affected by age-integration and others' behavior expectations. "Senility" may be conceived as a product of social definitions. This collection examines some of these environmental effects.

The book has two themes. One is concerned with three kinds of old age environment: physical, formal, and cross-cultural. These are considered in Parts I, II, and III, respectively. The second theme is environmental policy. Papers in Part IV deal with policy issues ranging from relocation to spiritual well-being.

Part I begins with Graney's discussion of factors that have been found to specify the relationship between physical aspects of elder environments (e.g. propinquity, density, homogeneity) and behavioral or attitudinal variables. He considers two kinds of specifying variables—normative and individual—and states that such variables must be considered in order to *explain* how the physical environment affects persons. Bultena's paper is a report of a study, the design of which includes an examination of the effect of several specifying variables (e.g. age, occupational status, health, friendship) on the relationship between age-segregation and life satisfaction. The last paper in Part I, by O'Rourke and Chevan, describes the factorial distribution of age groups in the United States based on 1960 census data. They consider several questions, e.g. which demographic characteristics of the population are most important in delineating between elders and other age groups, and how the older population differs from other age groups in the homogeneity of its distribution across the United States.

Part II deals with two environments which can be described as formal communities. One is a nursing home and the other a multi-unit retirement residence. Such communities are constructed purposely to house specific populations. Gubrium delineates the various definitions of patient care in a nursing home and how they influence what staff and patients do with their lives and to each other as participants in "care work." Ross raises the question of what kind of relationship exists between the internal social organization of an "embedded" community and the social organization of its context society. She explores the relationship in a retirement residence located in a Parisian suburb.

Part III shifts focus from small communities to relatively large ones. Cowgill's paper on age, culture, and modernization introduces this section of the book. He outlines a way by which to order these environments and their variations as they affect the status of the aged. Nahemow and Adams discuss the impact of continuity and change in Baganda society on its elders. Kiefer, on the other hand, examines the impact of cross-cultural experiences on elder Japanese-Americans on the West Coast.

Finally, Part IV takes up some issues in environmental policy. This section of the book contains four statements that each focus on separate dimensions of old age environments. Kahana constructs a scheme for evaluating the fit between environmental provisions and personal resources. Lieberman asks whether what we know currently about relocation provides us with a consistent rationale for formulating a relocation policy for elders who are in the business of moving. Hickey and Hodgson discuss the salience of the environment for how services are or might be provided to the elderly. And last, Moberg addresses some thorny questions involved in the study of elders' spiritual worlds and how to satisfy their spiritual needs.

Although all the papers in this book are concerned with some aspect of the environment of elders, they are by no means analytically consistent with each other. Some are implicit criticisms of others. Taken together, they perhaps raise more questions than they resolve. I am of the opinion that this is where we should begin, not with solutions.

To edit a collection of papers in social gerontology is to encounter a wide range of interests indeed—those of human scientists from psychiatrists to sociologists and anthropologists. I am grateful to all of those persons who shared their work with me, both that which appears in this volume and that which does not. The experience, I feel, was enriching.

On behalf of the contributors, I extend our collective appreciation to those elders among us who have served directly and indirectly as our "respondents." It is their lives, which are, in our reflections and work, at once subject and teacher.

The compilation of any book of this kind rests heavily on secretarial assistance. For countless letters typed and bibliographic services, I thank Mrs. Sharron Johns and Mrs. Diane Willette.

J.F.G.

CONTENTS

Page

Contributors v
Introduction vii

THE PHYSICAL ENVIRONMENT

Chapter
1. THE AGED AND THEIR ENVIRONMENT: THE STUDY OF
   INTERVENING VARIABLES
   Marshall Graney 5
2. STRUCTURAL EFFECTS ON THE MORALE OF THE AGED: A
   COMPARISON OF AGE-SEGREGATED AND AGE-INTEGRATED
   COMMUNITIES
   Gordon L. Bultena 18
3. A FACTORIAL ECOLOGY OF AGE GROUPS IN THE
   UNITED STATES, 1960
   John F. O'Rourke and Albert Chevan 32

FORMAL COMMUNITIES

4. ON MULTIPLE REALITIES IN A NURSING HOME
   Jaber F. Gubrium 61
5. LIFE GOES ON: SOCIAL ORGANIZATION IN A
   FRENCH RETIREMENT RESIDENCE
   Jennie-Keith Ross 99

CROSS-CULTURAL COMMUNITIES

6. AGING AND MODERNIZATION: A REVISION OF THE THEORY
   Donald O. Cowgill 123
7. OLD AGE AMONG THE BAGANDA: CONTINUITY AND CHANGE
   Nina Nahemow and Bert N. Adams 147
8. LESSONS FROM THE ISSEI
   Christie W. Kiefer 167

Chapter *Page*

ENVIRONMENTAL POLICY

9. MATCHING ENVIRONMENTS TO NEEDS OF THE AGED:
A CONCEPTUAL SCHEME
Eva Kahana 201

10. RELOCATION RESEARCH AND SOCIAL POLICY
Morton A. Lieberman 215

11. CONTEXTUAL AND DEVELOPMENTAL ISSUES IN THE EVALUATION
OF ADULT LEARNING: TRAINING IN APPLIED GERONTOLOGY
AS AN EXAMPLE
Tom Hickey and James W. Hodgson 235

12. SPIRITUAL WELL-BEING IN LATE LIFE
David O. Moberg 256

Index 281

LATE LIFE

THE PHYSICAL

ENVIRONMENT

CHAPTER 1

THE AGED AND THEIR ENVIRONMENT: THE STUDY OF INTERVENING VARIABLES[1]

Marshall Graney

Social gerontologists and others have developed an impressively large catalog of behavioral and attitudinal characteristics of the aged, and of correlations between pairs of such characteristics (see especially Riley, *et al.* 1968). But information about these parameters, either alone or in pairwise combinations, is merely descriptive and cannot, in itself, attain the conceptual level of scientific knowledge or theory. For this it is necessary that at least three characteristics be brought under analysis simultaneously.[2]

Analysis of this general kind is commonly found in sociological literature, although in too many instances it remains at the unreplicable subjective level of verbal analysis and deductions by individual investigators. This has been a serious problem of theory development in the sociology of aging. Further, when qualitative and quantitative multivariate analyses, and multivariate analyses of categorical data, are used they are often used in a descriptive manner rather than for obtaining the inductive inferences needed for empirically based theory. Thus, in only a few instances have multivariate data analysis techniques been

---

[1] This chapter is an expanded and extensively revised version of a paper prepared originally for presentation to the Annual Meeting of the Midwest Sociological Society, Kansas City, Missouri, April 21, 1972.

[2] Scientific knowledge or theory, as these are generally understood, imply explanation or prediction. In any case the knowledge involved consists of knowledge of process. Bivariate information alone is logically insufficient to illuminate processes which give rise to statistical associations. Thus the need for (a) third, fourth . . . or nth variable(s) which serve(s) to explain the association.

effectively used for their theory building potential in the sociology of aging. Some of these serve as examples in later sections of this chapter. The remainder of this preliminary section is devoted to clarifying the issues and studying a strategy for theory development accepted in sociology in general for application to the sociology of aging.

An important problem of effective use of inductive theory development techniques in analysis is the necessity of asking research questions involving multiple variables, while at the same time not overstepping the abilities of relevant statistical techniques to produce interpretable results from data analysis. Although it is necessary to consider at least three variables simultaneously in scientific research, this does not imply "the more the better." One reason for this constraint on elaboration is that there exists a point of diminishing returns where the most important variables are already included in the analytic model, and inclusion of additional variables would cost the investigator more in loss of parsimony than could be gained in predictive or explanatory power. Unfortunately there is no simple rule-of-thumb for determining when this point has been reached but, except in quantitative analysis in the form of multiple regression and closely-related techniques, elaboration beyond three or four variables is usually impractically cumbersome.

Multiple regression analysis allows efficient simultaneous study of relationships between many variables, and several different means to adapt qualitative and categorical data to multiple regression analysis are currently under study among methodologists and data analysts (Boyle, 1970; Heise, 1972; Labovitz, 1970). There is also work toward the development of independently motivated analytic techniques for these kinds of data (Theil, 1970). Thus, there are prospects of greater power and flexibility in data analysis in future research than is presently available. But in practical research projects of the past and present the liabilities of qualitative and categorical data analysis have often been ignored, yielding research products which are unconvincing and logically incomplete with respect to substantive theory. The principal liability of categorical and qualitative data is the restricted number of variables that can be included in practical data analysis. This has obvious implications for the kinds of theories that empirical research can be called upon to support.

Perhaps the most common failing in research in social gerontology is an overambitious list of variables whose simultaneous interactions are described and, ideally, are to be analyzed with empirical data. Most of the "classics" in social gerontology have had this common problem. It is clear that the results of this kind of ambitious research have been productive, but it is equally clear that their products do not include scientific theories. This is because systematic analysis of empirical data in the social sciences rarely produces results that are interpretable for more than three or four qualitative or categorical variables at a time. But it is precisely at these qualitative and categorical levels of measurement that many of the data of social gerontology are usually collected. Fortunately, interpretable techniques for statistical analysis of three-variable models are available at the present time for data collected at any level of measurement. For example, consider techniques in Zeisel (1968) and Van de Geer (1971). Anticipating their systematic use can and will produce effectively designed research projects whose results have more substantial importance as scientific theory than the results of overly-simple bivariate correlation analysis on the one hand, or uninterpretable complex studies on the other.

In contrast to the past, at present few complex and grand scale studies are initiated in the sociology of aging. The hazards to effective theory development now lie at the other end of the scale. scale studies are initiated in the sociology of aging. The hazards to effective theory development lie at the other end of the scale. The atheoretical nature of descriptive parameter estimation is obvious, but simple correlational analysis is more easily misunderstood as theory development.

Correlational analysis has a place in theory development, but if the catalog of bivariate relationships between all of the variables of interest to social gerontologists were finished, perfect and available today, it would (in itself, and without elaboration) contribute no scientific knowledge to the discipline—only potentially useful information. It is generally understood that such bivariate associations, relationships, and correlations are not the theories of science; but they are the apt subjects of its theories.

This present chapter suggests a data analysis strategy (seeking and using intervening variables in multivariate analysis) which more closely supports the investigator's scientific task than is possible in univariate or bivariate analysis, or in multivariate analysis when an excessive number of variables are included in the theoretical model. By an intervening variable we mean one that is introduced into analysis to explain (or explain away) an interesting bivariate association.

To start at the beginning of theory development: before attempting to construct useful explanations the theorist must assume that an empirical relationship has been established that warrants explanation. Establishing interesting statistical relationships which demand explanation is the contribution of correlational analysis to scientific research. Although the attempt to seek and use intervening variables in data analysis is perhaps ideally begun only when all bivariate relationships of interest are unequivocally established, the development of scientific theory cannot wait on that day. In scientific research one must accept that infallible data are never available for analysis. This is because science is an *ad hoc* human enterprise, based on fallible current practice in collecting observational data and in using them in making estimates of actual relationships between variables and, by implication, between concepts. All scientific findings are thus tentative, but these tentative findings can serve as a basis for further research.

The applied and theoretical interests in the field of aging require something more as the product of research than a catalog of bivariate relationships between pairs of variables. In addition, these relationships need to be explained in a useful way, such that prediction and, if appropriate, change or control may be ultimately possible. By providing information which specifies the conditions under which relationships hold or do not hold the study of intervening variables provides an important step toward this kind of scientifically and pragmatically useful knowledge.

In social gerontology one appropriately finds theories which emphasize social ecology, particularly the reciprocal relationship between selves and environmental factors. The elderly and their immediate social environment are almost always the topics of research interest, with inquiries aimed at learning how the elderly affect their environment and (more often) with how their environment, in turn, affects them. (This distinction serves to define the two major subdivisions of this chapter.) In expressing the latter question Schooler (1969:25) asks: "Does environment make a difference, and, if so, what is the process by which that difference is mediated?" Like Schooler, and many others, we adopt social well-being and/or subjective life satisfaction as interesting variables to be explained by other factors—but with the proviso that this adoption does not imply an endorsement of these variables as the proper long-term concern of theory in social gerontology. These are among the concerns that gave rise to social gerontology, but maturation of the subdiscipline is likely to lead away from early interests. The relevance of this discussion is not limited to these two topics.

Innumerable environmental effects on behavioral and attitudinal variables like these are, of course, plausible. Every aspect of older people's environment may potentially have direct effects on these measures on the older person, or may serve to specify conditions under which important relationships between these and other measured variables will be found. But it is important to note that but few of these plausible influences are likely to realize their potential as important explanatory factors and become relevant to social gerontology. Environmental characteristics are uninteresting to the social gerontologist except as they make a difference in personal lives. And, of these, it is the most influential that should be among those first studied.

Festinger (1951) has reported on research relating behavioral effects to housing arrangements of a youthful sample. Similarly, Deutsch and Collins (1951) have reported on research relating attitudinal effects to housing arrangements. These reports have long served the discipline as concrete general examples of social research which established the relevance of environmental variables to the attitudes and behavior of relatively young persons. It follows that environmental variables may influence the attitudes and activities of the elderly. Here Rosow (1967), Messer

(1967), Schooler (1969 and 1970), and others, all provide findings on the importance of environmental factors to the social well-being and subjective life satisfaction of elderly people.

We can consider the importance of environmental characteristics to elderly persons' happiness and well-being to be well-established in these studies. But how do environmental influences influence? How do they come to be meaningful? These questions ask how relationships between environmental characteristics and observed outcomes in personal lives can be explained.

In analysis of empirical data the study of intervening variables is well suited to the task of accomplishing this kind of explanation. Intervening variables explain (and sometimes explain away) bivariate correlations, and their discovery and inclusion in data analysis are critical to the development of a scientific sociology of aging.

The intervening variables of interest can be considered to fall under at least two broad subheadings, each of which may be analytically subdivided. The general subheadings emphasize the complimentary contributions of sociological and social psychological perspectives to theory. The first, current in the literature of social gerontology, are environmental characteristics used to explore how external influences can come to specify the normative meaning of behavior. Alternatively, taking another perspective, we can consider as a second set of intervening variables those characteristics of social selves that serve to define the meaning of the environment to the older person. Both kinds of intervening variable may prove to be useful in explaining social well-being or subjective life satisfaction in aging, the first emphasizing sociological explanations and the second emphasizing social psychological explanations.

ENVIRONMENT AFFECTS NORMATIVE MEANINGS

In the study of how environmental characteristics can come to influence the normative meaning of behavior, Messer (1967) has analyzed the value of a particular environmental characteristic in specifying the relationship between social participation activities and the subjective life satisfaction of aged persons.

In this research the degree of age concentration in the neighborhood is explored as an explanatory factor influencing alternative normative value systems among elderly people. According to Messer's findings, age concentration serves to qualify and specify social participation norms. Thus age concentration, or more precisely, the normative system associated with a specific degree of age concentration, acts as an intervening variable which mediates social participation activities into alternative kinds of outcome (in this particular instance, outcomes in subjective life satisfaction) among the aged. But, in addition to age concentration, other aspects of the neighborhood may also have important influences on the normative values of elderly people, and thus on their subjective life satisfaction or social well-being.

In actual research practice the physical location of the elderly person's dwelling can serve as a useful basis for defining "neighborhood." For example, one might define as "neighborhood" that area to which the older person has pedestrian access in leaving his dwelling, apartment, or room (compare Doxiadis, 1970). Observable characteristics of this neighborhood—like degree of age concentration—can be considered as situational variables, causally prior to their interpretation by the older person in his definition of the situation. Placing situational factors as intermediate between behavioral/attitudinal characteristics of social selves and the variables to be explained gives rise to sociological explanations.

In addition to the degree of neighborhood age concentration we should consider what other situational variables may be relevant to the older person. These variables may all be categorized into at least three broad subclasses of neighborhood characteristics: observations on the characteristics of neighbors; observations on the dwelling units in the neighborhood; and observations on the neighborhood as a large-scale physical plant —composed only in part of dwellings.

Observations on the characteristics of neighbors may include measurements on their degree of homogeneity in terms of age, sex, religion, ethnic derivation, and other relatively static personal characteristics. Other characteristics of neighbors, changing in relationship to those of the aging person, may also enter into the extent to which the elderly person can understand his neighbors, interact with them, and share their normative definitions. For example, research on the personal meaning of the elderly person's generally declining economic status *vis-á-vis* that of his neighbors may have important implications for public policy as well as for personal feelings and behavior.

Neighborhoods also differ in their degree of resident permanency and turnover. The elderly person is likely to be found to be a long term resident: does it make a difference if his neighbors are either similar, on the one hand, or, on the other hand, if they are comparatively transient and geographically mobile?

Dwelling unit characteristics may also be useful in specifying relationships between such independent variables as the older person's degree of social activity and important personal outcomes in the individual meaning that this activity may take on in social well-being and subjective life satisfaction in aging.

These socially relevant dwelling unit characteristics include both physical and more obviously social factors. Among the socially relevant physical characteristics of dwelling units are their floor plans and design features. Alcoves, stairs, halls, and mailboxes all provide potential settings for social interaction. These settings tend to situate social interaction in space. Important social outcomes in the lives of older people may be influenced as much by the provision of normatively appropriate environmental settings for social contact as by the elderly person's physical ability to gain access to these kinds of settings and his ability to utilize them successfully once access is gained.

More obviously social factors in the dwelling unit include the kind, quality, and quantity of private or personal space and space shared with others. These, too, may set the scene for alternative kinds of social interaction and thereby structure social reality for the older person in substantially important ways.

On a larger scale, socially relevant characteristics of the neighborhood as a macroscopic physical plant include its provisions for services and organizations. At the neighborhood level these are unlikely to extend to cover the range of resources necessary to sustain meaningful life in old age. The kinds of public transportation available and the neighborhood's location in the transportation network thus become important to older people. To some degree a lack of organizations and facilities sought by residents will cause the older person's own neighborhood to be less than a fully autonomous social unit, and transportation factors need to be considered. Other neighborhood characteristics that may take on meaning are planning variations, or layout (as demonstrated for a population of students by Festinger [1951]), and the neighborhood's changing state of blight, renovation, or maintenance. This latter characteristic may plausibly contribute toward establishing a neighborhood morale that modifies the importance of other causal and explanatory factors related to socially relevant aspects of aging.

SELVES AFFECT ENVIRONMENTAL MEANINGS

A second broad class of intervening variables tap those relatively personal characteristics of the self that may be important in defining the meaning of the environment for the older person. These, too, may be considered under three broad subheadings: physical ability, social resources, and personal orientations toward social participation. In a sense, all three of these kinds of indicators measure the older person's ability to cope with changes in the physical and social milieu. Observations on these personal characteristics may be useful in explaining the older person's potential to interact meaningfully with his environment. Gubrium (1970) provides an example of research using personal characteristics as variables intervening between environmental factors and "morale" (subjective life satisfaction). According to Gubrium's findings both health self-assessment and financial solvency serve as intervening variables which specify when a relationship between an environmental characteristic (age concentration) and "morale" will be found, and when it will not be found.

Observations on the older person's physical ability in perceptual acuity, mobility, and stamina all tap the individual's ability to gain access to social situations or to engage in social interaction once access is gained. These variables may well intervene, for example, between the provisions for specialized facilities and social services for the older person and the degree to which these resources are successfully utilized by the individual. How facilities, information, and services thus provided come to take on meaning in subjective life satisfaction and in social well-being may also involve psychological characteristics of the older person and other resources that he can bring to bear in gaining access to more specialized services. In general, placing personal factors as intermediate between environmental characteristics and variables to be explained gives rise to social psychological explanations.

Social resources like the family and personal economic resources, besides providing a means to access services, also provide means to alternatives to continued engagement in social situations which the elderly person finds to be unfavorable to his happiness or well-being. The ability to handle unfavorable interaction situations through either modification (negotiation of new shared meanings) or the search for alternatives (flight) brings social resources like the family and economic resources into play, as well as physical ability.

Psychological characteristics which should be considered include measures of both localism-cosmopolitanism and flexibility-routinism. Both of these kinds of indicators can provide measurements of the degree to which the older person can identify with the interests of his neighbors and their differing personal orientations toward socially relevant activities. Localism-cosmopolitanism, especially, may prove to be an important general indicator of the substantive content available in the interpersonal milieu and also of the personal orientation that the older individual holds toward social participation.

Both persons and alternative kinds of socially relevant communications activities can be classified in terms of localism-cosmopolitanism. The degree of consonance between the older person's personal orientations toward socially relevant activities and characteristics of the observable social milieu in which the older person is situated may act to specify rather precisely the potential for meaning that social activities in that environment can come to take on in his personal life. Once measurement on both persons and activity contexts are secured it is likely to be established that social activities in contexts outside the elderly person's domain of personal orientation are unrelated to important outcomes in aging. Other contexts may be found to be critically important: this will be a valuable finding with substantial theoretical and practical importance.

CONCLUSION

Research on subjective life satisfaction and social well-being among the aged is potentially valuable to both theory and practice in social gerontology. But the establishment of predictors of these outcomes does not, in itself, bring us substantially closer to our goals of explanation and understanding. Relationships between independent and dependent variables need to be considered in conjunction with additional variables to be substantiated and interpreted. When this is accomplished the additional variables may be found to specify conditions under which substantially important relationships hold, or do not hold.

We have considered a set of characteristics of housing and living arrangements that have potential value in situating our observations in research measurement in specific and understandable concrete situations. These environmental factors may also provide potential explanations by specifying various situations where relationships between the behavior of the older person and related outcomes in social well-being and subjective life satisfaction differ. The meaningfulness of the characteristics of the situation to the older person should not be developed by deductive arguments alone; empirical research can yield knowledge about the relationship of environmental characteristics to activities and behavior on the one hand, and to attitudes of subjective life satisfaction and indicators of social well-being on the other. Recent research findings in social gerontology suggest that environmental characteristics may be substantially important to the explanation of how these two aspects of the personal lives of elderly people are related to one another.

Simple cause and effect relationships can be more convincingly demonstrated for mechanical phenomena than for the social and social-psychological phenomena that are of interest to social gerontology. In seeking to explain how "environmental influences" come to be influential we can consider how the socially and social-psychologically important characteristics of the situation are mediated by the self into outcomes in subjective life satisfaction and social well-being. Intervening variables measured on physical, social, and social-psychological aspects of the self can help to explain the relationship between the observable situation and personal outcomes in aging.

The intervening variables mediating between the environment and these important outcomes are all potential resources to the older person for coping with aspects of his living arrangements and the social milieu of his neighborhood. These resources include physical ability, such as mobility and stamina; personal orientations, such as localism-cosmopolitanism or flexibility-routinism; and social resources, such as family and economic resources.

Physical abilities determine access to interaction situations; personal orientations are important to identification with other people and their interests; and social resources specify the degree of access to alternative situations available to the older person. The explanatory value of these intervening variables, measured on the social self, in building an understanding of the relationship between environmental influences and personal outcomes in social well-being and subjective life satisfaction is important to the development of scientific knowledge for both theory and practice in social gerontology.

REFERENCES

Boyle, R. P.: Path analysis and ordinal data. *American Journal of Sociology,* 75:461-480, 1970.

Deutsch, M., and Collins, M. E.: *Interracial Housing. A Psychological Evaluation of a Social Experiment.* Minneapolis, University of Minnesota Press, 1951.

Doxiadis, C. A.: Ekistics, the science of human settlements. *Science,* 170:393-403, 1970.

Festinger, L.: Architecture and group membership. *Journal of Social Issues,* 7:152-163, 1951.

Gubrium, J. F.: Environmental effects on morale in old age and the resources of health and solvency. *Gerontologist,* 10:294-297, 1970.

Heise, D. R.: Employing nominal variables, induced variables, and block variables in path analysis. *Sociological Methods and Research,* 1:147-174, 1972.

Labovitz, S.: The assignment of numbers to rank order categories. *American Sociological Review,* 35:515-524, 1970.

Messer, M.: The possibility of an age-concentrated environment becoming a normative system. *Gerontologist,* 7:247-251, 1967.

Riley, M. W.; Foner, A.; Moore, M. E.; Hess, B., and Roth, B. K.: *Aging and Society, Volume One: An Inventory of Research Findings.* New York, Russell Sage Foundation, 1968.

Rosow, I.: *Social Integration of the Aged.* New York, Free Press, 1967.

Schooler, K. K.: The relationship between social interaction and morale of the elderly as a function of environmental characteristics. *Gerontologist,* 9:25-29, 1969.

————: Effect of environment on morale. *Gerontologist,* 10:194-197, 1970.

Theil, H.: On the estimation of relationships involving qualitative variables. *American Journal of Sociology,* 76:103-154, 1970.

Van de Geer, J. P.: *Introduction to Multivariate Analysis for the Social Sciences.* San Francisco, W. H. Freeman, 1971.

Zeisel, H.: *Say It With Figures, Fifth Edition, Revised.* New York, Harper and Row, 1968.

CHAPTER 2

STRUCTURAL EFFECTS ON THE MORALE OF THE AGED: A COMPARISON OF AGE-SEGREGATED AND AGE-INTEGRATED COMMUNITIES[1]

GORDON L. BULTENA

INTRODUCTION

CONSIDERABLE STUDY HAS been directed to identifying factors affecting the morale of older persons in American society (Adams, 1971; Rosow, 1963). For the most part, these investigations have focused on individual and family attributes. Social-class standing, activity levels, and health status, in particular, often have been revealed to be important to the psychological adjustment of the aged.

More recently, attention has been directed to implications of alternative structural or social contexts for adjustment in old age. Cultural setting, size of community, age-composition of neighborhoods, and independent living versus congregate care arrangements have been proposed as important determinants of morale (Bultena, 1969; Neugarten, 1967; Rosow, 1967). The actual salience of alternative social contexts for morale, however, remains largely untested. In most cases social context serves as a backdrop for analysis rather than as a significant analytical variable (Bennett, 1970).

Findings reported here are from a study which explored

---

[1] This analysis is part of a larger study of post-retirement migration funded by the Administration on Aging, U.S. Dept. of Health, Education and Welfare.

implications for retirement adjustment of residence in two types of communities: "age-integrated communities" containing a full spectrum of age groups, and "age-segregated communities" in which younger persons are excluded as permanent residents.

THEORETICAL CONSIDERATIONS

Considerable speculation has been directed to implications of age-segregated living for the adjustment of the aged. The role of status-homophily in friendship selection (Laumann, 1966; Lazarsfeld and Merton, 1954) suggests the proposition that a physical concentration of retired persons may be advantageous to their social integration and accordingly may facilitate their maintaining high morale into old age.

A study (Rosow, 1967) of the relationship of age density to friendship ties partly supports this proposition in finding that elderly persons in age-segregated housing units were more effectively integrated in the social structure than those in age-integrated housing. Similarly, it has been found (Blau, 1961) that widowhood has a detrimental effect on friendship interaction in residential settings in which there are few widows, but not where they are more numerous.

A study (Bultena, 1968) of interaction patterns in age-integrated neighborhoods revealed that residential propinquity between age groups is insufficient for the development of viable intergenerational ties. Friendship interaction of older persons was directed primarily to age peers, with intergenerational ties being confined largely to children. Residence of older persons in age-integrated neighborhoods accordingly may serve as a potential source of social isolation and thereby foster demoralization.

It has been argued (Messer, 1967; Rose, 1965), from a different perspective, that age-segregated environments can facilitate the emergence of social norms among the aged which are better suited to the realities of their status in society than are the role expectations promulgated in age-integrated settings. Physical separation of the aged from younger persons is seen as insulating them from role definitions which find their locus in the work ethic, and in which personal worth is assessed on the basis of participation in productive or instrumental activities. Pursuit of a leisure life-style by retirees in age-integrated settings, being incongruous with these prevailing norms, may thus prove demeaning and ultimately result in their self-depreciation and demoralization.

Age-segregated environments, on the other hand, provide reference groups of age-peers who may serve to legitimize self-indulgence and consummatory activities, and for whom leisure may be defined as a dignified and preferred role in old age. It has been found in this regard (Bultena and Wood, 1969a; and Hamovitch, 1966) that leisure is elevated over work in planned retirement communities, and that there is a pronounced rejection of instrumental or work roles in these places.

That age-segregated environments may perform a positive function by facilitating the emergence of norms that are compatible with the structural realities of the retiree's situation also is consistent with the argument of Eisenstadt (1956) that the individual's adaptation to a set of new role behaviors, such as emerge at retirement, is facilitated by his involvement in social systems in which others are undergoing similar changes.

These two theoretical perspectives on the possible significance of structural patterns in housing for (1) friendship interaction and (2) the development of age-appropriate normative systems provide a rationale for hypothesizing that higher morale will obtain among persons retiring in age-segregated communities than for those settling in communities with mixed age groups. This conclusion is contrary to much prevailing public opinion that the physical separation of older and younger persons is inimical to the maintenance of good morale among the aged.

A test is made here of the proposition that structural effects on morale are mediated in retirement communities through increased opportunities for friendship interaction. It is hypothesized, first, that persons in age-segregated communities have higher morale than those in age-integrated communities. Second, that this higher morale is a function of the greater opportunity to establish desired levels of friendship interaction in old age in age-segregated environments than in other residential settings.

PROCEDURES

Sample

The data are from interviews with 521 males who had moved permanently to Arizona following their retirement in the Midwest. Three age-integrated communities were studied (Tucson, Mesa, Tempe). About 10 percent of the population in these places was 65 or older in 1970. The sample in these communities was drawn randomly from listings of retired persons in city directories. Screening interviews were used to identify persons in the initial sample eligible for inclusion in the study (i.e. persons who had moved at retirement from a North Central State). A total of 199 qualified respondents were interviewed in these three age-integrated communities.

Four planned retirement communities were studied (Dreamland Villa, Green Valley, Sun City, Youngtown). The samples in these places (N=322) were drawn randomly from records listing the home states of residents. Each of these communities is comprised exclusively of older persons. They are representative of a type of community which recently has grown to considerable prominence in several states.[2]

It should be noted that the retirement communities being studied hold considerable attraction for some migrants and that the residents in these settings generally have maintained independence in their living arrangements. Moves into other types of age-segregated environments, such as retirement homes and nursing facilities, may have a much different impact on the morale of their residents than is posited here.

Variables

Morale

Morale was measured by a modified form of the Life Satisfaction Scale. The procedures used to develop and validate the

---

[2] Barker (1966) found that the number of planned retirement communities in California had increased from none to 35 in the decade prior to 1966. Sun City, Arizona, one of the communities studied here, had grown in size since its founding in 1960 to over 12,000 aged residents by 1970.

original scale are described elsewhere (Neugarten *et al.* 1961). The modified scale used in this study contained thirteen agree-disagree items designed to measure respondents' satisfaction with their life-situations (Wood *et al.* 1969). The scores obtained by our respondents ranged from 3 to 26, with a median score of 20. The scores were used in their raw form in the correlational analysis. In the contingency tables they were categorized into: "low morale" (0 to 12), "medium morale" (13 to 21), and "high morale" (22 to 26).

Friendship

Friendship interaction was ascertained with the question: "How does the number of friends that you have in this community compare with the number you had in (home community in the Midwest)? Would you say that you have more, about the same number, or fewer friends here than in (home community)?"

Data on the number of friends of the respondents at the time of the interview as compared to their pre-retirement situation was used in the analysis rather than the absolute number of friends. This takes into consideration the criticism (cf. Rosow, 1963) that it is not the number of friends that is important to the maintenance of good morale in old age, but rather the extent to which continuity in friendship levels obtains between the pre- and post-retirement periods. Persons having few close friends throughout life are unlikely to suffer remorse over the prospects of limited social interaction in old age. On the other hand, it is anticipated that those who have enjoyed a wide circle of friends may be demoralized by a residential move which dissociates them from further contact with persons in their home towns without the compensatory development of friendship ties in their new communities.

Personal Characteristics

Other variables measured in the study, because of their previously-revealed association with morale of the elderly, included: age, occupational status (categorized using the U.S. Census Index of Occupations and Industries), educational attainment, income, and perceived health status (whether one's health was defined as being very good, good, fair, poor, or very poor).

Respondents in both the age-integrated and age-segregated communities were well established, having resided an average of four years in their present locales.

Chi-square, correlation, and partial correlation were used in the analysis of the data. Differences are reported as significant if at the .05 level.

FINDINGS

The data support the hypothesis of structural effects on morale in that residents of planned retirement communities evidenced higher morale on the whole than did their counterparts living in regular communities in Arizona (Table 2-I). Three-fifths (57 percent) of these persons choosing age-segregated places, compared to one-fourth (27 percent) in age-integrated communities, had high life-satisfaction scores. Conversely, a smaller proportion in retirement communities had low life satisfaction (3 and 10 percent, respectively).

This finding on differences in morale may reflect differential personal characteristics of migrants selecting these two types of communities rather than structural effects produced by age-grading. Indeed, the data indicate that migrants to retirement communities ranked considerably higher than those in regular communities on several characteristics which have been indicated in previous research to be associated with good morale.

TABLE 2-I

PERCENTAGE DISTRIBUTION ON LIFE SATISFACTION SCORES OF
AGED MIGRANTS IN RETIREMENT COMMUNITIES AND
REGULAR COMMUNITIES IN ARIZONA

Life Satisfaction Score	Retirement Communities (N=322)	Regular Communities (N=199)
Low	3	10
Medium	40	63
High	57	27
Total	100	100

$x^2 = 51.44$; df $= 2$; p $< .001$

TABLE 2-II

PERSONAL CHARACTERISTICS OF RESPONDENTS IN RETIREMENT
COMMUNITIES AND REGULAR COMMUNITIES IN ARIZONA

Personal Characteristics	Retirement Communities Percent (N=322)	Regular Communities Percent (N=199)
Age		
Under 60	2	14
60-64	10	15
65-69	32	28
70-74	35	24
75 or older	21	18
Not ascertained	—	1
Total	100	100

$x^2 = 37.04$; df = 4; P < .001

Pre-Retirement Occupation		
Professional or technical	20	19
Managerial	32	20
Clerical	9	6
Sales	4	8
Craftsman	19	23
Operative	6	15
Service	3	3
Farmer	6	6
Not ascertained	1	—
Total	100	100

$x^2 = 12.53$; df = 4; P < .02 (clerical and sales workers, as well as blue-collar workers, were combined in the statistical analysis)

Educational Attainment		
8 years or less	23	35
9-12 years	33	28
13 or more years	43	36
Not ascertained	1	1
Total	100	100

$x^2 = 8.65$; df = 2; P < .02

Current Income		
Under $3,000	12	26
$3,000-$4,999	30	27
$5,000-7,999	28	19
$8,000 and over	19	17
Not ascertained	11	11
Total	100	100

$x^2 = 16.94$; df = 2; P < .001

Perceived Health Status		
Very good	33	25
Good	42	34
Fair	23	25
Poor or very poor	2	16
Total	100	100

$x^2 = 36.93$; df = 3; P < .001

As reported in Table 2-II, migrants to retirement communities had higher educational attainment, higher incomes, came from higher status occupational positions, and perceived themselves as being in better health than did persons moving to the regular communities.

In order to better explicate the influence of structural effects, as versus individual factors, the variables of age, education, income, pre-retirement occupation, and perceived health status were controlled in testing the relationship between community type and morale. The initial relationship between these two variables (.36) was only slightly diminished when controlling on each of these factors in turn, or on all five simultaneously. Controlling on health status had the sharpest impact on the relationship of community type and morale (dropping it from .36 to .30), but the relationship nevertheless continued to be statistically significant (Table 2-III, column A).

TABLE 2-III

ASSOCIATION BETWEEN COMMUNITY TYPE, FRIENDSHIP TIES, AND LIFE SATISFACTION, CONTROLLING ON AGE, OCCUPATIONAL STATUS, INCOME, EDUCATIONAL ATTAINMENT, AND PERCEIVED HEALTH STATUS

Control	(A) Community Type and Life Satisfaction Score	(B) Community Type and Friendship	(C) Friendship and Life Satisfaction Score
Zero-order Correlation	.36	.23	.23
Control (partial correlation)			
Age	.34	.21	.22
Occupational status	.36	.22	.22
Educational attainment	.36	.23	.23
Income	.36	.23	.24
Perceived health status	.30	.20	.20
Simultaneous control on all five personal characteristics	.29	.20	.19

All of the zero-order and partial correlations reported in this table are significantly different from 0 at the .001 level.

Friendship Ties

The analysis reported above on the association of community type and morale is consistent with our hypothesis that residence in planned retirement communities contributes to good morale.

But the question remains as to the specific mechanisms through which these structural effects are mediated. Campbell and Alexander (1965) have demonstrated the value of a two-step model in testing for structural effects in which analysis is made, first, of the impact of structural patterns on the individual's situation and, second, of his psychological or behavioral response to that situation.

Following the two-step model, and in accord with the findings of previous research, it was hypothesized: (1) that friendship interaction of older persons would be expedited by age-segregated environments, and (2) that diminished friendship interaction following migration to a retirement state would be associated with low morale.

A test of the first hypothesis revealed that a smaller number of persons in age-integrated communities than in regular communities reported a decline in friendship ties following their move from the Midwest (Table 2-IV). Three-fifths (59 percent) of those in the regular communities as compared to one-third (35 percent) in retirement communities indicated they now had fewer friends than before; a larger proportion of those in retirement communities reported having as many or more friends now (65 and 41 percent).

Again, this finding may reflect a selectivity which characterizes migration to these two types of communities rather than structural effects. Previous research has indicated (Blau, 1961; Bultena, 1968; Cumming and Henry, 1961; Rosow, 1967) that friendship

TABLE 2-IV

PERCENTAGE DISTRIBUTION ON FRIENDSHIP TIES OF AGED
MIGANTS IN RETIREMENT COMMUNITIES AND
REGULAR COMMUNITIES

Number of Friends (Compared to Pre-retirement Situation)	Retirement Communities Percent (N=322)	Regular Communities Percent (N=199)
Fewer	35	59
Same	39	24
More	26	17
Total	100	100

$x^2 = 29.15$; df $= 2$; P $< .001$

interaction of the aged is associated with the attributes of age, social class and health status. Consequently, controls were applied on these variables in testing for structural effects. However, these controls had little impact on the initial relationship (.23) which obtained between community type and friendship ties (Table 2-III, column B).

The second hypothesis that a decline in friendship levels during retirement is associated with low morale also was supported by these data. A significantly larger proportion of respondents having fewer friends in Arizona than in their home communities in the Midwest (66 percent), as compared to those having as many or more friends now (44 percent), had low or medium life-satisfaction scores (Table 2-V). Controlling on the personal characteristics of the respondents did not materially alter this relationship (Table 2-III, column C).

These findings are consistent with our argument that the greater opportunities provided in age-integrated environments for friendship interaction may be important to the relationship which was found between community type and morale. It remains, however, to isolate the magnitude of the effect of friendship as compared to other possible influences on morale produced by age-grading. If friendship interaction is the salient mediating factor, controlling on friendship patterns should diminish the relationship that obtained between community type and morale. This control, however, produced only a slight reduction in the initial relationship (from .36 to .34). It thus

TABLE 2-V

PERCENTAGE DISTRIBUTION ON LIFE SATISFACTION,
BY FRIENDSHIP TIES

Life Satisfaction Score	Number of Friends		
	More	Same	Fewer
	Percent (N=117)	Percent (N=172)	Percent (N=228)
Low	4	3	7
Medium	37	44	59
High	59	53	34
Total	100	100	100

$x^2 = 26.21$; df = 4; P < .001

appears that the differential opportunity for establishing friend-ship ties is not a major factor producing the differences in morale which were found between residents in these two types of communities.

SUMMARY AND DISCUSSION

These data are consistent with the hypothesis that planned retirement communities facilitate the adaption of aged migrants to the retirement role. A larger proportion of retirees selecting planned retirement communities than those choosing regular communities had high life satisfaction. This finding could not be explained away by differences in the age, income, education, occupational standing, and health status of persons selecting these two types of retirement locales.

Contrary to expectations, the greater opportunity for friend-ship interaction evidenced in retirement communities was not revealed to be important to differences in the morale of residents. Unfortunately, comparative data on these communities necessary to test other theoretical propositions about beneficial effects of age-grading for morale were not available in this study. The argument (Eisenstadt, 1956; Messer, 1967; Rose, 1965) that a physical concentration of age-peers facilitates the emergence of social norms more appropriate to the retirement role than may otherwise obtain in age-integrated settings appears particularly fruitful for future analysis.

Exploration of the proposition that community norms are important to retirement adjustment would seem to require revision of our hypothesis about structural effects. Rather than a positive influence obtaining for all residents in retirement communities, as implied in our hypothesis on friendship, it would seem that these communities may be beneficial to some, but have deleterious effects for others. The specific effect would depend upon the personal orientations of residents toward work and leisure. Persons disposed to an active social life in old age and who are relatively permissive in their role definitions for retirement (e.g., place emphasis on leisure and expressive roles) are most likely to be psychologically benefited by the social atmosphere in planned retirement communities. On the other hand, migrants coming out of backgrounds typified by social isolation and who hold conservative viewpoints toward leisure and age-appropriate conduct may well be disturbed by the prominence of recreational behavior and the liberality of residents' views toward leisure in these places. The psychological adjustment of persons with conservative orientations toward leisure and age-appropriate conduct seemingly would be better served in residential settings in which the priorities of the greater society toward instrumental and consummatory activities are more faithfully mirrored in the behavior of age peers.

It appears that the issue of structural effects must be approached through a consideration of the types of persons who are most likely to be benefited, or harmed, in each type of residential setting. The impact of community type on life satisfaction likely reflects differential expectations of individuals toward the retirement role, particularly as regards the appropriate centrality of social and recreational activities in that role.[3]

The self-selection that operates in migration to retirement communities is important to a consideration of structural effects. Data reported in an earlier paper (Bultena and Wood, 1969b), indicate that most persons entering planned retirement communities have enjoyed active lives prior to their retirement and that they are more liberal in their views of acceptable conduct in old age, particularly as regards the legitimacy of a leisure role, than are persons who migrate to regular communities in Arizona, or than those who choose to remain in their home communities in the Midwest.

Persons most likely to benefit from a retirement community milieu thus appear to be those who are most often attracted to these places. Aged migrants with backgrounds predisposing them to more staid and traditional orientations toward age roles, and who might well become unhappy in the more liberal atmosphere of retirement communities, most often are drawn to age-integrated settings for their retirement.

---

[3] Attention increasingly has been focused in gerontology (Gubrium, 1972) on person-environment congruency approaches to understanding differential patterns of psychological adjustment in old age.

REFERENCES

Adams, D.: Correlates of satisfaction among the elderly. *The Gerontologist*, 2:64-68, 1971.

Barker, M.: *California Retirement Communities*. Berkeley: Center for Real Estate and Urban Economics, University of California, 1966.

Bennett, R.: Social context—a neglected variable in research on aging. *Aging and Human Development*, 1:97, 1970.

Blau, Z.: Structural constraints on friendships in old age. *American Sociological Review*, 26:429-439, 1961.

Bultena, G.: Age-grading in the social interaction of an elderly male population. *Journal of Gerontology*, 23:539-543, 1968.

————: Rural-urban differences in the familial interaction of the aged. *Rural Sociology*, 34:5-15, 1969.

Bultena, G, and Wood, V.: The American retirement community: bane or blessing? *Journal of Gerontology*, 24:209-217, 1969a.

————: Normative attitudes toward the aged role among migrant and non-migrant retirees. *The Gerontologist*, 9:204-208, 1969b.

Campbell, E., and Alexander, N.: Structural effects and interpersonal relationships. *American Journal of Sociology*, 71:284-289, 1965.

Cumming, E., and Henry, W.: *Growing Old*. New York, Basic Books, Inc., 1961.

Eisenstadt, S.: *From Generation to Generation*. Glencoe, The Free Press, 1956.

Gubrium, J.: Toward a socio-environmental theory of aging. *The Gerontologist*, 12:281-284, 1972.

Hamovitch, M.: Social and psychological factors in adjustment in a retirement village. In *The Retirement Process*, edited by Francis Carp. Washington: Public Health Service, U.S. Department of Health, Education, and Welfare, 1966.

Laumann, E.: *Prestige and Association in an Urban Community*. Indianapolis, The Bobbs-Merrill Company, Inc., 1966.

Lazarsfeld, P., and Merton, R.: Friendship as social process: a substantive and methodological analysis. In *Freedom and Control in Modern Society*, edited by Monroe Berger, *et al.* New York, D. Van Nostrand Company, Inc., 1954.

Messer, M.: The possibility of an age-concentrated environment becoming a normative system. *The Gerontologist*, 7:247-250, 1967.

Neugarten, B.: Disengagement reconsidered in a cross national context. Paper presented at the annual meeting of the Gerontological Society, St. Petersburg, 1967.

Neugarten, B.; Havighurst, R., and Tobin, S.: The measurement of life satisfaction. *Journal of Gerontology*, 16:134-143, 1961.

Rose, A.: The subculture of the aging: a framework for research in social gerontology. In Arnold Rose and Warren Peterson (eds.), *Older People and Their Social World*. Philadelphia, F. A. Davis Company, 1965.

Rosow, I.: Adjustment of the normal aged. In Clark Tibbits and Wilma Donahue (eds.), *Process of Aging*. New York, Atherton Press, 1963.

————: *Social Integration of the Aged*. New York, The Free Press, 1967.

Wood, V.; Wylie, M., and Sheafor, B.: An analysis of a short self-report measure of life satisfaction: correlation with rater judgments. *Journal of Gerontology*, 24:465-469, 1969.

CHAPTER 3

A FACTORIAL ECOLOGY OF AGE GROUPS IN THE UNITED STATES, 1960

JOHN F. O'ROURKE AND ALBERT CHEVAN

T HERE IS A LARGE amount of descriptive literature in the field of social gerontology which deals with the demographic and social characteristics of the older population. (Sheldon, 1958; Riley, Foner, *et al.* 1968, Part I)   In addition, there has been a considerable amount of study of the geographic distribution of the older population. (Council of State Governments, 1955; Sheldon, 1958; Sheldon, 1960; Rose and Peterson, 1965)   It is noteworthy, however, that the majority of these studies may be viewed as simplistic in the sense that they focus on single or small numbers of characteristics of individuals or on limited and noncontiguous geographic or ecological units such as cities and rural areas.   The result is that, in spite of the existence of large amounts of "analyzed data," the student of aging is left in doubt about several matters.   For example, of the many different demographic and social characteristics of the population, which are the most important in defining the difference between the elderly and other age groups?   Further, while we may assume that the older population is not homogeneously distributed across the United States, what *exactly* is the nature of the distributive heterogeneity which that population displays? Is it or is it not systematic?   And, how does the older population differ from other age groups in this respect?   Finally, there arise questions about the juncture between the attributive structure and spatial location of the population.   Do older persons who exhibit particular characteristics appear in certain types of places?

Whether or not this is so, is there characteristic continuity or discontinuity across age groups which inhabit particular types of places?

It seems clear that the answers to questions such as these would form the only adequate background against which significant sociological questions about aging and age groups in American society may be framed. It is also clear that without such a background the answers obtained for questions formulated at higher levels of theoretical abstraction must continue to be viewed as tentative. For example, the much heralded plight of the elderly in urban areas seems much more dramatically negative when cast in terms of a single variable such as income, or when considered in the context of one or two cities of doubtful representativeness. (Riley, Foner, *et al.* 1968, pp. 132-40; Maddox, 1970) In the final analysis, pain, isolation, dislocation and other socially problematic conditions are relative phenomena. Deprivation in terms of some single characteristic can be viewed realistically only when the interdependence of that characteristic and others is taken into consideration. Deprivation or satisfaction measured in terms of one or a cluster of variables in a single place takes on added sociological and practical meaning when viewed in the context of many different kinds of places. The analysis presented in this paper argues in favor of the use of multivariate analysis techniques as a means for gaining comprehensive but accurate pictures of some aspects of the condition of various age groups within our society.

In a previous paper we have shown that the correspondence between the characteristics of the older population and its geographic distribution is not obvious when depicted as a result of a multivariate analysis. (Chevan and O'Rourke, 1972). In that case it was demonstrated that the population of persons aged 65 and over in 1960 was distributed across the United States in a non-homogeneous but systematic fashion. Considering twenty-two characteristics of older persons, it was demonstrated that one could conceive of six "aging regions" of the United States or, in terms of the variables, that there were six elderly populations in the United States in 1960.

While that analysis was suggestive of the bases of differentiation within the older population and encouraging in terms of the utility of multivariate analysis in this field, it was less than satisfying in a sociological sense. The areal unit of analysis used in that study was the state; the states have less intrinsic social meaning than is desirable from a sociological point of view. In addition, an exclusive focus on the older population leaves out another dimension of the comparative stance advocated above. The data and analysis presented here are an attempt to refine and to extend the previous study with these shortcomings in mind. The "refinement" involves a shift from the single, politically meaningful unit, the state, to forty-one different ecological units which have more sociological meaning due to their greater degree of internal homogeneity. The "extension" consists of the inclusion of two other age groups in the analysis.

This investigation is an initial attempt to confront the question of the relationships between people viewed as members of age groups and the kinds of places which they inhabit. The analysis is synchronic in character, that is, it focuses on the location of groups having particular attributes in particular kinds of places at a *single* point in time. Thus, it may not address the important questions of how and why the relationships exist; it adds little to the study of aging as a *process*. However, the analysis shares the value of all adequate cross-sectional studies; it provides one kind of baseline against which change may be measured. In other words, it may contribute significantly to the study of age structure as a *product*.

The general question of the relationship between people and places implies two more specific questions, each of which may be divided into a set of operational questions.

1. What are the similarities and differences between age groups considering the attributes of their members and the kinds of places they inhabit?
   a. Which two age groups are most similar (or dissimilar)?
   b. Are some characteristics of their members more powerful than others in distinguishing between age groups?
   c. How are places related?
2. What are the similarities and differences between kinds of places

considering the age structures and characteristics of their inhabitants?

a. Do places cluster when considered from the point of view of particular age groups?
b. Are some of the characteristics of their inhabitants more powerful than others in distinguishing between kinds of places?
c. How are places related?

The answers to these questions will give us a more detailed and sociologically meaningful picture of the nature of "aging regions" of the United States.

THE STUDY DATA AND THE SELECTION OF VARIABLES

The data for this study were drawn from the One-In-A Thousand sample of the 1960 census. (U.S. Bureau of the Census, 1964). This sample provided 96,755 cases of individuals, aged 25 and over, in households. Extensive tabulations were carried out on these data resulting, finally, in the selection of twenty-nine variables for three adult age groups in forty-one ecological areas. The three age groups were 25-44 years, 45-64 years, and 65 years and older.

The forty-one areas chosen reflect two kinds of ecological influence: size of place and metropolitan location. Size of place for civil divisions has been shown to bear a distinct relationship to the characteristics of the populations who live at the various densities implied by the concept. (Duncan and Reiss, 1956) The fourteen place sizes available in the data permit a full classification of this dimension of ecological location. Metropolitan influence is only partially related to size of place and when cross-classified with size of place produces fine distinctions in the kinds of places in which the population lives.

We used three basic metropolitan locations: outside metropolitan areas, in central cities of metropolitan areas, and in the metropolitan rings (suburbs). Each of these three metropolitan locations was subdivided into five sizes of overall metropolitan population. Thus, for metropolitan locations, the areas are classified according to two size principles—the size of the civil division and the size of the metropolitan area in which the civil division is found.

The total number of persons in each of the forty-one areas analyzed is shown in Figure 3-I. In fact, sample populations were available for eighty areas, but only forty-one were retained after collapsing categories to insure an adequate sample size within each area and age group. The 65 year and over age group placed the most severe restriction on sample size, since only 15,405 of the total number of cases are in this category. For example, in area 39 which has a total of 484 cases, only sixty-six were aged 65 years and over. This is the area containing the lowest number of persons in the elderly category. It may also be noted that some of the areas could have been collapsed in other ways, but the choice is arbitrary within the sampling restrictions noted above.[1]

The first step in this analysis was the selection of twenty-nine variables from among a very large number of pieces of basic information which are available in the One-In-A-Thousand sample. Our intention was to construct a variable list which would represent a cross-section of the characteristics of the household population of the United States. In this we were constrained to select variables which are equally applicable to all individuals aged twenty-five years and older. Otherwise, it must be admitted that we had no certain set of criteria which determined the selection of variables. The list upon which we finally settled is shown in Table 3-I together with the probabilities of the F ratio for each variable for the forty-one areas and three age groups included in the study. It is evident that different areas of concern in sociological analysis are not equally represented in the variable list. For example, there are more variables in the area of economic status than in the area of fertility. This simply reflects the fact that the available data contain more information on economic status than they do on fertility. On the other hand, the available data contains an elaborately refined list

---

[1] For example, in an attempt to maintain some sort of symmetry, area 35 which has a large enough n was not subdivided. This was because areas 33 and 37 which have the same metropolitan location do not have comparably large n's.

METROPOLITAN LOCATION AND SIZE OF METROPOLITAN AREA

IN CENTRAL CITY

SIZE OF PLACE	OUTSIDE MET. AREA	UNDER 100,000	100,000-249,999	250,000-499,999	500,000-999,999	1,000,000+
RURAL FARM	1 · 6293					
RURAL NONFARM NOT INCORPORATED	2 · 9807					
RURAL NONFARM UNDER 1,000	3 · 1925					
RURAL NONFARM 1,000-2,499	4 · 2775					
URBAN NOT INCORPORATED	5 · 71					
2,500-4,999	2844					
5,000-9,999	6 · 3186					
10,000-24,999	7 · 4454	9 · 37	21			
25,000-49,999	8 · 3343	290	81	124	24	
50,000-99,999	90	10 · 653	11 · 2408	12 · 765	13 · 312	75
100,000-249,999			14 · 1611	15 · 2637	16 · 1064	81
250,000-499,999				17 · 749	18 · 3648	19 · 1586
500,000-999,999					20 · 652	21 · 5556
1,000,000+						22 · 10542

IN RING

SIZE OF PLACE	UNDER 100,000	100,000-249,999	250,000-499,999	500,000-999,999	1,000,000+
RURAL FARM	38	284	215	23 · 146	208
RURAL NONFARM NOT INCORPORATED	24 · 97	1132	25 · 1229	26 · 923	27 · 1525
RURAL NONFARM UNDER 1,000	8	69	61	35	69
RURAL NONFARM 1,000-2,499	6	156	171	77	214
URBAN NOT INCORPORATED	38	28 · 633	1106	29 · 1226	30 · 2237
2,500-4,999	5	31 · 164	275	212	32 · 655
5,000-9,999	6	33 · 197	289	344	34 · 1284
10,000-24,999	7	35 · 384	418	837	36 · 3387
25,000-49,999		37 · 75	372	546	38 · 3288
50,000-99,999		39 · 32	57	395	40 · 2869
100,000-249,999					41 · 1050

J. MAWSON

Figure 3-1. Location of sample population.

TABLE 3-I

THE ORIGINAL STUDY VARIABLES AND PROBABILITIES OF THE
F RATIOS FOR EACH VARIABLE BY AGE GROUPS AND BY AREAS

Variable No.	Variable Name	p AGE	p AREA
1.	% household population in age group	.000	1.000
2.	% household population, primary individuals	.000	1.000
3.	% household population living with spouse	.000	1.000
4.	% population in group quarters	.000	.371
5.	% household population born in state of residence	.000	.000
6.	% household population foreign born	.000	.389
7.	% household population nonwhite or with Spanish surname	.014	.000
8.	% household population in different house, same county	.000	.943
9.	% household population migrated to noncontiguous states	.000	.107
10.	% household population receiving income in 1959	.000	.994
11.	% household population with income under $3000	.000	1.000
12.	% household population, males in labor force	.000	1.000
13.	% household population, employed civilians, white collar	.137	.000
14.	% household heads in owner occupied units	.000	.000
15.	Median years education completed, household population	.000	1.000
16.	Household population, sex ratio, males/100 females	.002	.183
17.	Household population, mean children/ever-married female	.000	.016
18.	% household population single	.019	.000
19.	% household population married more than once	.000	.268
20.	% household population divorced or separated	.000	.002
21.	% household population in doubled-up families	.000	.918
22.	Median size household for heads of household	.000	1.000
23.	% household population living as non-relatives	.000	.266
24.	% household population, females in labor force	.000	1.000
25.	Median age at marriage, household population	.000	.983
26.	% household population, unemployed males	.014	.238
27.	% household heads in units of .76+ persons per room	.000	1.000
28.	% household heads living in unsound units	.006	.000
29.	% household heads living in 1 unit dwelling units	.562	.000

	n:	41	3
	df:	120	82

of information on housing quality; we include only two in our list. Thus, it is obvious that the process of variable selection was based on our experience with what sociologists view as important attributes of the population and intuitive rules of parsimony.

In order to ascertain whether our intuitions about the variables were correct two univariate analyses of variance were carried out, one for age and one for area. As has been noted, the probability of the F-ratio for each variable is shown in Table 3-I for each of the two analyses. There are three important finding in the analyses but, with respect to parsimony, the most important finding is that no variable fails to achieve a significant F-ratio in at least one of the two analyses. The analysis by age produces many more significant F-ratios. This indicates, at least preliminarily, that variations between age groups are more pronounced than variations between areas. This is not surprising in view of the fact that age is divided into three relatively gross categories, whereas area is divided into forty-one categories which are frequently very closely related. Finally, there are seven variables whose F-ratios have probabilities of .02 or lower on both age and areal distributions. Given any of the three patterns mentioned, it would be difficult to develop a compelling substantive rationale for any particular pattern. Clearly, a more sensitive analytic method is required to uncover whatever relationships there may be between the age distribution and the areal distribution of the population. The analyses of variance demonstrate that even if the variable list is not exhaustive, it is a list of characteristics of the population which must be regarded initially as discriminatory in terms of age, or area, or both.[2]

ANALYSIS AND RESULTS

The answers to the questions posed earlier were sought by two interdependent analyses. The first analysis is concerned with the structures of the age groups. The similarities between the three age groups were examined through the use of a conventional factor analytic treatment for each group. The three factor analyses speak most pointedly to the questions of the internal structures of the age groups; the similarities or dissimilarities between age groups may be described by comparing their factor structures. The comparison of factor structures of the age groups presents certain logical difficulties if an attempt is made to go beyond intuitive interpretations. Harmon (1960) proposed a statistic called the "coefficient of congruency" for this purpose; this method is used here. The next stage of this segment of the analysis deals with the question of how the age groups are related, giving particular consideration to the areal distributions of the populations. Age groups were correlated in pairs across

---

[2] A multiple discriminant analysis of the three age groups and three pairwise analyses of variance for each of the three pairs of age groups did not reveal substantially different results.

the twenty-nine variables in each area, leading directly to the second segment of the analysis.

The second segment of the analysis focuses attention more heavily on the relationship between places and the populations which inhabit them. We wish to ask whether the distinctions between kinds of places are made more manifest by some attributes of the inhabitants than others. At the same time we wish to retain the age group distinctions in the analysis. In order to do this a Q analysis was carried out for each age group. Q analysis transposes the original data so that the areas become variables and former variables become the units of observation. This yields groupings of areas which have similar configurations among the variables. In order to close the descriptive circle, mean factor scores were calculated for Q groups within each age group. These means supply the bases for interpreting Q groups in terms of the attributive characteristics of age groups.

Age Structure

The varimax solutions of the principal components analyses for the three age groups are shown in Tables 3-IIa, 3-IIb, and 3-IIc. In the initial run of twenty-nine variables it was found that six variables were unrepresented in any factor and had low correlations across all factors. These six variables also had communalities below 80.0 in at least two of the three age group test runs, and no communality above 82.0. For these reasons variables numbered 4, 8, 9, 12, 21, and 23 were eliminated from the analyses which are presented above.[3] The effect of this reduction in the variable list was to raise the percentage of the total variance accounted for in each of the three factor analyses.

In the population aged 25-44 (Table 3-IIa), five factors accounted for 87.0 percent of the total variance among the

----

[3] The elimination of these six variables provides a commentary on intuitive variable selection. The six variables were not eliminated because they were unrelated to age but, rather, because they were not strongly associated with *factors* containing variables generally assumed to be related to those eliminated. For example, the residential mobility variables (8 and 9) which were eliminated are generally assumed to be related to several of the socio-economic status variables which were retained.

TABLE 3-IIa

FACTOR ANALYSIS OF SELECTED CHARACTERISTICS OF THE
POPULATION AGED 25-44: VARIMAX SOLUTION

	Factor					
	I	II	III	IV	V	h^2
Percent variance accounted for:	37.0	30.6	7.2	6.8	5.4	
Variable name:						
Percent living with spouse	—.97	—.08	.01	.09	—.01	95.3
Percent primary individuals	.93	—.21	.03	—.07	.10	93.2
Percent in owner occupied units	—.93	—.23	.08	—.07	.04	93.5
Percent divorced or separated	.91	—.06	.25	—.01	—.07	90.8
Percent in 1 unit dwellings	—.90	.30	.21	—.07	.09	95.4
Percent single	.87	.08	—.32	—.18	.14	91.7
Median size household	—.83	.43	—.10	.22	.04	93.5
Percent females in labor force	.80	—.18	.20	—.24	—.26	84.3
Percent nonwhite or Spanish surname	.78	.18	.14	.46	.03	86.9
Percent receiving income, 1959	.70	—.37	.30	—.19	—.17	78.4
Percent in unsound units	.08	.95	—.14	.10	.08	94.1
Percent income under $3000	.16	.93	—.04	.00	—.17	91.8
Percent born in residence state	—.24	.88	.11	.01	—.04	85.1
Percent employed civilians, white collar	.10	—.87	.12	—.09	—.26	86.4
Percent in age group	—.15	—.85	.11	—.01	.15	78.0
Mean children/ever-married female	—.40	.84	.11	.22	—.01	92.2
Median age at marriage	.36	—.75	—.37	.02	.06	82.7
Median years education completed	—.11	—.73	.10	—.54	—.04	84.7
Percent foreign born	.33	—.66	—.58	.11	—.08	89.8
Percent married more than once	.40	—.21	.80	.23	—.01	88.5
Percent in units of .76+ persons/room	—.25	.27	.17	.79	—.09	79.2
Sex ratio, males/100 females	—.03	—.04	.00	—.03	.96	91.9
Percent unemployed males	.49	.26	.26	—.35	—.17	52.7

twenty-three variables. In all cases the extraction of factors was stopped when eigenvalues failed to exceed 1.0. When factor loadings of ± .60 are examined, two strong factors emerge. Factor I which accounts for 37.0 percent of the variance is a cluster of ten variables associated with family and living arrangements. The occurrence of the non-white variable in this factor is reasonable in family-living arrangement terms, and it may also be proposed that there is an implicit urban component in this factor. If that is so, the factor analysis for this age group produces the same two factors that have been found in several other studies. (Bell, 1955; Van Arsdol, Camilleri, *et al.* 1958; Hunter, 1971) The second factor, composed of nine variables, is very clearly an economic status factor. The population represented in this factor may be characterized as of low economic status,

TABLE 3-IIb

FACTOR ANALYSIS OF SELECTED CHARACTERISTICS OF THE POPULATION AGED 45-64: VARIMAX SOLUTION

| | Factor | | | | | |
	I	II	III	IV	V	h²
Percent variance accounted for:	31.1	26.7	13.1	8.6	6.5	h²
Variable name:						
Percent living with spouse	—.94	.03	.16	—.01	—.12	92.9
Percent primary individuals	.93	—.16	—.07	—.02	.24	95.0
Percent signle	.86	.15	—.25	—.17	—.03	86.0
Sex ratio, males/100 females	—.80	.13	—.01	—.11	.06	67.7
Percent in owner occupied units	—.78	—.03	.54	.08	—.11	92.8
Median size household	—.77	.39	—.21	—.17	—.21	84.3
Percent divorced or separated	.72	—.12	—.36	—.30	.20	78.6
Percent nonwhite or Spanish surname	.68	.29	—.09	.46	—.27	83.5
Percent in 1 unit dwellings	—.68	.20	.66	.08	—.10	95.8
Percent females in labor force	.66	—.45	.03	.11	.42	82.7
Percent in unsound units	.00	.93	.23	—.01	.00	90.0
Median years education completed	—.05	—.91	.06	—.02	—.18	86.9
Percent employed civilians white collar	.20	—.88	—.12	.05	—.08	84.0
Percent income under $3000	.19	.80	.47	.00	—.03	90.0
Mean children/ever-married female	—.30	.77	.38	—.01	—.01	82.9
Percent born in residence state	—.12	.77	.45	—.08	—.12	83.0
Percent receiving income, 1959	.48	—.66	.17	.07	.37	83.5
Percent foreign born	.12	—.45	—.81	—.22	.05	93.3
Median age at marriage	.21	—.39	—.77	—.05	—.30	87.5
Percent in units of .76+ persons/room	—.03	.58	—.12	.73	.00	88.4
Percent married more than once	.46	—.28	.12	.71	.12	82.3
Percent in age group	.45	.24	—.26	—.70	—.05	81.9
Percent unemployed males	.24	.16	.01	.03	.88	85.1

native born, and one which inhabits areas in which members of the 25-44 year age group are underrepresented. The latter point is the most important one in that it suggests the possibility of an implicit rural population. Other implications of these factors, including the fact that they absorb nineteen of the twenty-three variables, will be discussed below.

The factor analysis for the population aged 45-64 years (Table 3-IIb) presents almost exactly the same picture as that for the 25-44 year age group. Factor I which accounts for 31.1 percent of the total variance is again clearly the familistic or implicitly urban factor. The single difference in the structure of the factor is that the percent receiving income in 1959 drops out in the 45-64 year age group and is replaced by a low sex ratio variable. There are more significant changes in Factor II

TABLE 3-IIc

FACTOR ANALYSIS OF SELECTED CHARACTERISTICS OF THE
POPULATION AGED 65 AND OLDER: VARIMAX SOLUTION

	Factor							
	I	II	III	IV	V	VI	VII	h²
Percent variance accounted for:	26.3	14.5	11.1	10.7	8.7	7.8	5.4	
Variable name:								
Percent in unsound units	.95	—.11	.05	.02	.03	—.07	—.04	92.3
Percent income under $3000	.92	.16	.05	.07	—.06	—.12	—.15	89.8
Percent born in residence state	.89	—.06	—.05	—.16	—.13	.22	—.10	90.8
Percent foreign born	—.80	—.11	.13	.30	—.13	—.25	.22	88.1
Mean children/ever-married female	.78	—.16	—.15	—.16	.02	—.29	.21	80.7
Percent employed civilians, white collar	—.76	.24	.10	—.23	.29	.03	.21	82.7
Median years education completed	—.69	—.03	—.20	.03	.41	.37	—.10	83.2
Median size household	—.08	—.92	—.02	—.08	—.03	—.02	—.20	89.2
Percent primary individuals	.01	.87	.12	.22	.34	—.04	—.02	94.0
Sex ratio, males/100 females	.18	—.76	—.08	.09	.22	—.43	.09	86.7
Percent living with spouse	.18	—.70	—.28	—.01	—.02	—.48	—.04	82.8
Percent in units of .76+ persons/room	.04	.06	.87	.09	—.06	.00	.04	77.7
Percent nonwhite or Spanish surname	.37	.29	.72	—.01	.15	.14	—.33	89.3
Percent divorced or separated	—.27	—.06	.63	.00	.04	.46	.19	72.3
Percent in owner occupied units	.39	—.37	—.63	—.41	—.10	.04	—.12	87.6
Percent single	—.14	.11	.16	.89	—.06	.15	—.04	87.9
Percent in age group	.35	.20	—.22	.70	.33	.13	.02	82.7
Percent receiving income, 1959	—.09	.12	—.05	.20	.84	.13	.04	78.7
Percent married more than once	—.16	—.02	.16	—.23	.81	—.18	.07	80.8
Percent females in labor force	.05	.32	.14	.16	—.04	.82	.14	83.2
Percent unemployed males	—.10	.09	.02	—.08	.10	.12	.91	88.4
Percent in 1 unit dwellings	.58	—.33	—.40	—.56	.06	.06	.03	92.2
Median age at marriage	—.51	—.16	.11	.55	—.07	—.09	—.16	63.3

for this age group in which, in comparison with the 25-44 year group, only six of the original nine variables are replicated and one new variable appears: percent receiving income in 1959. The two which are lost are the percent of the population in the age group under study and percent foreign-born. Once again there are three peripheral factors which, taken together, include seven variables. As in the case of Factors III, IV and V for the 25-44 year age group, each of these factors includes too small a number of variables to permit easy labeling of the factor structure.

Three meaningful factors were produced in the analysis for the group aged 65 years and over (Table 3-IIc) along with four factors of lesser importance. The seven factors account for 84.6 percent of the total variance in this age group. The picture presented by the structures of the three main factors differs somewhat from that which developed in the younger groups. In this group the economic status factor appears as the principal factor and accounts for 26.3 percent of the total variance. Its internal structure replicates that of the 45-64 year age group almost exactly. The outcome becomes interestingly different in Factors II and III for the elderly group. Here it appears that the "familistic" factors of the two younger age groups has been split along the lines of living arrangements and, possibly, color. Factor II reflects mainly the isolated living arrangements of a segment of the elderly population. Factor III has an internal structure which is more difficult to summarize, but could easily take its name from the correlation of non-whites with this factor.

In summary, it is possible to make several observations about this factor analysis:

1. The factor structures for the two younger age groups bear a stronger resemblance to one another than either does to the oldest age group.
2. The lack of comparability between the factor structures for the oldest age group and the two younger age groups results from a progressive change in the composition of factor structures and a decrease in the substantive clarity of the factor structures as the age of the group under study increases.
3. However, even considering these changes in factor structures, it remains true that there is more similarity across age groups than might have been expected on the basis of the aging literature and considering the rapidity and profundity of social change in the United States during the past century.[4]
4. In comparison with studies of the factorial ecologies of populations which have already been mentioned, it is important to note that the economic status factors and family-living arrangement factors found before continue to appear even when widely

---

[4] It should be emphasized here that the technique of variable selection used in this study would tend to maximize *similarities* between age groups. Thus, the differences which do occur may be regarded as the more remarkable.

disparate types of ecological areas are included in the analysis. Perhaps not surprisingly, the ethnic segregation factor of the older studies does not appear here, unless Factor III for the 65 year and older group can be so labeled.

As is usually the case in factor analysis, the comparisons of factor structures and the conclusions based on these comparisons are highly intuitive in character. Some validation of these interpretations is provided by the coefficients of congruency between pairs of age groups shown in Table 3-III. Overall, it is

TABLE 3-III

COEFFICIENTS OF CONGRUENCY BETWEEN NOMINALLY SIMILAR
FACTORS FOR PAIRS OF AGE GROUPS

Nominal Factor Type		Age Groups Compared		
		25-44 and 45-64	45-64 and 65+	25-44 and 65+
Economic Status:	Factor Numbers Compared*	II-II	II-I	II-I
	Coefficient of Congruency	.87	.85	.78
Family:	Factor Numbers Compared	I-I	I-II	I-II
	Coefficient of Congruency	.92	.82	.68
Family:	Factor Numbers Compared		I-III	I-III
	Coefficient of Congruency		.57	.60

* In all cases the factor numbers presented in this table refer to the factor numbers for the three age groups as shown in Table 3-II. The left-hand factor numbr in each comparison in this tbale always designates the factor for the younger age group.

apparent that, regardless of the substantive characters of factors, that is, whether they are economic or familistic, the degree of congruency declines markedly as the disparity between age groups increases. Thus, for two of the factor types, economic status and the first family factor, the coefficients are consistently high when adjacent age groups are compared but drop sharply when the youngest and oldest age groups are compared. The highest level of congruency, .92, is found in the first family factor between the youngest and middle-aged groups. However, the economic status factor exhibits the most highly consistent congruency overall. The second family factor found in the 65 year and older age group exhibits very low levels of congruency when compared with the single family factor in either of the two younger age groups. If we bear in mind that, in the analyses upon which these coefficients are based, the factor structures are derived from data aggregated on the basis of age within ecological areas, these findings hint at but do not really demonstrate an increasing lack of population homogeneity within areas as age increases. Within the limits of correlational analysis, these coefficients do seem to supply some validation of previous conclusions.[5]

Area Structure

In order to sharpen our interpretive focus upon the factor analytic outcomes, it is useful to shift our attention back to the fact that the areal designations may be presumed to have a strong influence on the outcomes. As a preliminary way of assessing the particular influence of each type of area, a correlation coefficient was calculated across the twenty-three variables for each pair of age groups within each area. These coefficients are presented in Table 3-IV.

As might have been anticipated from the analysis of variance outcomes in Table 3-I, there is considerable variation in the relations between age groups within areas. If, for the sake of discussion, the mean of the coefficients for each age group is taken as a dividing line between high and low orders of correlation, it develops that in only fourteen of the forty-one areas do all three pairs of age groups correlate highly across all the variables. Seven of the areas have low orders of correlation in all three pairs. It is noteworthy that in the case of these consistent groups, whether high or low in correlation, there are no readily apparent patterns of areal type. The means of the

---

[5] A canonical correlation analysis of factor scores for each age group was carried out following Koons (1962). The analysis showed that the greatest predictability occurred between the 25-44 and 45-64 year age groups; the least predictability occurred between the 45-64 and 65 year and older age groups. However, the differences in the degrees of predictability as shown by the correlations of the age group factor scores to the canonical variable was not great. Also, the logical expectation for least predictability between the 25-44 and 65 year and older age groups was not realized. In general, the canonical correlations did not produce as clear a picture of decrease in population homogeneity with increase in age differences as do the coefficients of congruency.

TABLE 3-IV

CORRELATIONS OF CHARACTERISTICS OF MEMBERS OF PAIRS OF
AGE GROUPS WITHIN ECOLOGICAL AREAS (23 VARIABLES)*

	Age Groups Correlated		
Area Number**	25-44 and 45-64	45-64 and 65+	25-44 and 65+
1	.893	.917	.827
2	.954	.848	.870
3	.616	.832	.340
4	.338	.776	.057
5	.432	.504	—.288
6	.552	.740	.222
7	.667	.639	.502
8	.493	.476	.358
9	.046	.019	.171
10	.292	.245	.189
11	.814	.780	.456
12	.739	.300	.322
13	.688	.102	—.069
14	.851	.202	.121
15	—.200	.503	.438
16	.410	.177	.436
17	.772	.550	.659
18	.932	.633	.633
19	.743	.665	.646
20	.804	.716	.746
21	.922	.875	.838
22	.884	.912	.789
23	.685	.740	.639
24	.757	.341	.306
25	.765	.813	.661
26	.682	.525	.520
27	.744	.698	.435
28	.570	.638	.243
29	.326	.582	.137
30	.689	.767	.545
31	.150	—.163	.647
32	.818	.062	.157
33	.516	.529	.267
34	.707	.630	.433
35	.038	.310	.456
36	.839	.677	.451
37	.288	.299	.292
38	.723	.795	.471
39	.652	.436	.375
40	.732	.754	.713
41	.817	.779	.520
Xr	.613	.553	.428

* Based on standard score transformations.
** Area numbers refer to blocks as numbered in Figure 3-I above.

correlation coefficients tend to correspond to the factor analytic outcomes in that the weakest occurs between the oldest age group and the two younger age groups. The complexity of outcomes which is so evident in this table argues that the apparently clear distinctions of the factor analysis must be re-examined from an areal point of view. The factor analyses, taken by themselves, give no hint of the degree of areal variation which occurs within and between age groups.

This observation implies several specific questions which may be answered on the basis of the Q analysis presented below:

1. How many Q groups (discreet groupings of areas) are formed in each age group?
2. Do the Q groups have internal areal consistency which would allow them to be nominalized?
3. Does the number of Q groups formed vary within age groups?
4. Is there comparability between Q groups across age groups?

The Q analyses for the three age groups ranging from youngest to oldest are shown in Tables 3-Va, 3-Vb, and 3-Vc, respectively. In presenting the outcomes for these analyses we display only those areas (here treated as variables) which have factor loadings of ± .600 or higher. Each area which loads in a Q group is numbered with reference to Figure 3-I and is designated as a member of a gross ecological type. Areas 1-8 in Figure 3-I are those outside metropolitan areas (OMA) irrespective of size; areas 9-22 are central cities (CC); and areas 23-41 are suburban ring places (R). Three well defined Q groups appear in the two younger age groups and four Q groups were formed in the 65 year and older age group.[6] It is reasonably clear that, in all three age groups, Q groups I, II and III are each dominated by a particular type of ecological area. Q group I is composed mainly or entirely of suburban ring places. Q group II is predominantly a central city configuration. And, Q group III is composed mainly or entirely of places outside metropolitan areas. Closer inspection

---

[6] Table 5 excludes from consideration Q groups in which fewer than three areas loaded at ± .600. In the 25-44 year age group, areas 9 and 22 failed to load at all. In the 45-64 age group, areas 9, 12, 24 and 25 failed to load. And, in the 65 year and older age group, areas 11, 12, 14, 19, 32, 37, and 39 failed to load.

TABLE 3-Va

Q ANALYSIS OF 41 ECOLOGICAL AREAS BY SELECTED
CHARACTERISTICS OF THE POPULATION AGED 25-44:
VARIMAX SOLUTION

Q Group

	I			II			III	
Area Number	Area Type	Factor Loading	Area Number	Area Type	Factor Loading	Area Number	Area Type	Factor Loading
10	CC*	.711	1	OMA*	—.764	2	OMA	.633
12	CC	.634	8	OMA	.704	3	OMA	.940
15	CC	.638	11	CC	.911	4	OMA	.911
24	R*	.670	13	CC	.861	5	OMA	.844
25	R	.697	14	CC	.873	6	OMA	.894
26	R	.862	17	CC	.732	7	OMA	.724
27	R	.833	18	CC	.938	23	R	.684
28	R	.894	20	CC	.892			
29	R	.962	21	CC	.907			
30	R	.987	41	R	.662			
31	R	.735						
32	R	.893						
33	R	.796						
34	R	.899						
35	R	.726						
36	R	.929						
37	R	.808						
38	R	.949						
39	R	.810						
40	R	.937						

* In this and Tables 3-Vb and 3-Vc, the designations OMA, CC and R are used to designate areas according to the locational aspect of their ecology, that is, outside metropolitan area, in central city, and in ring, respectively. For specification of the two size dimensions of each area, the reader must refer by area number to Figure 3-I above.

reveals that the patterns of internal consistency which are implied by these labels must be qualified in several ways when comparisons are made between age groups. For example, Q group I for the 25-44 year age group includes three central city areas; this is not true of Q group I in either of the two older age groups. Q group III contains the most consistent list of areas. Q group II is perhaps the most interesting from both within- and between-age group standpoints. It presents a picture of bi-polarity which becomes increasingly strong as age increases, with central cities on one pole and rural areas on the other. In the 65 year and older age group there is also a fourth Q group which is a second central city complex. Area 41 which includes the largest of the

TABLE 3-Vb

Q ANALYSIS OF 41 ECOLOGICAL AREAS BY SELECTED CHARACTERISTICS OF THE POPULATION AGED 45-64: VARIMAX SOLUTION

Q Group

	I			II			III	
Area Number	Area Type	Factor Loading	Area Number	Area Type	Factor Loading	Area Number	Area Type	Factor Loading
27	R	.682	1	OMA	—.911	3	OMA	.895
28	R	.774	2	OMA	—.713	4	OMA	.948
29	R	.638	11	CC	.680	5	OMA	.914
30	R	.888	13	CC	.632	6	OMA	.859
32	R	.942	14	CC	.692	7	OMA	.871
33	R	.743	15	CC	.605	8	OMA	.862
34	R	.941	17	CC	.842	11	CC	.652
35	R	.685	18	CC	.874	31	R	.734
36	R	.964	20	CC	.896			
37	R	.865	21	CC	.860			
38	R	.916	22	CC	.624			
39	R	.755	23	R	—.789			
40	R	.830	41	R	.767			

TABLE 3-Vc

Q ANALYSIS OF 41 ECOLOGICAL AREAS BY SELECTED CHARACTERISTICS OF THE POPULATION AGED 65+: VARIMAX SOLUTION

Q Group

	I			II	
Area Number	Area Type	Factor Loading	Area Number	Area Type	Factor Loading
27	R	.807	1	OMA	.642
28	R	.830	2	OMA	.684
29	R	.807	9	CC	—.761
30	R	.929	17	CC	—.739
33	R	.603	21	CC	—.788
34	R	.862	22	CC	—.766
35	R	.622	25	R	.616
36	R	.883	26	R	.629
38	R	.712	31	R	.761
40	R	.736			

	III			IV	
Area Number	Area Type	Factor Loading	Area Number	Area Type	Factor Loading
3	OMA	.915	15	CC	—.714
4	OMA	.879	18	CC	—.834
5	OMA	.879	20	CC	—.700
6	OMA	.880	41	R	—.684
7	OMA	.877			
8	OMA	.812			

suburban ring places falls consistently into the central city groupings.

There are other areas which display atypicality from the point of view of the typology being used here. Area 8 which includes the largest places outside metropolitan areas tends to appear in nominally different Q groups depending on which age group is studied. For example, in the 25-44 year age group, area 8 is associated with central city places whereas, in the two older age groups, it is associated with places of its own type. Similarly, area 23, which includes rural farm places which are distinguished by being located in rings, appears more consistently in the two younger age groups in Q groups in which rurality rather than ring location is the dominant feature. The fact that area 23 loads by itself in the 65 year and older age group points to the ambiguity of the typology as it applies in this age group and at least hints at the possibility of the existence of two distinct elderly rural farm populations. Finally, area 31 which includes the smallest urban places in rings loads differently in each age group.

On the basis of inspection there is a high degree of comparability in Q structures among the three age groups in spite of the discrepancies which have been cited. As in the cases of the factor analyses, the greatest discrepancies occur between the oldest age group and the two younger age groups. In the 65 year and older age group there are fewer areas included in each Q group and, as has been noted, the elderly group appears to have two distinct urban populations and, possibly, two distinct rural farm populations. In making these inter-age comparisons it is important to bear in mind that the thing which determines the Q group into which a particular area falls is the composite structure of the characteristics of the members of the age group who inhabit the particular area. When this consideration is given its due weight it becomes quite apparent that the factorial ecologies of the areas are very much a function of the age structures of their populations. It is also important to note that the ecologies rely no more on the *percentage* of persons in an age group who inhabit a particular area than they rely on the social and economic characteristics of those persons. Previous studies which have used the percentage age distribution of the population in an area have failed to demonstrate the complexity of the juncture between the aggregate characteristics of members of age groups and the places they inhabit. This is particularly true with respect to the findings for urban areas. To our knowledge no previous study has demonstrated the existence of two distinct urban populations of elderly people and the fact that there is a bi-polarity in urban populations which increases across age groups.

Neither of these findings is explicable in terms of the factor analysis or the Q analysis viewed separately. It is necessary to find a means of determining how the salient outcomes of the factor analysis merge with those of the Q analysis. The mean varimax factor scores for the Q groups within each age group serve this purpose; they are shown in Table 3-VI. Mean varimax factor scores are obtained by computing factor scores for factors such as those in Table 3-II for each area, summing the factor scores for the areas within each Q group, and dividing the sum

TABLE 3-VI

MEAN FACTOR SCORES AND FACTOR SCORE STANDARD
DEVIATIONS FOR Q GROUPS

Q Groups		Factor: Type:	25-44 II Ec.St.	25-44 I Fam.	45-64 II Ec.St.	45-64 I Fam.	65+ I Ec.St.	65+ II Fam.	65+ III Fam.
I	Mean		—.57	—.69	—.90	—.88	—.75	—.54	—.42
	S.D.		.60	.45	.46	.46	.46	.48	.52
II(+)	Mean		—.09	1.32	—.21	1.21	—.38	.11	1.13
	S.D.		.43	.53	.51	.26	.50	.30	.85
II(—)	Mean				2.45	—1.11	1.28	—.90	.18
	S.D.				.49	.16	.88	.81	.53
III	Mean		1.24	—.28	.39	.58	.94	.97	—.92
	S.D.		.58	.24	.38	.24	.56	.26	.53
IV	Mean						—.69	.56	.52
	S.D.						.51	.55	.93

by the/ number of areas within each Q group. (Chevan and O'Rourke, 1972, p. 124) Where Q groups exhibit bi-polarity at the level of two or more areas on each pole the means are presented separately. For example, the bi-polar Q group II in the 45-64 year age group is shown under the headings II(+) and II(−) in Table 3-VI.

The findings in the youngest age group are consistent with previous research. (Schnore, 1965; Duncan and Reiss, 1956) Suburban areas and rural areas are at opposite poles of the economic status factor with central cities in between. "Young" people in the rural Q groups have particularly low status on Factor II. The significant aspect of the findings on economic status in this age group is that the picture presented by the factor analysis for the age group most aptly describes those who live in rural areas. Not unexpectedly, the classic picture of a group of poor whites who show high fertility, low age at marriage, poor housing, low education and low geographic mobility is a rural picture. Suburban areas (Q group I) are nearly the opposite of rural areas on the economic status factor.

The means for the Q groups on the family-living arrangement factor distinguish between the three types of ecological areas. Once again, the findings are not unexpected. The mean of −.69 for those living in suburban areas reflects a conventional familistic pattern whereas, for central cities, almost the opposite pattern obtains. Rural areas fall between these two but tend to be more like suburban areas than central cities. In summary, the extreme comparison between types of ecological areas occurs between suburban and rural areas in terms of economic status but between urban and suburban areas in terms of family-living arrangement structures.

The emergence of the bi-polar Q group II is the most salient feature of the factorial ecology of the 45-64 year age group as compared to the 25-44 year age group. Specifically, as was suggested by the Q analysis, we find a distinction between urban and suburban areas but, more importantly, a breakdown of areas previously called "rural." One of these is more strictly rural in the conventional sense and the other is composed of places of a rural character outside of metropolitan areas. In the urban-suburban comparison (Q groups II+ and I) of both the economic status and family-living arrangement factors the resemblance in the array of means between the 45-64 year age group and the 25-44 year age group is striking. On both factors the differences between the two Q groups for ecological areas outside of metropolitan areas (Q groups II— and III) are almost as large as the differences between rural areas and central city areas (Q groups II+ and II—).

To the extent that one can make comparisons between the different age groups in this kind of an analysis, it is important to note that the ecological structures of the age groups become more complex as the comparison focus moves from younger to older age groups. The ecological complexity reaches its highest level in the 65 year and older age group. In this group, in addition to the bifurcation of Q group II, we now have a bifurcation of the family-living arrangement factor and a new Q group (IV) composed of central cities and the largest ring cities. The ecological structure of the 65 year and older age group involves two non-metropolitan populations (Q groups II— and III), two urban populations (Q groups II+ and IV), and a suburban population.

Continuity is maintained between the 65 year and older age group and the younger age groups in the ring populations and primarily in terms of economic status. The key to the two bifurcations mentioned above is that within the oldest age group there appear to be populations in both urban and non-metropolitan places which are distinguished from one another in terms of family-living arrangement variables and, also, in terms of economic distinctions similar to those which obtain between the younger age groups. Thus, the oldest age group has the most highly differentiated ecology, that is, there are at least five discrete elderly populations which differ from one another in economic terms, family-living arrangement terms, or both.

CONCLUSION

This paper reports the results of a study of the factorial ecology of three age groups in the United States in 1960. An attempt was made to establish relationships which might obtain between populations as defined by age and the kinds of places they inhabit through the application of techniques of multivariate analysis. The characteristics of the members of the three age groups were described in a list of twenty-nine variables (reduced to twenty-three in the process of the analysis), and related to forty-one types of ecological area defined by size and metropolitan location.

The major findings of the study may be summarized as follows:

1. Considered separately, there is greater variation between age groups than between ecological areas.
2. Factor analyses of the characteristics of the members of the three age groups show that while there is gross comparability between age groups in terms of the types of factors which emerge, the composition of the factors varies markedly between age groups. There is also a reduction in the clarity of factor structures in older as compared to younger age groups.
3. An analysis of the correlations between age groups within areas shows that among those cases where the correlations between age groups are consistently high or low within an area, there are no obvious patterns of relationship between areas. If areal patterns are to become evident, they must do so in terms of the selective characteristics of their inhabitants.
4. The Q analyses for the three age groups show that, in gross terms, each of the groups has a distinctive ecology. As in the case of the factor analyses, there is general similarity between the Q groups for different age groups. However, the numbers and the compositions of the Q groups differ from one age group to the next. Q groups take on the identity of traditional ecological areas.

These findings have implications for the kinds of questions which are asked about age groups and for the aged in particular. Questions of whether age strata exist are logically prior to discussion of age stratification as a process. Clearly discrete strata do not appear to be reflected in the ecological patterns which emerge in this study. On the one hand, the gross dissimilarities in the ecologies of the age groups which have been shown in the analysis argue in favor of the conclusion that a system of age stratification existed in the United States in 1960. On the other hand, the fact that the ecologies of the age groups were not perfectly dissimilar mitigates against this conclusion. It should be observed that the requirement of perfect ecological dissimilarity to demonstrate the existence of age strata is valid only if it can be asserted that the logical requirements for the existence of discrete classes have direct ecological implications. To the extent that aging is a continuous process, there is overlap between broad age groups in their characteristics. This comes about, primarily as a function of the fact that all of the age groups studied have had at least twenty-five years and as much as sixty-four years of common social experience. Under these conditions it is unlikely that when the aging process is stopped analytically, as it is in this type of synchronic analysis, perfectly discrete age strata will be identified and be describable in ecological terms. This, however, is at least no greater a difficulty than that which has been found commonly on broader studies of social stratification. In any event, the epistemological and ontological problems of the relationship between structure and process cannot be resolved on the basis of this analysis.

Regardless of these outstanding problems, the outcomes of the study have relevance for other theoretical issues in the field of aging and social gerontology. One issue which has been the subject of a lengthy polemic among gerontologists is the question of the status of the aged as a minority group or as a subculture. (Rose, 1962; Streib, 1965) In the light of the increasing but systematic heterogeneity which this study demonstrates between the youngest and oldest age groups, it seems reasonable to conclude that the contradictory answers to these questions proffered by previous analyses result from two difficulties. The first is methodological in character and may be expressed simply by asserting that previous conclusions about the minority status of "the elderly" have been based on evidence which was far too fragmentary. Our analysis which suggests the possibility of six different sub-populations of the elderly in the United States raises the question whether all of the previous conclusions based on limited evidence were in fact correct and not contradictory.

The second difficulty, ironically, is one about which there

has been much concern, especially in the applied gerontological literature. This is the problem of "stereotyping" the elderly; in methodological terms this takes the form of overgeneralizing from fragentary evidence also. Without indicting previous writers on the subject and, granting the inadvertance of previous generalizations, this study indicates that sweeping statements about *the* elderly as a minority group are no more warranted on ecological grounds than they have been regarded to be on social psychological grounds. The only supportable generalization seems to be that there are several age-graded populations in the United States.

REFERENCES

Bell, W.: Economic, family and ethnic status: an empirical test. *Am. Sociol. Rev.*, 20:45, 1955.

Bureau of the Census: *One-In-A-Thousand Sample Description and Technical Documentation.* Washington, D.C., United States Government Printing Office, 1964.

Chevan, A.. and O'Rourke, J. F.: Aging regions of the United States. *J. Gerontol.*, 27:119, 1972.

Council of State Governments: *The States and Their Older Citizens.* Chicago, Council of State Governments, 1955.

Duncan, Otis D., and Reiss, Albert J.: *Social Characteristics of Urban and Rural Communities, 1950.* New York, Wiley, 1956.

Harmon, Harry H.: *Modern Factor Analysis.* Chicago, University of Chicago Press, 1960.

Hunter, A.: The ecology of Chicago: persistence and change, 1930-1960. *Am. J. Sociol.*, 77:425, 1971.

Koons. P. B., Jr.: Canonical analysis. In *Computer Applications in the Behavioral Sciences,* edited by H. Borko, Englewood Cliffs, Prentice-Hall, 1962.

Maddox, G. L.: Themes and issues in sociological theories of aging. *Hum. Dev.*, 13:17, 1970.

Riley, Matilda W.; Foner, Anne; *et al.*: *Aging and Society, An Inventory of Research Findings.* New York, Russell Sage, 1968, vol. I.

Rose, A.: The subculture of aging: a topic for sociological research. *Gerontologist*, 2:123, 1962.

————, and Peterson, Warren E.: *Older People and Their Social World: The Sub-culture of Aging.* Philadelphia. F. A. Davis, 1965.

Schnore, Leo F.: *The Urban Scene: Human Ecology and Demography.* New York, Free Press, 1965.

Sheldon, Henry D.: *The Older Population of the United States*. New York, Wiley, 1958.

————: The changing demographic profile. In *Handbook of Social Gerontology: Societal Aspects of Aging*, edited by Clark Tibbits, Chicago, University of Chicago Press, 1960.

Streib, G. F.: Are the aged a minority group? In *Applied Sociology*, edited by A. W. Gouldner and S. M. Miller, Glencoe, Free Press, 1965.

Van Arsdol, M., Jr.; Camilleri, S., and Schmid, C.: The generality of urban social area indexes. *Am. Sociol. Rev.*, 23:277, 1958.

FORMAL

COMMUNITIES

CHAPTER 4

ON MULTIPLE REALITIES IN A
NURSING HOME[1]

JABER F. GUBRIUM

FORMAL ORGANIZATIONS THAT serve an internal clientele (e.g. prisons, hospitals, nursing homes) usually compile official reports about the quality and quantity of services they offer and the processing and progress of their clientele in relation to such services. These reports constitute administrative definitions of organizational relevance. Reports are written by some persons in the organization about other roles and activities in it.

Official reports are portraits of the organization which assume, for all practical purposes, that persons within the organization define it in an official way and act in terms of this. If, on the other hand, such an organization is not conceived, analytically, as an official one, but rather, as a formally structured set of situations containing a variety of role complexes, then the sociological problem arises of what organizational relevances are systematically omitted in official reports (cf. Berger and Luckmann, 1966:79-80). This problem assumes that formal organizations contain situations that generate multiple realities about what people do and think within them.

There is another sociological problem implicit here that is an important aspect of conceiving of a formal organization as a situation of multiple realities. Given that the varied definitions of particular realities have been delineated, there is still the problem of accommodation. Although a formal organization may

---

[1] Field work for this study was supported by a Summer Faculty Fellowship, Marquette University, Milwaukee, Wisconsin.

be composed of situated role complexes that differentially influence the concerns and actions of their incumbents, insofar as these roles are organized, differential concerns and actions must somehow be accommodated. This is conceived here largely as a problem for actors within an organization.

In this paper, I shall be dealing with the nursing home as an organized setting of role complexes centered on long-term care. Three sociological problems will be examined, both together and separately: (1) the constraints of situations as they influence, (2) definitions of the reality of patient care in the nursing home, and (3) the accommodations that actors with different definitions make to each other.

Our behavioral focus is on actors, variations in their situated definitions, and the processes by which they resolve conflicts in definition (accommodation). The actor is not conceived as a completely unrestrained agent of his actions. Rather, he is considered to be constrained by the structure of an organized setting but at the same time sufficiently separate from it so as to deal with the problems it poses for everyday living (See Gerth and Mills, 1953).

SITUATED CONSTRAINTS ON PATIENT CARE

Murray Manor[2] is a year old, non-profit, church related nursing home located in a middle-sized midwestern city. It has accommodations for 360 patients and residents on six floors. At present its census fluctuates around 130, one third of whom are residents and the rest patients. Residents occupy the first floor. This floor houses individuals in need of residential, but not nursing care. Patients occupy the third and fourth floors currently. They are in need of various levels of skilled nursing care. The mean age of patients and residents is just over 80 years; the home is formally recognized as a geriatric care facility. In this paper, I am concerned only with patients and the staff that cares for them.

There are three role complexes, the situations of which

_____

[2] References to places and persons throughout are pseudonyms.

generate various definitions of care at Murray Manor. Two of
these are staff complexes, namely, the administrative (or top)
staff and the floor staff. The third is the complex of patient roles.

The administrative staff, which conceives of itself as involved
in patient care, especially patient care policy, consists of the
administrator, director of nursing, assistant director of nursing,
occupational therapist, activity director, medical director, chaplain, and social worker. Although these persons all think of
themselves as directly involved in patient care, the job requirements of their positions place such administrative demands on
their time that they rarely appear on patient floors. When any
of the administrative staff does appear on the floors, it is usually
in a capacity that does not involve the patient as a person. For
example, the medical director makes periodic physical examinations on his particular patients; the administrator may provide
a guided tour of the building for an interested outsider; the
social worker shows off the facilities to the family of a potential
patient; or the director of nursing makes a relatively brief
check of nursing routines.

There is a further constraint that prevents top staff from
being directly involved in patient care. Murray Manor is an
organization that is about a year old. In order to remain solvent,
pressures are being felt to increase the patient census rapidly
while conserving the growth of the top staff. This increases top
staff's administrative responsibilities, which in turn, increasingly
directs its attention away from the everyday life of patients.

Because the patient care aspect of administrative roles is
primarily one of policy-making, there is a situated constraint
other than the pressure of administrative work that affects top
staff's view of patients. The everyday routines of patient lives
and patient care that it does see are perceived through the eyes
of policy-makers. Thus, what little there is that is directly known
by the top staff about patients' everyday lives on the floors tends
to be understood in terms of policy standards and not in their
own rights.

The business of patient care for the top staff involves: (a)
formulating care policy that is (b) presumably based on accurate
knowledge of patients and their everyday floor life in the home,

while (c) facing administrative job requirements that increasingly constrain them to direct their attention elsewhere. These
organizational constraints (formulating care policy, knowing the
everyday lives of patients, and administrative pressures) must
be dealt with by top staff personnel in such a way that visible
evidence of care policy develops, since each top staff position
depends upon such evidence to carry on its work. For example,
the administrator is accountable to government licensing and
funding agents, which is dependent on evidence of patient care
as compiled by other staff members.

Given the constraints that the top staff faces, how is care
policy formulated to everyone's satisfaction? One very important
way that this is dealt with by top staff personnel is to construct
definitions of the realities of patient life on the floors and to
formulate policy in terms of these definitions. There is no
evidence that this is a deliberately deceptive thing. Rather, it
is an unwitting outcome of persons attempting to "work" through
their jobs and make them reasonable. Before delineating top
staff's definitions of the realities of patient life and how these
are practically accommodated to other realities, the characteristics of two other role complexes at Murray Manor that constrain
persons to generate other definitions of patient care will be
discussed briefly.

The floor staff, like the top staff, also considers itself to be
involved in the business of patient care. Furthermore, top staff
continually informs floor personnel that the main goal of Murray
Manor is:

> . . . to provide quality care for the convalescent and aging person
> in an atmosphere conducive to meeting the optimum physical,
> emotional, social, and religious needs of the residents and patients.

Floor personnel are reminded of this both informally in conversation with administrative staff and in such formal settings as
in-service training classes and patient staffings. Floor staff includes: the charge nurses on each of the two patient floors, sup-
porting nursing personnel (usually LPN's), and nurse's aides.
The floor staff is exactly that; their jobs do not primarily involve
them in administrative matters (except perhaps for some of the

charge nurse's work) but rather in directly caring for patients assigned to them. Their time is spent on the floors where they constantly come into contact with individual patients and their circumstances. Their work does not involve formulating official care policy, but rather is considered by the top staff to be putting policy into practice.

Floor staff roles constrain their personnel to direct their attention both toward the most physical aspects of patient care and to patient behavior and desires. This is a result of three organizational pressures felt by the floor staff. The first is an outcome of how top staff evaluates good care in practice (which contrasts with their ideals). The second is an outcome of a chronic shortage of nursing personnel. And the third is a result of the fact that floor staff is constantly involved in the everyday lives of patients.

Since top staff is increasingly bound by growing administrative responsibilities, its evaluative function as work supervisors becomes a process of judging patient care in terms of quickly observed conditions on the floors. Good care becomes a matter of cleanliness and physical order (e.g. beds made, patients dressed, absence of odors). The most visible aspects of patient care are what matter to the top staff, in practice. The floor staff knows this and frequently mentions it directly in talking about their work. For example, they'll caution each other about such things as "not spending too much time with the patients but rather getting your work done." One aide, who had been talking to a patient, noticed me and said to the patient: "Well, I didn't really take much of a lunch hour, or my morning break, so we can sit down and talk a bit." This legitimized her "sitting down on the job," since it was presumably being done on her own time.

A second organizational condition that constrains floor personnel to attend primarily to the physical needs of patients is a chronic shortage of and high demand for nurses and aides in the labor market. It is not unusual at Murray Manor for half the number of expected aides to appear for work on some shifts. This places a burden on those aides who do report to work, increasing their need to attend to the highly visible aspects of having done a job. The patient becomes largely a matter of bed-and-body.

There is another kind of constraint which affects floor personnel's definition of the realities of patient care. This is the fact that, in contrast to top staff, they constantly encounter and must deal with patient peculiarities and demands. Their work is directly involved with patients and their social relationships. Since they work with patients, they feel constrained to do something for them. At the very least, if a patient is to be ignored, something must be done so that he is manageably ignorable.

The situation in which floor personnel find themselves induces them to define the realities of patient care somewhat differently than do top staff personnel. Their definition is more complex than that of top staff since it is constrained by and is accountable to both top staff and patients. Floor staff's definition of patient care is two-sided. Floor staff conceives of one set of patient care relevances important in its relations with top staff and another set as important in its relations with patients. Because floor staff experiences the personal behavior and social relationships of patients every day, and experiences them rather intimately, it knows that (as one aide said), "there's more to these people than toileting and feeding, you know—but what can you do?" It's obvious from this statement that floor staff has both top staff and patients in mind when thinking about patient care. Their view of patient care is, to a great extent, an attempt to deal reasonably with a situation taken as given.

Patients, like the administrative and floor staff, are constrained by their situation in the nursing home in such a way as to produce definitions, specific to them, of the reality of care. Because the nursing home structures the lives of its patients rather extensively, they come to depend upon it for making a gamut of spatial and temporal decisions. This structures their everyday lives and influences their conception of care. Another structured constraint is located in contingencies of the social relationships that patients develop among themselves and with the floor staff.

After spending a number of weeks living with the organizational routines of the home, most patients come to realize that many of the decisions which they made for themselves before entering the home now are made for them. Take the business of deciding when to perform such routine tasks of everyday life as getting up, eating, and going to bed. In the working world, these routines generally involve the necessity of keeping track of time in order to properly sequence them with other events of daily living. Now what would happen to time-keeping if daily living were composed largely of the events of getting up, eating, and going to bed? What would happen to it if a person were guaranteed that regardless of clock time, the proper sequencing of events in daily living would occur and be managed by someone else? One would expect that clock time would become irrelevant to such persons. This is one way the nursing home as an organized situation constrains the lives of its patients. Their situation tends to make irrelevant what to non-patients is a rather important aspect of daily living. This also affects patients' conceptions of the relevances of patient care.

Patients who are able to come into contact with other patients may form social relationships with them. Many of these relationships are such that they influence definitions of self that are contingent on the relationship. For example, some patients become rather close friends. Such persons tend to face the actions of both top and floor staff as companions rather than as separate individuals. Their social ties lead to a shared concern over their common welfare. For persons with such ties, patient care is not completely a staff-to-individual affair.

There is another very important way that the social relationships of patients affect their conceptions of patient care. This is that nursing home patients recognize that all share the same overwhelming everyday dependence on the staff. Such recognition underpins a rather intense sympathy that some patients have for others in the kinds of physical, psychological, and social trials that any one of them might face at any time. There is a felt solidarity that is sustained by the fact that patients are clientele, but exceptionally dependent ones. This solidarity, like friendship but more general, supports a specific definition of the reality of patient care.

Some patients, by no means all of them, are so dependent on the floor staff that their specific patient-staff relationship spawns peculiar definitions of care which allow these patients to deal with the constraints imposed by the relationship. Patients whose medications make them physiologically dependent on the frequent help of the floor staff exemplify this relationship. One patient, whose physician had ordered a diuretic for her, was given the medication a few times daily, making it necessary for her to be assisted relatively frequently to the toilet. The staff shortage meant that a floor aide had to ignore her other assigned duties (many highly visible to top staff) in order to attend to her. This demand caused an obvious degree of impatience and impertinence in the aide when dealing with this patient. The patient, understanding the connection between her diuretic and the ornery aide, realized that her care as a patient necessitated dealing with the situation so as to alter it for, as she put, "my own peace of mind." Patient care, to her, became a dilemma between her own sensibilities and her physical needs—a definition arising out of the situated contingencies of her relationship with floor staff. She resolved the dilemma by not taking, but hiding the medication that had been ordered for her. She would take it only when she felt aides would be most receptive to her needs for frequent toileting.

DEFINITIONS OF PATIENT CARE

The various situations in which staff and patients find themselves make for differences in their perceptions of and interests in patient care. Any one relevant world of care is a world that is constrained by the organized structure of a particular situation. Within this nursing home, there exist multiple realities of patient care—sometimes visible to each other and sometimes not. How are these realities defined?

Top Staff

Top staff is concerned with patient care in that it formulates policy and instructs the floor staff on the procedure for carrying it out. This is a task that it is required to do, but in a circumstance that allows for relatively little direct and continuous experience with patients. In order to do its job, top staff constructs its own definitions of the realities of care.

There are two important settings at Murray Manor in which top staff's conceptions of patient care are clearly visible. One of these settings is a policy-formulating meeting, "patient care conferences" (PCC), at which once per week, top staff gathers to evaluate the physical and social problems of one to four patients who have been suggested by top staff members as in need of "staffing."

Most of what the top staff knows about the particular patients that are chosen for staffings comes from three sources, none of which involve top staff's direct observation of everyday lives on the floors. These are: (1) information on patient's charts, either medical in nature or nurses' notes that are administratively-oriented descriptions of the daily behavior of patients, chart entries being required of floor personnel on each shift; (2) top staff's anecdotal knowledge of certain patients, comprised of curious and idiosyncratic accounts that are part of the daily talk of top staff members about their work and its trials or rewards (cf. Emerson, 1970:75); and (3) an occasional "serious personal interview" (open chat) undertaken by one top staff member with a patient to be staffed, such "interviews" rarely lasting more than ten or fifteen minutes, with the interviewer subsequently serving as resident-expert on the patient in the staffing.

Another setting in which top staff's conception of patient care emerges is what is referred to at Murray Manor as the "reality orientations" (RO). These are daily classroom-like sessions involving a floor aide as instructor and usually five patients as students. The instructional materials and their content are provided by the administrative nurses, but with top staff's approval. Materials consist of a chart which lists the name of the nursing home, its location, the date, the day of the week, and the state of the weather; and a cardboard instructional clock that can be set readily to teach time-keeping.

What do these settings show as evidence of top staff's definition of patient care? Top staff's conception of the patient and his care has three dimensions. One is the definition of the patient as an individual, with little or no serious concern with the social nature of his life on the floors. Another dimension is top staff's ideas about "total patient care" which, as one staff member said, involves "taking care of the emotional needs of the individual patient as well as giving good nursing care." The third dimension involves top staff's conception of what a sound mind is, or as they would say—"mentally alert."

All of top staff's sources of information about patients leads to an individualistic conception of them (cf. Ichheiser, 1970: 45-50). Chart information is about single patients and such personal acts of each as sleeping, eating, voiding, and mood. Anecdotes about patients usually refer to a single person's own idiosyncratic behavior or remarks that allegedly "typify" him as an individual. Interviews with patients usually begin with the question, "How are you today?", and remain focused on various aspects of the patient's mood at the time.

Top staff has a rather simple language which it uses to diagnose the individual behavior of patients, this diagnosis serving as the basis for treatment, or as they would say, "writing a patient care plan." This language is composed of three words: agitated, disoriented, and confused. Individual patients are diagnosed by referring to them by any one or combination of these terms. By the way the terms are used, it is obvious that they refer to *individual* patients and individualistic explanations of their behavior because they describe individual states of mind and not the personal effects of situational contingencies.

In the patient care conferences, top staff rarely considers patient behavior as rational components of a social situation. First of all, the staff's sources of information about patients do not provide data about such matters. Second, nursing personnel are usually trained to deal with patient care on an individualistic basis, i.e. training does not take serious consideration of the total social situation of patients, which involves patients as well as staff. The target of nursing care is the patient and not the situation in which he acts.

After top staff has conducted what it considers an adequate appraisal of the patient being staffed, it concludes by deciding on a plan of care. Like the evaluation of the patient, this care plan is individualistic, that is, it prescribes dealing with the patient himself so as to alter his behavior in such a way as to make him, as they would say, "more aware of reality." This means to orient him properly to the routines of daily life in the home as defined by top staff, and thereby to reduce his apparent confusion.

Care plans written by the top staff are based on the following rationale. First, plans assume that what is planned will be carried out by the floor staff. Second, it is taken for granted that patients will respond to treatment by changing their behavior toward more "realistic lines." And third, it is assumed that patients will react to treatment as individuals and not take other patients into account in receiving their own care. The care plan model does not seriously consider the social contingencies of treatment from the patient's point of view. For example, in altering a patient's diet by omitting some part of it that is thought to be medically detrimental, a plan assumes that food prepared for this patient will reflect its directive and that the patient will respond by eating whatever is provided for him for "his own good." It does not consider that a patient's friendship ties with other patients at a common table often obligates them to share food with him when he is "short-changed." Floor staff knows of such incidents but the condition is not taken by them nor by top staff as an integral component of constructing a care plan.

Treatment, then, like diagnosis, also is defined individualistically by the top staff. The model that top staff has in mind when it constructs care plans is one that considers the patient as being individualistically-oriented to care when it is put into practice. If anything goes wrong, top staff has two places in the model to find cause, the application of the plan and the individual reception of the patient. Problems of patient receptivity are defined as individual patients being unrealistic or confused.

Top staff not only considers patient care as an individual affair on the patient's side, but also conceives of this care as "total." Top staff is concerned that the patients at Murray Manor are not only receiving the proper medical attention but also that their so-called emotional needs are being fulfilled. "Emotional needs" refers to whatever else besides medical care is involved in maintaining an elderly person at what is said to be his optimum level of everyday living.

Because of this emphasis on total patient care, the patient care plan is not simply a plan for what might traditionally be called nursing care. It also includes a section on "behavioral problems and needs" and the "approach" to be taken in alleviating these problems. The total care plan is placed both in the patient's chart and on his personal card in the Cardex. Patients' charts and the Cardex are readily accessible to all floor staff personnel. Top staff assumes that the practice of patient care proceeds along the lines noted in the care plan.

Top staff's entries under behavioral problems and approach show an obvious individualistic orientation to the so-called emotional needs of the patient. It is common for the plan to list such directives as "give moral support," "remind patient of time and day of week," "use a positive approach," and "get patient to accept reality." There is little evidence that top staff conceives of behavioral problems and needs as having social dimensions. Behavioral problems and their treatment are individualistic and the total care plan reflects this.

Although top staff is concerned with total individual patient care, it is clear that both in the discussions at patient care conferences and in care plan entries, the emotional side of the care plan is given less attention than the medical side. Entries under behavioral problems and approach are always sketchier than medical ones. This certainly reflects the content of discussions at patient staffings. Staffings begin with a review of the medical condition of a patient. This is done quickly and easily with occasional questioning and commentary by the administrative nurses and medical director. But, discussion soon becomes exasperating to staff attending the PCC as the patient's behavior is considered. Each staffing ends with a rather grueling process of developing an approach to the patient's emotional needs. Staff feels pressure to write something down and always does.

The approach usually prescribes treating the individual

patient in a supportive manner for his alleged confusion and/or disorientation. Compared to the total number of patients who have been staffed so far, it appears that there is very little or no variation in approach to emotional needs. Entries for behavioral approach on the care plan for each patient staffed tend to be quite similar. This contrasts with the relatively varied entries listed dealing with the nursing needs of the patient. The relative uniformity of approaches to the emotional needs of patients reflects situational constraints on the top staff, constraints that homogenize their conceptions of the variability between patients' behaviors, especially the cause of each patient's actions.

Besides treating the patient as an individual and developing relatively homogeneous plans to care for everyone's "emotional needs," top staff also constructs definitions of the relevances of his everyday living. Top staff's definitions are quite apparent in the reality orientation sessions.

To the top staff, an alert patient is one who keeps track of and is readily aware of such features of daily living as the time of day, the day of the week, the location of the place where he lives, its name, and the state of the weather. If a patient shows evidence of knowing these things, he is considered alert. Top staff does not raise the question among themselves of whether these presumed everyday relevances are salient aspects of living a "reasonably normal" everyday life as a patient in a nursing home. Since top staff has little direct knowledge of the floor life of patients, it assumes that the relevances of everyday life in its own work-a-day world are the same as those of patients. This has led the top staff to have the RO sessions conducted on a daily basis for patients who show evidence of not keeping track of time, day, and place but who presumably are rehabilitatable.

The RO sessions consist of drills by a nurse's aide of materials provided by the top staff. Attending patients are asked to read a chart and then quizzed on its contents. The instructor next sets the instructional clock to official times of the day when patients are awakened, fed, brought to class, and put to bed. Each patient then is asked what happens at those particular times of the day. Correct answers to all of these questions, to the top staff, means that patients are "accepting reality."

Top staff, then, defines patients as individuals and works out plans for their care that are based on this definition. The defined reality of patients and patient life is the basis for diagnosing and explaining their behavioral problems as well as prescribing their treatment. The situated constraints by which top staff are bound make the generation of such definitions a "reasonable" process.

Floor Staff

Because of their position between top staff and patients, the floor staff has a view of patient care that is influenced by the double contingencies of their situation. On the one hand, what they consider relevant about patient care is what they perceive as important to top staff, namely, the appearance of "good patient care." On the other hand, their close daily contact with patients makes them aware that the quality of their work is dependent on dealing with patients to some extent on the patients' terms. How does this affect floor staff's definition of the relevances of patient care?

Like the top staff, there are specific settings in the nursing home where the floor staff's view of patient care is evident. One of these is the nurses' notes on each patient's chart. A second is in the conduct of the RO sessions and talk about the progress of patients in them. A third setting is the floor itself, and floor staff's routine work with patients.

The nurses' notes on each patient's chart is the one setting that the floor staff knows is completely oriented to the top staff. The notes are defined by top staff as a running record of what the floor staff considers to be the important events of daily care. Nurse's aides are required to "chart" each of the patients assigned to them. This is done at least once at the end of every work shift.

Inspection of the language used by floor staff in charting shows evidence of a high degree of consensus about what aides believe the staff feels is important about patient care. Regardless of highly variable floor behavior between patients, a perusal of the nurses' notes (written mostly by aides) in the patients' charts provides evidence that patients are considered both personally and socially homogeneous—so much so that if one did not know that different patients were being charted, one would conclude that a single, or at best a very few, patients were being described.

A second setting in which the floor staff's view of patient care emerges is in the RO sessions. The behavior of aides in relation to patients while conducting the sessions is notably different than their behavior with patients while on the floors. When conducting the sessions, even in the absence of top staff, aides seriously demand patients to act in terms of what top staff defines as realistic everyday patient relevances. While in the RO setting, aides are quite vehement with patients who do not answer questions "realistically" (i.e. in RO chart-oriented terms). On the floor, an entirely different criterion of patient realism is used by aides. Patient realism thus depends on the setting in which it is considered.

Routine floor work with patients is the third setting in which the floor staff's definition of patient care is evident. Top staff is rarely on the floors observing patient care. In the absence of top staff, patient care tends to take serious account of the patient as a person, separate from top staff's conception of him. A wholly different idea of patient realism characterizes care on the floor. Rather than patient realism being defined in terms of top staff's conception of individuals "keeping track of time and place," patients are considered realistic when their demands and behavior do not exceed what the floor staff feels can be reasonably met and handled within the bounds of "normal working routines."

Normal working routines include dealing with two kinds of contingencies. First, there are the bed-and-body demands that floor staff defines as meeting the practical expectations of top staff. Floor staff often will comment that they "just have to get their jobs done" before they can spend any time with patients. Second, not only does the top staff place demands on normal working routines, but so do patients. Floor staff knows that part of the normal work routine of providing patient care is to deal with patient demands that go beyond fulfilling bed-and-body needs—such things as making telephone calls for patients,

listening to their opinions, getting them their cigarettes and
sitting with them while they smoke, taking them outdoors for a
walk, and being considerate of their social relationships (both
positive and negative). Floor staff knows that a certain minimal
degree of mutual respect between themselves and patients allows
them to be flexible in locating the bounds of normal routine, e.g.
patients are more likely to be "patient" with their demands when
they know that "they'll get what they want as soon as work
permits." On the floor, whether or not patients keep track of
time and place is usually considered an irrelevant aspect of their
behavior. Rather, it is by the standards of normal work routine
that floor staff defines patients as "realistic" or not.

Out of the social constraints and contingencies of its work,
floor staff constructs a specific definition of the realities of patient
care. There are two aspects to floor staff's definition. One of
these is a conception of the relevances of patient care that
emerges from the constraints that top staff places on the work
of floor personnel. The other is a definition of relevance that
emerges from what floor staff considers to be normal floor routine.

Nurses' notes show evidence of a conception of patients and
patient care that is largely focused on the most mundane aspects
of daily living. When aides enter descriptions of what they have
done for the patients in their charge, they outline how well or
poorly any of the following were performed by patients: eating,
defecating, urinating, sleeping, bathing, and walking. When any
of these activities were performed in what the staff conceives as
admirable form, it is noted in the charts, e.g. as good appetite,
good B.M., slept through the night, etc. When any are performed
poorly, they are likewise noted as poor. If none of these activities
was perceived as either noticeably poor or good, aides tend to
omit mention of them on the charts and simply write, for instance,
"usual routine" or "a.m. cares given."

The impression one gets from these entries on the patients'
charts is that floor personnel consider the relevances of care to
be limited to the care of the physical person. This contrasts
notably with top staff's conception of total patient care. In spite
of this, physical care is that aspect of their work which the floor
staff perceives top staff to be "checking up on," especially in

relation to itself. Top staff, however, does not consider this to be their first priority in patient care, notwithstanding the fact that it uses the visible conditions of these things as indicators of quality of care. Thus, top staff's *practical* consideration of patient care coincides with floor staff's charting relevances.

Another feature of charting that attests to the top staff-oriented, physical definition of patient care held by floor personnel is the kinds of acronyms frequently used in making chart entries. The use of acronyms in any work routine is a clue to those aspects of work that most concerns personnel. They may be considered as indicators of work relevance.

Acronyms most commonly found in the nurses' notes section of patients' charts are the following: W/C, B.R., B.M., D/R, S.O.B., and C/O. These stand for, respectively: wheelchair, bathroom, bowel movement, dining room, short of breath, and complains of. It is clear from the references of these acronyms that, at least in charting (which is top staff-oriented), the bed-and-body aspects of patient care are the critical ones. Even C/O, which could refer to a range of complaints from physical to residential and administrative, does not. It most typically is followed by descriptions of bed-and-body complaints and what may have been done for them.

The suggestion that the common usage of bed-and-body acronyms is a clue to what floor staff considers relevant about patient care in relation to top staff does not mean to imply that the usage is an exclusive result of floor staff's particular work situation. Certainly, floor staff is trained (by in-service, for one thing) in charting procedures. What is significant, though, is that it is also told, both by top staff and during in-service training, that its job is the total care of the patient. It is informed that total patient care not only refers to the physical needs of patients, but to social and emotional ones as well. In spite of this, there are no acronyms used with such referents. Moreover, chart entries typically do not describe social features of a patient's daily routines—even though they are often quite noticeable when one is in the company of floor staff and patients. They are noticeable in that a significant share of what floor staff deals with *on the floor* involves the social aspects of patients' everyday lives in the nursing home.

Occasionally, chart entries will refer to the mood of a patient. For example, he may be said to be in a good or bad mood, or in good or bad spirits. Where such descriptions appear in the chart, the context is fairly clear in showing that mood references indicate how easily floor staff proceeded through bed-and-body routines with specific patients. If such routines were considered to have consumed a large share of floor staff's time due to what they refer to in the charts as uncooperativeness, then patients are described as having been in a bad mood on that particular shift. This charting interpretation occurs in spite of the fact that, when one systematically observes floor staff-patient interaction, there are a number of other obvious explanations for so-called bad moods. For example some bad moods arise from aides too loosely interpreting the bounds of mutual respect between staff and patient, which thus *induces* bad moods.

The one setting where floor staff attends to non-physical aspects of patient care on top staff terms is the RO sessions. The training in reality that presumably goes on in these sessions assumes that one of the tasks of total patient care is to make the patient "realistic" as to time and place. Evidence of realism is considered to lie in patients keeping track of clock time and knowing where they reside.

After the patients attending the RO sessions have been exercised in the reality program, they are quizzed. If a patient does not know the answer to questions about the specific time and place of events in his life at Murray Manor, the presiding aide will refer to that patient as disoriented today—even when systematic observation of the interaction between patients and teacher makes it evident that patients sometimes deliberately make errors. For example, one male patient who did not want to attend the RO session that particular day, was irritated at having been wheeled to the session against his will and deliberately made errors when he was being quizzed. The patient's deliberate errors were said by the teacher to be evidence of his confusion. Immediately after such sessions, it is not uncommon for the presiding aide to mention to other aides that a particular patient "is just not in reality today."

Labeling patients as "confused," "disoriented," or "not in reality" when errors are made in the RO sessions is based on an important assumption about patient behavior: that patients have no independent rational self-interest. Consequently, they are either institutionally-oriented or irrational. This is a purely official conception of subordinates.

The reality of patient care on the floors contrasts rather sharply with that evidenced by nurses' notes in the charts and in the RO sessions. Floor reality ignores concern with time and place as top staff defines them. This affects the labeling of patients. The bed-and-body care of patients is a main concern of floor staff. But, rather than each patient being systematically cared for, equally and individually, floor staff varies bed-and-body care. Variations are contingent on two aspects of routine care on the floor, namely, what may be readily visible to top staff when it makes relatively rare rounds on the floors, and the demands of various patients.

In the process of doing its work, floor staff follows the informal stages of what it considers to be normal routine. The following are treated as stages of normal routine: a.m. cares (awakening, dressing, and toileting), feeding, treatments, doing beds, bathing, and retiring. Most patients, after living in the nursing home for a few days, follow the normal stages of this routine too. Patients proceed from one stage to another depending on two conditions: (1) when the floor staff is generally ready for them and (2) floor staff definitions of how difficult it is to move specific patients from one stage to another.

Although it is not completely inconsistent with clock time, floor staff tends to get patients through daily routines as "their" time permits. "Their" time is consistent with clock time only to the extent that distinction is made beween things to be done early in a shift and things to be done later.

Some patients are more difficult to move from one stage of daily routine to another. For example, work on patients who require extensive personal care usually begins earlier than on self-care patients. This is done so that all patients tend to arrive at any stage of daily routine simultaneously. Some patients complain more than others. They usually are readied for any stage of daily routine much earlier or much later than other patients, personal care capacities being equal. If their complaints usually implore staff to ready them, the floor staff tends to attend to them much earlier than other patients in order to, as they would say, "get them off my back." If their complaints express sentiments against being involved in some stage of daily routine, they are readied much later than other patients. Overall, in dealing with specific patients, one "just has to be realistic," as floor staff says.

The characteristics of individual patients that floor staff takes into account in its routine work contrasts with the homogeneous conception of the patient that tends to dominate top staff's considerations. The patient that top staff usually "sees," however, the charted patient, is one that coincides with top staff's practical conception of patient care.

Since the normal routine of floor work and getting from one stage of it to another are what is considered the reality of patient care on the floor by the floor staff, only floor behavior that makes this routine unduly difficult is considered problematic patient activity. For instance, what are considered to be unrealistic statements in the RO sessions are largely ignored on the floors. The criterion for patient realism on the floor is entirely different from its criterion in the RO sessions. Should a patient mention that the day is Sunday when it is Wednesday, it depends on if he's in the RO session or on the floor whether he is referred to as confused and disoriented. In the RO session, he'd be confused. On the floor, he'd be ignored or acknowledged, but not usually labeled disoriented.

In sum, the realities of patient care as defined by the floor staff are related to the constraints of the situation they face in the nursing home. The dual relevances which they define emerge from a situation that is bounded, on the one hand, by individualistic, time-place centered policies of patient care, and on the other by patient-contingent care and routine-dependent patient lives.

Patients

Patients also are situated in the nursing home in such a way that particular definitions of patient care are generated out of the contingencies of their everyday routines. Two social settings provide evidence of what patients consider the realities of care. One of these is the RO sessions. Not all patients participate in them. Presently at Murray Manor, five patients participate regularly. There are other sessions currently in the works, however. The floors on which patients carry on the routines of daily living are the second setting. Each floor is made up of several different kinds of space which provide varying contexts for exploring patients' definitions of care. Floors are divided into the following spaces: patients' rooms, dining room, day rooms, bathroom (separate from each patient's private toilet), and a nurse's station.

The reality of care from the patients' point of view has four dimensions. One of these is their feeling that they are not simply patients, but also persons. Both floor staff and patients take this into account in their interactions. This feeling varies in intensity from patient to patient. Second, patients form social relationships with each other. Such relationships influence their definitions of what is considered good patient care. A third dimension of care that is relevant to patients is the contingencies of normal routine on the floor as it operates in practice. The fourth aspect of care involves judgments by patients about the relative contributions that floor and top staff make to their well-being in the home.

In any organized setting involving clientele, officers of the organization generally structure work in relation to the *collection* of persons constituting clientele. The planning of work and the facets of its procedure are defined in terms of the set of persons to be serviced. Even when a policy exists to provide "personalized service" to clients, the official organization's basic conception of clients is as *the* clientele which is to be given personalized service. From the organization's point of view, it would be considered absurd and redundant to formulate a "general" service policy that was *only* an aggregation of separate individual plans and procedures for each client. This would tend to make the organization less than what it characteristically is, namely, organized—which implies that there is some general mechanism linking its parts. When such a general mechanism exists, an organization of disparate elements emerges. Elements become parts of an organization. For example, a person becomes a patient. The very fact of organization means that persons involved have a more general life than their own individual ones and that the organization *per se* must treat individuals, to some minimal degree, as clientele or some other organizational category. It cannot do less and still be organized.

The same is true of the nursing home as an organization. Despite staff members' awareness of personal needs, persons who are serviced are always to some extent patients. There are organizational limits to "personalized" nursing care. However much the staff tries to make the organization less "institutional" for patients (and at Murray Manor, they try) it is limited by the organized constraints of their common circumstance.

From the patients' point of view, their interests as persons are at stake in the nursing home. The activation of such interests is what matters to the floor staff, for then they must somehow deal with it as part of normal work routine. Patients vary in the extent to which they actively demand personal interests to be considered by the floor staff.

A very important feature of care to patients is the degree to which they perceive it as being respectful of themselves as persons who have dignity in their own right, separate from the institution. To them, this is *rational* self-interest and not merely an aberration or some sign of confusion.

There are various places on the floor where this patient conception of respectful care is made evident. Take the following example. Sometimes as much as an hour and a half before it is time to eat, patients begin to be readied to be taken to the dining room. Staff takes into consideration the time needed to bring a variety of patients to table. Some patients are almost completely dependent on the physical assistance of their aides. And, patient calls for other than dining needs must be attended to. As patients are readied, they are wheeled into the dining room. Some, then, must sit at their table for an hour or so before all patients are present and their trays are brought up from the kitchen. Through experience, floor staff knows that it can minimize complaints and hostility about "letting us sit for hours in the dining room" by readying the non-complainers first and the complainers last. Occasionally, a problem arises, which may not be floor staff's mistake but for example, a result of trays arriving late. In such a circumstance, it is not uncommon to hear patients in the dining room comment hostilely that "that's no way to treat a person," or that "we're not cattle, you know, rushing us in here and making us wait."

When events occur on the floor that affect the personal dignity of several patients and all are aware of being collectively affected, the setting which most clearly provides evidence of the patients' concern for the personal dignities of patient care is the day room. Those patients who are physically able gather there and review their common indignity. Typically, this involves a detailed recollection of various aspects of the event. In relating these details to each other, each person's description is supported by every other person's acknowledgement. In this way, each member of the gathering is reinforced in his or her feeling of having been treated disrespectfully.

Such talk between patients about various indignities is not simple recollection. It is repeated reinforcement of at least two aspects of patient identity. One of these was described above, namely, the basic contention of each patient that he is also a person and deserves a certain degree of human respect from the staff. Further, patients are "sure" that they deserve basic respect because they are, "after all, elderly and ill." As they would typically say: "That's no way to treat a sick person. They should be ashamed," or "Who do they think they are? I've lived a lot longer than them and I should know better."

Patients' feelings about personal dignity are further evidenced in their sentiments about remuneration. Again, this follows from their assumption that they have rational self-interests. When patients talk about various indignities which they say they have experienced, they'll often state that they "don't deserve that because we pay plenty for being here." As one elderly man stated, "They're here to serve us. I don't know what the hell they think they're doing. We're not getting what we pay for. I'll tell you that much." Occasionally, a single patient will become indignant at some disrespect which he personally has experienced. For example, an elderly woman, who had a diarrhea problem, frequently needed help with toileting and would call the aides for assistance. She felt that she was being ignored more than the other patients. When she related her feelings about aides not respecting her personal needs, she cried: "Why don't they come. I pay here like everyone else. That's not asking too much."

Not only do patients define care in terms of personal respect and aid proportionate to payment rendered, but care, in their minds, has a social dimension. Patients who develop close friendship ties tend to judge care in terms of the relationship rather than personally. For example, two men who are roommates at Murray Manor, are avidly concerned for each other's welfare. When one is "shortchanged," the other will see to it that "he's taken care of." They like each other's company and are "grateful that they moved us into the same room." It has been suggested by one member of the top staff that one of these men could be moved to the first floor since he is ambulatory. Top staff usually takes an individualistic view of patient care. If such a move were implemented, it would be, as top staff would say, "for the good of the patient." The two roommates, however, define the good of patients to some extent as their common good. Patient care for them involves their common care. This is one example out of many in which top staff's definition of care contrasts with the more socially-oriented view of patients. From these roommates' perspective, moving one of them would be wanton disregard for a relationship from which they mutually benefit.

Avoidance relationships between patients also affect definitions of care from the patient's point of view. Between those who avoid one another, good care is considered to result from staff's efforts to keep them separated. From the patients' perspective, staff should be aware of this in dealing with them. Nevertheless, top staff often makes decisions that are ignorant of such relationships. Floor staff may indicate to their superiors that they are having problems with certain patients which they cannot handle themselves. However, in formulating solutions for such patient problems, the floor staff is rarely consulted. For example, top staff may decide to make a roommate out of a person who desires not to share a room with some other patient. One or both of them usually becomes quite indignant at such a decision. This generally prolongs difficulties for floor staff's normal routines. It is sometimes corrected by floor personnel further persuading top staff to alter the situation. Whether, in fact, it is corrected may be more fortuitous than rational.

Top staff usually cooperates with the floor staff in the long run after a request is made for some patient change. But, top staff's conception of patients as, first and foremost, individuals is always apparent. Typically, top staff personnel will remark: "I don't know what's the matter with her." or "These patients are just going to have to learn to live with each other."

A third dimension of patient care, from the patient's point of view, is what they see as the practice of normal routine on the floor. Normal routine is dependent both on patients' and floor staff's actions. It is an interactive process of moving from one point in daily living on the floor to another. These points are stage-like in that both floor staff and patients distinguish between groups of things that are done earlier in the day and other things that are done later.

Patients' time is structured by the routines of daily living, much like anybody's else's time. One main difference between patient time and time in the work-a-day world is that patients are dependent on floor staff for keeping track of it, while in the work-a-day world it is assumed that a person keeps track of time himself. Keeping track of time, then, is a social demand. If it is socially necessary, then not keeping time makes for problems in social interaction. Likewise, if it is not socially necessary, then keeping time also may produce problems in social interaction.

On the floors at Murray Manor, those patients who depend upon the floor staff and their routine readiness for proceeding through the stages of daily living pose relatively few problems for social interaction between them and the staff. This is most patients. It is common for patients, who are quite intelligible, to not know the day of the week or the time of day. When asked whether knowing such things is important, they typically respond that "it doesn't matter, anyway." The few patients that do keep track of clock time, but still depend on floor routine for being ready, may say that "it's nice to know what time it is," or something to that effect. Keeping time for them is something done out of habit and enjoyment. Some of them keep track of time because they have varied daily social ties with persons outside the nursing home. Patients who maintain such ties explain that they keep track of time because their "people expect them to be on time."

There is an occasional patient at Murray Manor who keeps track of clock time and seriously uses it to structure the routines of daily living. Proper care, to such patients, means providing care readily and on schedule. Floor staff considers such patients as impatient. They tend to hamper the flow of floor routine both for floor staff and other patients. For example, a patient who is being given a treatment may have to be momentarily left unattended in order to fulfill the "scheduled" request of a time-oriented patient. Such patients, however, are not typical.

Time-orientation also has a longitudinal aspect. Many patients, when they first enter the nursing home, keep track of time. This seems to subside as patients become accustomed to floor routine. This initial time-keeping is part of the reason that some patients are referred to as "agitated" by the floor staff in their first days in residence. This reference tends to disappear along with floor staff's annoyance as patients become dependent on floor routine.

Given the typical irrelevance of keeping clock time on the floor and the problems that keeping clock time poses, it seems ironic that an attempt is being made in the RO sessions to train patients to keep track of time. When this seeming contradiction is placed in the context of the situations that brought it into existence, however, it is understandable. As was mentioned above, top staff's view of patients and their care needs is an indirect product of how official patients are defined as well as constraints on its own time. The first of these makes for a work-a-day conception of patient actions while the second prevents this conception from being contradicted. Both of these factors tend to put top staff in the business of training patients for an irrelevant world.

It should be noted here that the reason that many patients do not keep track of clock time is not that they cannot. It is that it does not seem reasonable for them to do so. When it is reasonable, they become time-oriented. For example, one woman who is a regular attendant at the RO sessions is rarely correct when she is quizzed about the time of various events in a typical day at Murray Manor. To her, "all of this is crazy." She usually is said to be disoriented. One day, as she was trudging past the nurses' station, I asked her (with a mild sense of urgency) if she happened to know the time. She immediately looked at the clock above the nurses' station and said it was ten minutes past two.

A fourth dimension of patients' definition of care is located in their judgment about the relative contributions of top and floor staff to their well-being. Whenever patients feel that the quality of their care is getting poor, they blame both the top and floor staff, but for different reasons. Floor staff is blamed for not doing their job, which patients refer to as "service."[3] Top staff is blamed for not doing their job, which patients say is to see that things are "going right" on the floors.

When patients are angry about the quality of service, they initially blame the floor staff for any indignities which they've suffered. Patients will name specific aides whom they feel are poor workers. Aides cited vary from patient to patient. When patients are probed further on the general quality of aides, they typically refuse to generalize to all of them and usually state: "Well, they're not all bad. Some of them are very good." What follows from this, however, is commonly a general statement

---

[3] The fact that patients call "service" what staff calls "care," is further evidence of patients' rational interest in themselves as persons separate from the organization. For a theoretical treatment of the absence of this kind of distinction as a criticism of functionalism, see Alvin Gouldner's discussion in his paper "Reciprocity and Autonomy in Functional Theory" in Gross (1959).

about the top staff. It is usual for such statements to refer to "the lack of proper management here." As one patient said: "If they'd [top staff] do their job right, the nurses[4] would be nicer or they'd ship 'em out."

Patients justify their general opinion about the lack of management by the top staff through one of two examples. One involves the administrator of the nursing home and the other refers to its medical director. These are the people on the top staff whom they know by position. Other top staff positions typically are not delineated by patients.

The administrator is generally said to be the reason why "everything's not on the up-and-up." One patient stated that the "big boss" couldn't possibly know what's going on because "you just never see him around." Another patient said that the only time she ever sees him, "he's running around with papers in his hand." These are typical comments made about the administrator. Generally, patients say that he's not available when you want to see him and that they never see him in the hall. This, to patients, "is obviously why the care here is not up to snuff."

Some references are made to the medical director that place blame on him for problems that patients have with aides, especially those that are related to feelings of being neglected medically. Patients will say that ever since they had to change doctors when they entered the nursing home, "things have never been the same." They typically will complain that the doctor hardly visits them or that they haven't seen him in a month, and "when I do, he does a real rush job—in and out—just like that."

As with top and floor staff, patients' definitions of the realities of patient care are understandable when their situation in the nursing home is delineated. The situation in which they carry on their daily living makes reasonable a view of care that differs from the reality of others. All are reasonable in the contexts in which they occur.

----

[4] Patients usually refer to floor personnel as "nurses," not differentiating between RNs and LPNs (nurses) and nurse's aides.

ACCOMMODATIONS BETWEEN DEFINITIONS

Social organizations that differentially constrain persons within them make for concomitant variations in their views of the organization, and their relationship to it. Murray Manor is a long-term care organization with three fairly distinct complexes of roles, the actors of which perceive patient care differently and define relevances that coincide reasonably with their perceptions. Variations in patient care realities are rational when they are considered analytically from their respective situated points of view.

Stating that all three patient care realities discussed above are rational is reasonable from a sociological point of view. But, from the point of view of actors located in any particularly situated roles, the rationality of definitions of patient care tends to be situation-specific. Since actors carry situation-specific definitions of patient care, on the one hand, and are organizationally constrained to interact with one another, on the other, a major situational problem for them is dealing with varying definitions of patient care. In what ways is accommodation accomplished by actors?

Three structural conditions influence definitional accommodations at Murray Manor. One of these is the administrative and floor constraints that usually keep top and floor staff working in separate areas of the nursing home (with the exception of some patient care conferences). This separation of workplace tends to make for less pressure on personnel to deal with varied definitions of patient care than would be the case if top and floor staff "worked together." A second structural condition is the hierarchical relationship that exists between top staff and floor staff. Top staff has authority over floor staff. Because of this, definitional accommodation is a more serious problem for floor personnel than for the top staff. Floor staff tends to deal with the definitional differences between itself and top staff rather than the reverse. A third structural condition influencing accommodation is the location of the floor staff between the official organizational hierarchy and its clientele. The work of floor staff is constrained by both top staff directives and patient demands. On the floors, these often become antithetical constraints on normal work routine. Floor staff knows that it is bound by top staff's policies, but it also "knows the realities" of patient life in a way that top staff does not. Top staff and patients rarely encounter each other. Because of their location in the organization, the business of accommodating definitional realities devolves largely upon the floor staff in working with top staff or patients.

Practical Rule-Breaking

Top staff issues a variety of directives about patient care procedure. These directives are based on its particular view of the realities of care. This view considers patients to be individuals who are to be provided by the floor staff with total patient care. The floor staff, in dealing with patients on the floors, must take into account the social contingencies between patients as well as the relationship between patients and its own work routines. Top staff's individualistic conception of total patient care sometimes clashes with social contingencies between patients, and between staff and patients on the floor. In these circumstances, floor staff, temporarily, will break rules made by top staff in order to resolve what they know is a patient care dilemma.

Rule-breaking is conceived by the floor staff to be a practical and circumstantial procedure used to resolve care dilemmas. It is not considered to be permanent. Floor staff knows it is breaking rules momentarily, but it usually feels it is justified "for the good of all concerned." As one aide mentioned: "This way, no one suffers. We do what we can for the patient and when it's all over, no one knows what went on anyway."

In temporarily breaking rules, floor staff does not consider itself to be undermining directives. On the whole, floor staff has great respect for its superiors, especially the administrative nurses. Rather, floor staff's attitude toward its superiors when breaking rules is one of both sympathy and appreciation: sympathy for what they consider are the fine intentions of the administrative nurses, but appreciation of the fact that top staff "simply doesn't know some of the things we face on the floor."

In the minds of floor staff personnel, practical rule-breaking is made possible by two conditions of floor life at the nursing home. First, rule-breaking depends significantly on the relative absence of top staff from the floors. Second, the floor staff usually does not break rules unless it feels that it has a justification that top staff will accept, should the latter encounter the practice. The following examples of practical rule-breaking should illustrate these conditions.

Top staff feels that good patient care involves attending to the total needs of each individual patient. When a patient buzzes for a nurse, this means that the floor staff should attend to the call. This directive ignores both the routine tasks with other patients in which floor staff is involved as well as excesses in patient demands.

There is a female patient at Murray Manor who is known on the floor as a "nag." She is capable of attending to a variety of personal needs herself but will call the nurses to attend to them. When she makes what the floor staff considers a reasonable request, she is most often told that it will be handled shortly if floor-timing makes it difficult to fulfill at the moment. For instance, this patient often requests to be taken to occupational therapy (OT) in the morning, but does so before the therapists have begun their work with patients. In spite of being told of this she continues to regularly buzz the nurses to be taken to OT. It is common for her to put her buzzer on and then to proceed to another room to visit a friend, whereupon the aides will simply turn her buzzer off. This "nagging" does not depend upon nor does it make any concessions to the timing of normal work routines on the floor.

This patient's calls often are ignored on the floors, except when the call is from the patient's toilet (which is a buzzer that sounds different than the room buzzer) or when the call coincides with normal work routine. When asked what they would say if the top staff knew that this patient were being ignored, floor staff personnel typically will mention one of two justifications. They'll answer, with nonchalance, that "they're never around anyway." When probed on what they'd do if top staff were around, they answer that "everyone knows what that patient is like—they [top staff] can ask anyone on the floor."

Murray Manor has one patient in residence who is not elderly. She is a 27 year old terminal diabetic. When she first entered the nursing home, she was given privileges not commonly given to other patients—partially because she is young and partially because she is explicitly diagnosed as and knows that she is terminal (cf. Glaser and Strauss, 1965: 206-207). She was allowed to eat anything that she desired and to smoke in her room. Whenever the aides move her in the slightest way, she grimaces and agonizes over her pain. When she is being wheeled about in her chair, the slightest jar makes her groan and cry.

Sometime after her initial entrance to the home, top staff informed the charge nurse on the floor that the patient was now to be treated like the other patients. This meant that any smoking was to be done only in the dining room. The charge nurse informed the other floor personnel of the new directive.

The new directive did not dramatically change floor staff's routine treatment of the patient. Allowing her to smoke in her room had coincided well with normal work routine. They sympathized with her desires and at the same time, taking her to the dining room to smoke would have meant that one aide's bed-and-body work would have gone unattended. An aide would not only have had to go through the slow, agonizing process of taking the patient to the dining room but also sit with the patient until she finished her cigarette. When the new directive was issued, some of the aides saw no reason why something that had worked so well before should now be discontinued.

Floor staff took advantage of three conditions in continuing this patient's old routine. First, top staff (especially the administrator, who issued the new directive) is rarely on the floor. Second, the patient's room is immediately next to the nurse's station where "we can keep an eye on her anyway." And third, there is evidence that some aides would plead ignorance of the new directive if necessary.

Accommodating Patients

Patients hold a definition of themselves as persons as well as patients. They feel that part of good care ("service") involves respect for that definition. Most patients depend on normal floor routine to structure their lives. From the patient's point of view the bounds of dependence on and patience with normal floor routine hinge on how seriously they consider their demand for respect as persons. Those patients who most seriously consider their interests as persons tend to be the least patient with normal floor routine; those who show little or no evidence of being self-interested tend to be the most patient and dependent on normal floor routine. Thus, the extent to which patients make distinctions between themselves as patients and as persons, influences where they set the bounds of (tolerance for) normal routine.

Floor staff knows of these individual differences between patients and tries to accommodate them within the bounds of what they themselves consider normal floor routine. The general bounds which floor staff considers to encompass normal routine are usually wide enough to accommodate a broad range of patients.

The general bounds defined by floor staff vary somewhat between the two patient floors at Murray Manor. They are wider on the third than on the fourth floor. Aides will often say that "it's hard to work with patients on the third floor because some are so alert." They feel constrained to handle a wider range of patient demands than on the fourth floor. Consequently, from floor staff's point of view, patient demands that are treated as normal routine on one floor may be considered excessive on the other. In such cases, it is common to hear an aide say of a patient that "she just doesn't belong up here."

Within the bounds of what they consider normal floor routine, staff accommodates patients' variable personal demands by sequencing them. Demanding patients' tend to be dealt with first while staff feels that it can afford to leave less demanding ones until later in any stage of daily living. As one aide remarked: "She's sharp as a whip. You can't push her around and make her wait like some of the others." This sequencing of patients maintains the "normality" of both floor staff's and patients' definitions of routine respectability.

Accommodating Top Staff

Top staff considers patients as individuals. Whenever they receive reports of patients acting "peculiarly," they usually locate the cause in the individual patient. Such patients are said to be acting the way they are because they are confused, disoriented, or agitated—or simply not in reality. Top staff's formal considerations of patients occurs in their patient care conferences. In this setting, patients are reviewed, their behavior is diagnosed, and an approach is formulated. All of this is done with an individualistic conception of the patient in mind.

Occasionally, top staff will invite a member of the floor personnel to a staffing so as to get what top staff calls "the floor staff's point of view." When a floor aide or nurse attends a staffing, she sits "alone," i.e. she is the sole representative of a world the routine contingencies of which are largely unknown to or not aligned with the conceptions of the top staff, especially the non-nursing administration which includes the administrator, medical director, social worker, chaplain, and occupational therapist. Not only does the floor staff member represent the floor on her own, but she faces her employers, some of whom command considerable public prestige independent of their status as employers, namely, the physician and the chaplain.

The level at which conversation is carried on in the PCC is well above the usual level of floor talk engaged in by aides and floor nurses. After their experience at a PCC, floor personnel often will comment that they "couldn't understand half of what was going on at that staffing." They never admit this publicly at the PCC nor do they ask for clarification of something they do not understand. Typically, floor staff members invited to the PCC remain silent during much of what is informal discussion of patients by top staff.

When a member of the floor staff is invited to comment on the proceedings, she faces a quite formidable audience: professionally, educationally, and administratively. Typically the aide or nurse will agree with what has been said, acknowledging top staff's diagnosis and prescription for the patient being considered. She may even add anecdotal credence to the discussion by citing instances of patient behavior that exemplify what top staff has discussed during the staffing. This is always warmly appreciated by the top staff. For example, the medical director is quite indulgent in expressing gratitude for the "light that you've shed on this case," as a floor staff member is thanked for offering her "expertise" to the staffing. Thus, patient care policies developed by the top staff emerge from and are corroborated out of the same ground, namely, the patient care world as defined by top staff.

During the PCCs, floor staff never contradicts the behavior diagnoses of and approach to particular patients formulated by the top staff. In the context of the PCC, the floor aides or nurses witness the development of a rationale for some approach that it to be taken with the patient being staffed, and accept it seriously. Floor staff accommodates itself to the patient care world of top staff.

In actually dealing (behaviorally) with patients on the floors, however, a whole set of other relevances are taken into consideration by the floor staff. Normal floor routine, with its varied social contingencies, is at stake. There is little behavioral transfer from the context of patient care at staffings to its context on the floor. However, there is some linguistic transfer. Floor staff may "explain" a patient's behavior to themselves and each other in the same language heard at staffings. But, they *act* in terms of a more social model of patient care. This difference between the transfer of patient care language and patient care behavior from the staffing conference to the floor is not apparent when floor staff is simply asked about patients and their relations with them. The difference must be observed.[5]

---

[5] For a more analytic discussion of the difference between talk about and the practice of everyday life, see Aaron Cicourel's paper "Basic and Normative Rules in the Negotiation of Status and Role," in Sudnow (1972).

Accommodating Floor Staff

In its work with patients, floor staff occasionally will be pressured by one of them to change rooms. Although most new or reassigned patients do not request room changes, when requests are made, they tend to occur soon after a new patient has been assigned to a room or an old patient has been reassigned to another one.

Patient demands on floor staff usually build up gradually. At first, floor staff does not respond significantly to this pressure. There is a certain degree of pressure from patients that floor staff will tolerate within the bounds of normal work routine. Floor staff tries to accommodate patients who desire room changes by "telling them that they can live with each other if they try." Sometimes, floor staff will try to explain to such patients that they have no authority to change patients' rooms (which is true) and that "if some patients had their rooms changed as they wished, then everyone would want their rooms changed." This, of course, is not true since several roommates are good friends and prefer sharing a room with each other than with anyone else.

As patient demands for room changes go beyond what floor staff feels it can handle within the bounds of normal routine, requests for room changes are referred to the top staff. Top staff usually considers such patients' requests unrealistic. It is not uncommon for top staff to remark that "these patients will just have to face reality," the request for a room change being denied. With continued complaints from floor personnel, top staff usually comes around and reassigns rooms. This may accommodate the floor staff as far as normalizing floor routine, if reassignments happen to make for patient accommodation.

Such patients tend to be defined as unrealistic by top staff personnel long after their problematic floor behavior has been resolved for the floor staff. After a patient's room has been changed, top staff may even have a staffing on him because of his unrealistic demands, and plan an approach to him. This approach, ostensibly, is to be carried out on the floor as a way to "bring the patient over to a more realistic attitude." The approach is rarely implemented, because (1) floor staff often is not told directly about a new approach decided upon in the PCC, the new approach being placed in the patient's chart and (2) when they are told, they may agree to its rationale but it does not usually become part of normal floor routine (which is not individually structured). Because patients often "settle down" after a room change has been made, top staff's new approach to such patients is not put into practice on the floor since it "would be a waste of time" or "simply is no longer needed."

CONCLUSION

When the varied situations of an organization, such as a nursing home, are examined sociologically, multiple definitions emerge of what is officially defined as a common concern. These definitions are rational conceptions of the internal world of the organization as seen from the perspective of various situations structured within it. Situations constrain actors differently. They constrain them to define the importance of various kinds of behavior in ways that may be at odds with one another. Because of these variations, actors make attempts to accommodate their definitions so that each can get on with the business of their own work. In this paper, I have discussed three major dimensions, both simultaneously and separately, of the social organization of multiple realities in a nursing home.

The multiple realities of patient care at Murray Manor are sustained by the structure of the organization as well as the accommodations that actors in various situations make with each other. Any new care policies promulgated by the top staff are confronted by the compound resistance of organizational structure and actor accommodations. Because of this, they tend to congeal as policy (cf. Scheff, 1961). The context of policy-making remains separate from the context of patient care practice.

When the multiple realities of a nursing home are examined in terms of their place in the everyday lives of persons that hold them, the rationality of each definition becomes apparent. We come away from the nursing home with the conclusion that its social constraints make for several normal worlds, one of which is official and the others not. Within each of these worlds, life goes on. Between them, actors try to accommodate themselves to what they often feel are irrational demands on their lives in the organization. They do so because they know that the integrity of their own worlds and lives depends on it.

REFERENCES

Berger, Peter, and Luckmann, Thomas: *The Social Construction of Reality.* New York, Doubleday, 1966.

Cicourel, Aaron: Basic and normative rules in the negotiation of status and role. In Sudnow, David (Ed.): *Studies in Social Interaction,* New York, Macmillan, 1972, pp. 229-258.

Emerson, Joan P.: Behavior in private places: sustaining definitions of reality in gynecological examinations. In Dreitzel, Hans Peter (Ed.): *Recent Sociology No. 2,* New York, Macmillan, 1970, pp. 74-97.

Gerth, Hans, and Mills, C. Wright: *Character and Social Structure.* New York, Harcourt, Brace & World, 1953.

Glaser, Barney G., and Strauss, Anselm L.: *Awareness of Dying.* Chicago, Aldine, 1965.

Gouldner, Alvin W.: Reciprocity and autonomy in functional theory. In Gross, Llewellyn (Ed.): *Symposium on Sociological Theory,* New York, 1959, pp. 241-270.

Ichheiser, Gustav: *Appearances and Realities.* San Francisco, Jossey-Bass, 1970.

Scheff, Thomas J.: Control over policy by attendants in a mental hospital, *Journal of Health and Human Behavior,* 2:93-105, 1961.

CHAPTER 5

LIFE GOES ON: SOCIAL ORGANIZATION IN A FRENCH RETIREMENT RESIDENCE

JENNIE-KEITH ROSS

BECAUSE AGE IS universally available as a principle of social organization and yet is put to a wide diversity of uses as a social border through life cycles or within societies, it fits perfectly into the paradigm for cross-cultural research.[1] One particular use of age as a marker of social separation is a new development in several modern industrial societies where retirement villages, hotels, communities, cities or "worlds" represent an explicit residential separation by age. Because these residential settings for retired people are restricted by age, and because they are embedded in the context of complex societies, they seem to be structurally similar to other embedded communities which are homogeneous in terms of at least one characteristic, such as those

[1] This is a revised version of a paper presented to the session on Anthropology of the Aged chaired by Professor Jane Murphy at the 70th annual meeting of the American Anthropological Association, New York City, November 21, 1971. The research on which the paper is based was carried out from June 1969 to August 1970 and supported by National Institute of Mental Health Fellowship and Research Grant MH-37442. The research would not have been possible without the permission and active assistance of M. Y. Pergeaux, Director General of the Caisse Nationale de Retraite des Ouvriers du Batiment et des Trauvaux Publiques, of M. le Docteur J. Huet, Anthropological and Medical Consultant to the C.N.R.O., of M. O. de Moussac, Director of the Centre de Gerontologie Sociale, and of M. J-P. Guérillon, former Director of the Residence Les Floralies at Bagnolet. I am very grateful to them and to Professor Ethel Shanas who introduced me to the C.N.R.O. The retired residents of Les Floralies were not only willing and generous informants, but also made us feel comfortable and at home among them. Professors Marc Howard Ross and Roger Cobb made very helpful comments on both versions of this paper.

which develop inside prisons and mental institutions, or through utopian experiments. The same general theoretical question which has been raised about these communities needs to be directed toward retirement residences: what are the relationships between the internal social organization of these embedded communities and the social organization of their context society? Since it requires description of social organization in a retirement community, the answer to this question may also provide a basis for objective evaluation of popular images of these residences as "fogey farms," "human scrapheaps" or "waiting rooms for death."

RESEARCH SETTING

The retirement residence where this research took place is in Bagnolet, France, a working class suburb just across the eastern city limits of Paris. France has a range of retirement housing comparable to that in the United States, sponsored by various levels of government, by unions, religious groups and private developers (Pergeaux, 1968; Haut Comité, 1962).

The "Residence Les Floralies" at Bagnolet is a thirteen story glass and concrete building which represents a dramatic transplant in physical setting for the residents, who are all members of a retirement fund for construction workers (Caisse de Retraite National des Ouvriers du Batiment and des Travaux Publiques), ranging from road pavers to painters and masons. Only fourteen of the 127 residents could afford to pay the six dollars (30 NF) per day for a private apartment, all meals and complete medical care; the others were paid for by government assistance (L'aide Sociale). Except for two floors reserved for individuals who were not well enough to do their own housekeeping, every apartment had a small kitchen and a private bathroom.

This residence was especially suited to research on sources of social organization for several reasons. First, its location near bus and subway stops made contact with friends and relatives possible for the residents, who had all spent most of their adult lives in the Paris region. These circumstances make it reasonable to consider patterns of social contact outside the residence in terms of choice, without too much concern about the constraints of distance which are obvious in more isolated retirement housing. Second, the central dining room in this building provided a public arena where all residents saw each other at least once a day, since they were required to eat the noon meal there. Especially in the early stages of the research, this public scene was crucial for making contacts, as the residents otherwise spent a great deal of their time in their individual apartments. Also, the residence was not full when we arrived, and about fifty people arrived during our stay. It was consequently possible to observe the socialization process in detail, by going with the driver to pick up the new-comers at their homes and then following them closely through observation and interviews during their first months.

There were 127 residents at Les Floralies by the end of our year in Bagnolet. The youngest person was sixty-one, a woman married to an older man. The oldest was ninety-one, and the average age was seventy-five. There were eighty-one women and forty-six men. Fourteen married couples lived in the residence, eighty-seven widows and widowers, and twelve people who were single or divorced. Fifty-seven percent lived alone before entering the residence, 20 percent alone with a spouse, and 5 percent with children (Table 5-I).

TABLE 5-I

SOCIAL CHARACTERISTICS OF RESIDENTS*

Characteristic	
Average Age	75
Female	64%
Martial Status:	
Married	22%
Widowed	69%
Divorced or Single	9%
Receive Government Assistance to Meet Costs of Living in Residence	90%
Have Children	47%
Average Length of Time in Residence	12 months

———
* The figures in this table are based on data for the total residence population of 127.

An eighty-six year old man walked out of the residence one morning, leaving behind a note saying he was going to live with his mistress in Paris. This "run-away" did not really have to run away; he walked out the front door into the daylight with his suitcase in his hand. The residence is always open. The people who lived there came and went at all hours, although they were asked to notify the nurse if they planned to be away for more than a few days. The director, the business manager, a secretary, the nurse, four nurse's aides, and a chauffeur lived in a separate wing of the residence building and ate either at home or in the staff dining room. Four waitresses, two cooks, a medical secretary, an accountant, two cleaning women, and a laundress came in to work every day. A doctor, a physical therapist, and a pottery instructor followed a regular schedule of visits to the residence.

Attitudes toward the staff varied from a view of them as benefactors to the opposite perception of them as employees of the residents. These attitudes tended to correspond with the two political factions in the community. Except for the director and the nurse, staff members did not exercise great control over the residents. The other employees knew that they were likely to be fired if they did not get along with the old people; and the residents knew that their complaints were taken seriously. Even the director and the nurse did not have complete control since the residents could leave permanently if they wanted. The residence is consequently not a total institution as Goffman defines it, since it lacks the characteristics of restricted access to the outside and caste-like dominance of the staff (Goffman, 1961).

HYPOTHESES ABOUT SOCIAL ORGANIZATION

The possible relationships between the internal social organization of the embedded community and the social organization of its external context can be expressed concisely in terms of three alternative hypotheses: 1) that the internal social organization will be as far as possible a reflection of the external. Inmates of a women's prison in West Virginia, for instance, recreated a detailed version of the American kinship system—including spouses, children, brothers and sisters, grandparents, cousins, aunts and uncles (Giallombardo, 1966). The internal social organization of a community embedded in a wider society may also represent 2) a reaction against some aspect of the external social organization, in particular the external significance of the characteristic in terms of which the embedded community is homogeneous. Its significance would then be reversed into a "first shall be last and last shall be first" pattern. Hutterites, for example, have organized independent communities called Bruderhof where members of the sect live in a communal, spiritual, pacifist way. The social organization of a Bruderhof is explicitly dedicated to overcoming the individualistic, materialist and violent values which Hutterites feel dominate the wider American society (Hoestetler and Huntington, 1967) 3) The external significance of a social characteristic may also be simply refused in a pattern which makes the characteristic irrelevant to internal social organization. In a condominium residence for retired people in northern California, community members exerted strong sanctions against attempts to make external social status relevant to life in the community. One man who insisted on calling attention to his wealth by expanding his housing unit to distinguish it from the others and who tried to demand respect on the basis of his previous occupation as a stock broker was finally deposed from a position on the elected governing committee. The widely expressed explanation for his removal from office was his desire to "live in the past" and consequently to threaten the solidarity of the community in the present (cf. Ross, 1968, Chapter 8).

INVESTIGATION OF THE HYPOTHESES

The first step toward evaluation of these three hypotheses in terms of social organization at Les Floralies was to identify the basic outlines of social behavior in this community. Participant observation is the method ideally suited for discovery of this initial map of social relations. The first stage of participant observation is a mutual search for comfortable, consistent patterns of social contact between a researcher and people who often participate in a different culture and speak a different language. Young researchers in a community of old people face an additional difference in generation. The role of a staff member seemed to offer too narrow a view of life in the residence, so I chose the more general role of a person interested in the problems of old people. We moved into an apartment on one of the regular floors of the residence. Eating in the dining room every noon, at a different table every day, led to invitations to visit most residents. Seating arrangements also provided a natural map of social relations since people tended to keep their seats at tables for four unless strong attraction or rejection motivated a change. These early contacts in turn led to participation in a variety of regular activities: meetings of the social committee of six elected residents; card games with the men after lunch; sewing and knitting with a women's group; work with residents in the kitchen, office, garden, laundry room; sitting in the clinic waiting room on the doctor's visiting days; trips to the nearby cafe for a morning glass of white wine and to the twice-weekly open market in the town; watching movies or television in the public lounge. Some extraordinary events also occurred during this period, such as Christmas celebrations and a highly conflictual election of representatives to the residents committee.

This initial period of observation first of all revealed that there is social organization in the residence: there are both informal and formal groups, clearly defined and persistent factions, norms for behavior distinct from rules imposed by the administration, and a distinctive socialization process through which new residents are inducted into the community. In addition, these early observations suggested other kinds of evidence for evaluation of the hypotheses about sources of social order in the residence.

Specific aspects of the organization of social life at Bagnolet were formalized into variables for which every resident could be given a score. Rating every resident on such characteristics as frequency of leaving the residence, performance of work roles, popularity or unpopularity made my observations more rigorous because it required a commitment to a relative ranking for every individual. This method was also a precaution against a dangerously eager group of volunteer informants, predominantly leaders of the political factions trying to make sure that I saw things clearly, and from their point of view. Gaps in the information also became very obvious early enough in the field work that there was still time to fill them in. The last advantage of this technique is that it provides data which can be analyzed quantitatively (cf. Ross and Ross, 1974).

Detailed information about location of friends and relatives outside the residence and amount of contact with them, as well as a variety of attitudes about life in the residence and in the world in general, were obtained from a questionnaire. Scores on the dimensions of participation, questionnaire responses, and the results of continuing participant observation provide the information needed to evaluate the alternative explanations of social organization in an embedded community in the specific setting of Les Floralies. Social status, general level of internal interaction, participation in formal groups, work roles and visiting with other residents represent patterns of social behavior inside the residence. Age, health, contacts with family and friends outside the residence, and former roles such as occupation, marriage, and political identification represent external sources of social identity which may be reflected, reversed or irrelevant in the social organization of the residence.

Sources of Social Organization—Age

'He really looks out for our interests because he knows how to talk to the big wheels' and 'Just because he's on a committee he thinks he's better than the rest of us' are representative of frequent and contradictory comments about the president of the Residence Committee. Relative statuses were clearly present at Les Floralies; some residents were perceived, sometimes with admiration and sometimes with resentment, as being more important than others. How to attach concrete markers to social ranking in the residence was not at all clear, since the familiar

measures of status—occupation, income, and education—are
washed out by the relative homogeneity of the community in
terms of all these criteria. Friendships did not follow the lines
of specific jobs within the construction trades. Differences in
education and income were minimal, and most residents knew
very little about each other in these terms. The basic assumption
was that everyone had very little schooling, and that except
for a few "rich" people who could pay for themselves, everyone
was poor. Although residents knew that a few people paid
their own fees, none could identify more than one or two of them.[2]

Observation and questioning suggested three measures of
social rank in the residence: formal and informal leadership
roles; popularity, or being liked by a large number of other
residents; and visibility, or being known and recognized by a
large number of other residents.[3] Everyone in the community
was given a score on each of these characteristics, and the total
is a measure of his social status. The three hypotheses about
sources of internal organization in embedded communities then
can be interpreted as explanations for different levels of social
status: the first explains it as a reflection of status outside, the
second explains it through the reversal of external standards,
the third predicts their irrelevance. In the setting of a retirement
community the reflection hypothesis suggests that the individuals
with higher social status should be those with the characteristics
that are positively valued in the wider society. Since old age
is negatively valued, the younger members of the community
should have higher status. The alternative hypotheses predict
either that values on age should be reversed, so that the oldest
among the old should have high status, or that residents should
escape from the values placed on age outside by making it
irrelevant to social organization inside. The table of correlations

---

[2] Paying fees as opposed to welfare sponsorship was weakly correlated with
social status, but when the intervening effects of political identification were
controlled for, the relationship was greatly reduced and was no longer significant.

[3] Factor analysis of my ratings on these three characteristics showed that
they cluster together as a single dimension.

(Table 5-II) shows that at Les Floralies age is not at all related to social status.[4]

TABLE 5-II

CORRELATIONS BETWEEN SOCIAL STATUS, INTERNAL INTERACTION, FORMAL GROUP PARTICIUATION, POSSESSION OF A WORK ROLE, VISITING OTHER FAMILY, CONTACTS WITH FRIENDS OUTSIDE RESIDENCE, STRENGTH OF POLITICAL IDENTIFICATION AND FACTIONAL ALLEGIANCE[a]

	Social Status	Internal Interaction	Formal Group Participation	Possession of Work Role	Visiting Other Residents
Age	.03 (126)	—.13 (125)	.05 (120)	—.13 (120)	—.11 (64)
High Self-Evaluation of Health	.14 (73)	.15 (73)	.21* (68)	.27** (68)	.00 (65)
Contact with Family	.07 (45)	—.04 (45)	—.10 (42)	—.02 (42)	.20 (40)
Contacts with Friends outside Residence	.11 (67)	.04 (67)	—.20 (63)	—.10 (63)	—.05 (64)
Strength of Political Identification	.66** (126)	.50** (126)	.15 (121)	.17* (121)	.32** (65)
Factional Allegiance (Communist vs. Non-Communist)	—.03 (126)	—.09 (126)	—.23** (121)	—.02 (121)	—.04 (65)

Sample sizes in parentheses
* Significant at the .05 level
** Significant at the .01 level
[a] The variables are measured in the following manner:
1) *Social status* is a scale based on scores on my rankings of individuals according to observation of their leadership roles, popularity, and visibility.
   A high score on *leadership* indicates that according to my observations an individual was often seen as a task, emotional, or opinion leader by other residents. A medium score indicates that an individual was sometimes seen as a leader; a low score indicates that he was rarely or never seen as a leader.
   Popularity scores are based on my observations of the numbers of people by whom an individual was liked and the intensity of their expression of this attitude. Individuals were scored separately on numbers and intensity, and then the scores were combined; a high on numbers and a low on intensity would produce a popularity score of medium.
   Visibility scores (high, medium, low) are based on my observations of the extent to which an individual is known in the community, either by name or by an outstanding characteristic or activity.

---

[4] Friedman reports that age and seniority (length of residence) combined were sources of popularity in an American home for aged Episcopalian women (Friedman, 1967).

2) *Internal interaction* scores are based on my observations of both frequency and intensity of an individual's social interaction with other residents. A high score indicates either a high level of interaction or several close friends or a combination of these. Medium indicates several social contacts or at least one close friend. Low indicates few social contacts and no close friend.

3) *Formal group participation* refers to institutionalized public contact with other residents through participation in regular public groups, e.g., the residence committee, the sewing club, television in the lounge, pottery class, card games. A high score indicates my observation of an individual's formal group participation about five times a week; medium score indicates participation about once a week; low score indicates rare participation or never.

4) *Possession of a work role* is defined by both participation in work activities and identification by other residents as having a work role. High score indicates that according to my observations an individual works regularly and is clearly identified in a work role. Medium indicates that an individual works occasionally when needed, but identification with the work role is not strong. Low indicates that a person never or very rarely works.

5) *Visiting other residents* is an index based on responses to two questionnaire items:
   a) When was the last time you visited another resident? Within the last week? Within the last month? More than a month ago?
   b) When was the last time another resident came to see you? (Same response categories.)

6) *Age* is chronological age in July, 1970, as reported in the residence records.

7) *Self-evaluation of health* is based on responses to a questionnaire item:
   By comparison with other people your age, do you think that your health is excellent, good, fair, or poor?

8) *Contacts with family* is an index constructed from the following questionnaire items:
   a) When was the last time you saw one of your children? Within the last week, during the last month, during the last year?
   b) When was the last time you saw one of your grandchildren?
   c) When was the last time you saw one of your sisters?
   d) When was the last time you saw one of your brothers?
   (same response categories as above)
   The score on contacts with family is the highest (most recent) response to any of these items.

9) *Contacts with friends outside* the residence is scored on the basis of response to a questionnaire item:
   When was the last time you saw a friend who does not live in the residence? During the last week, during the last month, during the last year?

10) *Strength of political identification* is a score based on my observations of the extent to which an individual was identified by other residents as being aligned with either the Catholic-Socialist coalition or the Communist opposition. A high score indicates that an individual was clearly identified, medium that he was partially or vaguely identified, low that he was not identified at all.

11) *Factional allegiance* is a score based on my observations of the direction of an individual's political identification: not Communist, tendency toward being not Communist, neutral, tendency toward being Communist, Communist.

Satisfying routines of regular social contact may exist with or without the formalities of public meeting places, specified meeting times, and explicit shared goals. Various jobs in the residence, sewing on one afternoon a week, the pottery class, the Residence Committee, the Menu Committee, afternoon card games and television in the public lounge offered possibilities for formal group participation. Visiting with other residents, usually in the privacy of an apartment, was the major kind of informal social activity. A resident's age had no effect on his or her tendency to belong to formal recreational or work groups, or on the extent of visiting with other members of the community. In the case of age, description of external sources of organization as irrelevant seems the most adequate.

Sources of Social Organization—Health

One eighty year old woman shuffled her painful way to a chair near the dining room door every morning, her worn flannel robe always contradicted by the beret that showed she was "dressed." Although she shouted insults at anyone who sat in the chair she thought of as hers or who left open the door into the hall, "La Mama" was surrounded by an attentive group of residents before and after every meal. Rather than being a source of social isolation or low status, this woman's frailty may explain her prominence. Since she could not wash or dress herself or clean her own apartment, she needed a great deal of care from the staff, and the subject of many conversations in the group gathered around her every day was the latest gossip she had obtained from the nurse who dressed her that morning. Hours spent at her station in the lobby also added to her store of information. Residents often used "La Mama" to transmit messages to each other; and those who did not volunteer information were closely observed or interrogated. The fact that frailty and immobility could become means to information may explain the lack of correlation between health conditions and social status at Les Floralies. Excellent health has been proposed as a plausible attribute of status among retired people (Rose, 1965) and could also be derived logically from the hypothesis of external sources for internal social organization. Residents' evaluations of their own health in comparison with that of others in their age group were not correlated with social status, which suggests that external values about health were neither reflected nor reversed inside the residence; again, they seem irrelevant. Differences in physical condition were very visible, and in addition they were emphasized by the spatial separation of the least strong in apartments without kitchens on the first two floors. The example of "La Mama" suggests that in terms of social status access to information through unusually frequent contact with staff members or through constant observation of other residents may balance or cancel out some of the disadvantages of physical disability (cf. Caudill, 1958).

Residents who reported poorer health were less likely to take work roles or to participate in groups, but their visiting with other residents and their general level of social activity do not distinguish them from other members of the community.

Sources of Social Organization— Contact With the Outside

A walk to the neighborhood café to buy a glass of white wine and a newspaper was a morning routine for several men in the residence. Twice a week the outdoor market in the town square attracted many of the women. Many residents also left Les Floralies for meals, visits or vacations with friends and relatives. The presence of guests in the residence was especially obvious at the noon meal on Sunday, when grandchildren ran around the dining room and there were often gift bottles of wine or desserts on the tables. These kinds of direct contact with the outside world, either through leaving the residence or through guests coming in, have been proposed as a source of social status in retirement communities (Kleemeier, 1954). Social status derived from contact outside the residence would be evidence in support of the hypothesis that internal social organization in general has external sources. Residents were asked when was the last time they had seen a child, a grandchild, a brother, a sister or a friend from outside the residence. Visits to or from family and friends showed no relationship to social status or to frequency of visiting with other residents, participation in groups, working inside the residence or general level of social activity there. Leaving the residence for other purposes such as shopping or going to a café was also unrelated to participation in the social world of Les Floralies. Direct contact with the outside appears irrelevant to the internal social organization of the residence.

Sources of Social Organization— Previous Roles

A common stereotype of residents in retirement communities is that they are waiting out leftover lives. They are seen as frozen into the roles they had before entering the new residence, and they are consequently expected to struggle to maintain these social identities inside it. In terms of the hypothesis that the major sources of internal social organization in an embedded community are external, roles which individuals acquired before moving in should be important sources of internal status. Occupation before entering the residence, for example, should remain an important determinant of association patterns inside.[5] Since wide class differences did not exist at Les Floralies, the only occupational identifications available to influence association patterns were specific jobs within the construction trades. No former jobs provided higher prestige inside the residence than others. The individuals with formal leadership roles had not had more skilled occupations; and previous occupation did not predict to the other components of high status, popularity and visibility. A more general application of the relationship between occupation and status did appear at Les Floralies, but in the present tense, rather than in the past. Taking work roles inside the community offered higher status than the more complete "retirement" of participation only in social and recreational activities.

"I was so sure it was written all over my face that I couldn't go downstairs to dinner for a week." "It" was the happiness the woman speaking felt about having begun an affair with a man across the hall. They soon shared a household, using one apartment for a bedroom, the other for a living room and kitchen.

----

[5] In three retirement communities in Arizona, Bultena found that among residents of various occupational backgrounds, men tended to choose as their three closest friends other men with similar previous occupations, indicated by general occupational groups such as professional, clerical-sales, blue collar, managerial-proprieter (Bultena, 1969).

They attended almost all public events together, and the other residents called them Mr. and Mrs. Several couples formed in the residence, some sharing public companionship as well as domestic and sexual relationships, some only companionship, some companionship and a joint household without being sexual partners. Residents described the two kinds of non-sexual relationships as "just for companionship," and recognized the individuals as a couple; but the titles Mr. and Mrs. were extended only to those relationships acknowledged by the partners to be sexual as well. Marriage is an important source of roles in adult life, and marital status is certainly an identity from the past which residents bring with them into Les Floralies. In this community however, present social relationships assert themselves even in terms of martial status, as couples who are not married in the eyes of the outside legal system are addressed and responded to socially as Mr. and Mrs. All couples were reluctant to marry legally either for fear of what their children would think or to avoid losing the widow's pension rights.

Sources of Social Organization—Seniority

Several residents considered themselves pioneers because they entered the community before all the construction was completed. They protested loudly and bitterly when participants for a special excursion were chosen by a lottery. The old-timers claimed that they "deserved" to go more than newcomers to the residence. Seniority in an organization is often used as a source of prestige and power in the society outside the retirement community.[6] Translated into the internal social organization, seniority measured in terms in length of time in the residence might be a source of high status. However, attempts to use seniority as a basis for priority at Les Floralies were not successful. Only the very newest residents seemed to be influenced by these demands. One recently arrived couple, for instance, felt obliged to buy drinks for the more senior residents on a

---

[6] Friedman reports that seniority (length of residence) combined with age as a source of popularity in an American home for aged Episcopalian women (Friedman, 1967).

trip in order to show their appreciation for being chosen to go in spite of their newness in the community. In general, length of time in the residence had no significant relationship to social status, or to frequency of visiting, working or general level of social activity. Residents who had been in the community longer were more likely to participate in formal groups.

Sources of Social Organization—
Political Identification

"He's one of ours" was a common comment about a new resident, meaning he was a Communist or a non-Communist, depending on the point of view of the speaker. In the present social life of Les Floralies, political identification was the single most well-known and salient social fact from the past. Virtually the first thing residents tried to find out about a new person was to what union he or she had belonged, which revealed political affiliation.[7] This information was used to steer new residents into a series of contacts with established residents of the same political background (cf. Ross, forthcoming). Communist vs. non-Communist was the crucial distinction, so Catholics and Socialists formed a tight anti-Communist coalition for most purposes. Socialization into the residence consequently took place in two separate channels; and two factions became progressively more sharply defined through this process. The very high status of the leaders of these two factions is reflected in the correlations between strength of political identification and social status. Probably because the mutual negative attitudes of the two factions cancel each other out, the direction of political identification is not at all related to status.

The faction leaders stood out sharply from the social landscape, each fortressed by ideological certainty and surrounded by a small group of highly committed followers. Political identification was less visible and less salient in the daily lives

---

[7] In France unions are focused on political affiliation rather than on occupation, so that several unions of different political orientations may represent workers in one industry or occupation. Union membership was consequently used by residents of Les Floralies as an indicator of an individual's political sympathies.

of most other residents, but was always available as a basis for mobilization when a conflict defined between the faction leaders reverberated out through the community. Strength or visibility of political identification, whether Communist or non-Communist, was correlated with levels of participation in work roles, visiting and overall social activity in the residence. Communists were less likely to participate in formal groups than members of the non-Communist faction, which reflects the dominance of anti-Communists in the formal organization of the residence, derived from their majority in the Residence Committee. The President of the Committee was the leader of the non-Communist faction; when we moved into the community in summer 1969 only one Committee member was Communist and she was not re-elected.

Although identification as a Communist or a non-Communist is clearly derived from the past lives of the residents, it was put to use for purposes strictly internal to the residence. Political identification is a social cue which provides a shorthand summary of several crucial facts about the past lives of the retired people at Les Floralies. Because of its link to union affiliation, political allegiance indicates patterns of association throughout the occupational lives of these construction workers. Identification as Communist or non-Communist also reveals an individual's participation in events which were traumatic not only for individuals in this generation, but for French society as whole. Communists pride themselves on their role in the Resistance against the German occupation of France in World War II. They accuse non-Communists, especially Socialists, of having been at best passive, and at worst active supporters of the Vichy regime. Non-Communists refute these accusations with aspersions on the Communists' actual role in the Resistance or with references to the French lives that were saved by the restraint of the non-Communist political leaders. In addition, retired workers of this generation lived through the strikes of the 1930's where once again Communist vs. non-Communist confrontations left the borders of political identification sharply marked in most memories.

"Where were you during the Resistance?" was the question that signaled escalation of an argument between residents to the level of serious hostility. Although the question calls into focus a summary statement about many of a resident's past social identities, it was inevitably used in a quarrel about present activities in the residence, how social funds should be spent or who should be elected to the Committee (See Ross, n.d.). Residents rarely reminisced with each other about their past political lives, and most showed little interest in contemporary French national politics. Elections to the Residence Committee however elicited intense interest and wide participation. The day of the election a ballot box was placed in the dining hall. Forty minutes after the first vote was cast, all but 13 residents had not only voted, but sat waiting to hear the votes counted, wearing the berets and gold watches or high-heeled shoes and gold brooches that signalled their "best."

The non-Communists controlled the Committee during our stay; the Communist minority was the vocal opposition. The Communists tried to compensate for their lack of influence on the Committee by organizing a Social Committee to plan dances and entertainment, even searching the Catholic calendar of festival days to find excuses for celebration. The controlling faction refused to give the Social Committee a meeting room for fear they would set up a "satellite" government.[8] Christmas decorations were also a source of factional conflict because the Communists bitterly complained about spending social funds to buy a baby Jesus for the manger.

CONCLUSION: LIFE GOES ON

Social organization inside Les Floralies appears to be neither a reflection of the outside world nor a reaction against it: such external sources of social identity or prestige as age, occupation, health, contact with the outside or seniority rather appear to be irrelevant. The two external sources of social identity which are used in the community are modified in important ways. Political identification is derived from, and in a sense summarizes,

---

[8] An indignant letter from the former president of the Committee informed me that the Communists had "taken over" the residence since the leader of their faction had been elected president in December, 1971.

the past lives of the residents, but it acquires almost exclusively internal functions. Work vs. retirement seems to be used internally very much as it is externally as a marker of social status; however, in this case the source of the identity is strictly internal, not external occupation.

To consider social organization at Les Floralies in its own terms, it is necessary to investigate the way its various aspects are linked to each other and to the attitudes and demographic characteristics of the individuals who participate in it. Social status in the community is related to a high level of participation in community affairs. There are two styles of participation, one formal and one informal, which provide two roads to the combination of popularity, visibility and leadership which indicates high status in the residence.[9] People who participate in groups such as the sewing club, the pottery class or the Committee are also likely to have jobs in the residence kitchen, garden, laundry or office, as is shown by the correlation between group participation and work roles in Table 5-III. Residents who participate

TABLE 5-III

CORRELATIONS BETWEEN SOCIAL STATUS, INTERNAL INTERACTION, GROUP PARTICIPATION, POSSESSION OF WORK ROLE, VISITING OTHER RESIDENTS AND MONTHS IN RESIDENCE

	Social Status	Internal Interaction	Group Participation	Possession of Work Role	Visiting Other Residents	Months in Residence
Social Status	1.00					
Internal Interaction	.69** (126)	1.00				
Group Participation	.25** (121)	.44** (121)	1.00			
Possession of Work Role	.34** (121)	.46** (121)	.50** (121)	1.00		
Visiting Other Residents	—.34** (65)	.29** (65)	.16 (61)	—.09 (61)	1.00	
Months in Residence	.13 (126)	—.06 (125)	.16* (120)	.007 (120)	.18 (65)	1.00

Sample sizes in parentheses
* Significant at the .05 level
** Significant at the .01 level

[9] Factor analysis of the variables representing social organization (shown on Table 5-III) revealed these two styles.

very actively through these relatively formal channels are likely to have high status. Those whose social lives are organized around more informal contacts with other residents may also achieve high status if they have either a large number of friends or a few whom they visit very frequently. Women are more likely to visit with other residents than men, which may reflect the fact that during most of their lives these women found most of their social contacts in informal ties with relatives and neighbors. The formal and informal styles of participation in the social life of Les Floralies do not overlap; there is no tendency for people who do a great deal of visiting also to belong to groups or to work. The fact that frequent or extensive informal contacts are a source of social status helps explain why individuals who don't feel well enough to work and Communists who are excluded from many formal groups are still able to acquire prestige.

The social world of Les Floralies appears to be largely autonomous from its external context. Acceptance of this fact consequently seems to be prerequisite to happiness in this community. The residents who feel most happy are those whose social lives and emotional energies are focussed on the community. They are also most loyal to the residence. (Table 5-IV) The residents who are happiest at Les Floralies have achieved high status in the community, but they are not distinguished by any specific level or style of participation. (Table 5-V) People who visit a great deal or who have a job or who participate in groups are not more likely to be happy in the residence than others. The key to happiness is not the amount or type of social activity, but a general accepance of the community as the focus of day-to-day social life.[10]

Life goes on at Les Floralies. Social organization in the community is neither a reflection of the world outside nor a reaction against it. The social lives of its residents represent their adaptation to a context which is not only new in their

---

[10] In a study of midwestern retirees in Arizona, those in retirement communities had higher morale than those in mixed-age communities (Bultena and Wood, 1969).

TABLE 5-IV

CORRELATIONS BETWEEN LOYALTY TO RESIDENCE, IMPORTANCE OF
RESIDENCE TO INDIVIDUAL, AND HAPPINESS[a]

	Loyalty to Residence	Importance of Residence	Happiness
Loyalty to Residence	1.00		
Importance of Residence	.23[*]	1.00	
	(67)		
Happiness	.24[*]	.40[**]	1.00
	(69)	(69)	

    Sample sizes in parentheses
[*] Significant at the .05 level
[**] Significant at the .01 level
[a] Variables are measured in the following way:

    1) *Happiness* is an index constructed from the following questionnaire items:
Would you describe your life these days as very happy, fairly happy or
not very happy?
In general does the life you lead now seem happier, less happy or about
the same as the life you used to lead?
Does the life you lead now seem happier, less happy or about the same
as the life you led before moving into the residence?
In general, is your life in the residence better than you expected, worse
than you expected or about the same as you expected?

    2) *Importance of Residence* is a score (high, medium or low) based on my
observation of the subjective salience of the community to an individual,
as indicated by tendency to make social judgments in internal terms, to
express strong loyalty or criticism, to show strong affect or commitment
to the community in any way.

    3) *Loyalty to Residence* is an index constructed from the following question-
naire items:
Everyone who is able to should take a job in the residence in order to
contribute to the life in community. Agree, disagree, neither.
People who have a tendency to criticize the residence are basically
ingrates. Agree, disagree, neither.

experience, but new in the experience of the wider society in
which it is embedded. Individuals who are happiest in the
residence are those who most clearly accept this fact. The extent
and the enthusiasm of participation in the details of daily living,
in the friendships and the battles, force their way into view
even through the filter of stereotypes: Les Floralies is not a
fogey farm or a waiting room for death. The patterns of social
life created by residents of Les Floralies and other residential
settings for retired people (cf. Bultena and Wood, 1969) should
contribute to a clearer definition of retirement both as a new
stage in the life cycle and as a new social border in industrial
society.

TABLE 5-V

CORRELATIONS BETWEEN LOYALTY TO THE RESIDENCE,
IMPORTANCE OF THE COMMUNITY OF THE INDIVIDUAL, HAPPINESS
AGE AND SEX BY SOCIAL STATUS, GROUP PARTICIPATION,
POSSESSION OF WORK ROLE, VISITING WITH OTHER RESIDENTS,
MONTHS IN RESIDENCE AND FACTIONAL ALLEGIANCE

	Social Status	Group Participation	Possession of Work Role	Visiting With Other Residents	Months in Residence	Factional Allegiance (Communist vs. non-Communists)
Loyalty to the Residence	.19 (71)	.22* (67)	.32** (67)	.09 (64)	.07 (69)	—.21* (71)
Importance of of the community to individual	.61** (122)	.36** (120)	.41** (120)	—.09 (63)	.01 (121)	.09 (122)
Happiness	.26* (72)	.12 (67)	—.12 (67)	.08 (64)	—.01 (72)	.07 (72)
Age	.03 (126)	.05 (120)	—.13 (120)	.11 (64)	.41** (125)	—.16* (125)
Female Sex	—.03 (127)	—.05 (121)	.01 (121)	.25* (65)	—.09 (126)	.00 (126)

Sample sizes in parentheses
* Significant at the .05 level
** Significant at the .01 level

REFERENCES

Bultena, G. L.: Relationship of Occupational Status to Friendship Ties in Three Planned Retirement Communities. *Journal of Gerontology*, 24: No. 4, 461-464, 1969.

Bultena, G. L., and Wood, Vivian: The American Retirement Community: Bane or Blessing. *Journal of Gerontology*, 24: No. 2, 209-217, 1969.

Caudill, William: *The Psychiatric Hospital as a Small Society.* Cambridge, Harvard University Press, 1958.

Cobban, Alfred: *A History of Modern France.* Middlesex, England, Penguin Books, 1963.

Friedman, E. P.: Age, Length of Institutionalization and Social Status in a Home for the Aged. *Journal of Gerontology*, 22:474-477, 1967.

Giallombardo, Rose: *Society of Women.* New York, John Wiley and Sons, 1966.

Goffman, Erving: *Asylums.* Garden City, New York, Doubleday, 1961.

Haut Comité Consultatif de la Population et de la Famille. *La Politique de la Vieillesse.* Paris, La Documentation Francaise, 1962.

Hoestetler, J. A., and Huntington, G. E.: *The Hutterites in North America.* New York, Holt, Rinehart & Winston, 1967.

Kleemeier, R. W.: Moosehaven: Congregate Living in a Community of the Retired. *American Journal of Sociology*, 59:347-351, 1954.

Pergeaux, Yves: *Réalities du Troisième Age.* Paris, Dunod, 1968.

Rose, Arnold: The Subculture of the Aging. In Rose, Arnold and Peterson, Warren: *Older People and Their Social World.* Philadelphia, F. A. Davis and Co., 1965.

Ross, Jennie-Keith: *The Culture of Retirement.* Unpublished doctoral dissertation, Northwestern University, 1968.

    (a) *Learning to Be Retired: Socialization into a French Retirement Residence. Journal of Gerontology,* 29:211-233, 1974.

    (b) *"What Did You Do During the War?" Community Conflict in a French Retirement Residence.* Unpublished manuscript.

Ross, Jennie-Keith, and Ross, Marc Howard: Participant Observation in Political Research. *Political Methodology,* Winter, 1974.

Shanas, Ethel: *The Health of Older People.* Cambridge, Harvard University Press, 1962.

CROSS-CULTURAL

COMMUNITIES

AGING AND MODERNIZATION: A REVISION
OF THE THEORY

DONALD O. COWGILL

THE BOOK, *Aging and Modernization* (Cowgill & Holmes, 1972), developed a theory of aging in cross-societal perspective. The theory emerged from a comparison of the role and status of older people in fifteen different societies which differed widely among themselves in degree of modernization and modernization was utilized as the chief independent variable. Thus the theory as it emerged was essentially a descriptive statement of the changes in role and status of older people with increasing modernization.

However, it was expressed in twenty-two discrete propositions each of which enunciated a correlation between a pair of of variables. In thirteen of those propositions modernization was explicitly used as one of the paired variables and it was assumed to be the independent variable. Thus modernization was declared to be associated with later onset of old age, increased use of chronological criteria, increased longevity, aging populations, increased proportions of females and widows in the population, increased proportions of grandparents, lower status of the aged, decline in leadership roles of the aged, decline in power and influence of the aged, increased ambiguity of the role of widows and an increase in the extent of disengagement of older people from community life. In eight further propositions, modernization was not explicitly made one of the paired variables, but the independent variables were assumed to be closely related to modernization if not integral aspects of it.

Thus rapid social change, mobility, urbanization, literacy, decline of ancestor worship, break up of the extended family, loss of useful roles for the aged and increased proportions of aged in the population were declared to be associated with lower status of the aged. Reexamination indicates that only one of the propositions utilized an independent variable which could not be subsumed under the general rubic, modernization. An individualistic value system appears to be at least partly independent of the forces of modernization.

This article is an attempt to refine that theoretical statement in several ways: (1) a more precise explication of concepts, (2) differentiation between major or primary variables and intervening variables, (3) more explicit attention to functional relationship among the variables, and, most importantly, (4) an effort to develop the interrelation among all of the variables within a single integrated system. Such a revised statement should provide a more meaningful and significant theoretical formulation.

THE CONCEPT OF MODERNIZATION

Stated in its most general form, utilizing the most general independent and dependent variables, the theory holds that with increasing modernization the status of older people declines. However, such a proposition cries out for explicit definition of the term "modernization."

However, one will search the literature in vain for a single, concise, generally accepted definition of this much used term. One gains the impression that the meaning is so broad and all-encompassing that most authors avoid an explicit definition and merely give illustrative facets of what must be viewed as a more general process. I plead guilty to this approach in our book where the nearest we come to a definition is to state that it encompasses level of technology, degree of urbanization, rate of social change, and degree of westernization (Cowgill & Holmes, 1972:2). Such a statement is useful in that it points to significant aspects of the process, but it is not a definition.

Some, in valiant attempts to define the term get caught up

in what appear to be tautological statements. For example, Dore (1969) defines modernization as ". . . the transformation of one's own society or segments of it in imitation of models drawn from another country or society." Bendix (1968) is only a little more explicit in indicating what kind of countries are the models when he says that it is a process whereby "backward" countries imitate "advanced" countries. Nettl (1968:56-57) is not much more helpful: "Modernization is the process whereby national elites seek successfully to reduce their *atimic* status and move towards equivalence with other 'well-placed' nations." Such statements are little better than the assertion that modernization is the process of becoming modernized.

Others who have sought to give more meaningful referents in their delineations have usually been trapped by their limited disciplinary perspectives. Perhaps the most common perspective is an economic one which holds that modernization is primarily a matter of technology, a succinct illustration of which is the following: "A society will be considered more or less modernized to the extent that its members use inanimate sources of power and/or use tools to multiply the effects of their efforts." (Levy, 1966:11) Those who have this perspective tend to equate modernization with economic development or at least that stage of development which is characterized by "self-sustaining growth" (Rostow, 1963). This tends in turn to lead to the employment of a vast array of economic indicators to measure it. These include not only the usual GNP per capita and kilowatts of electricity per capita but indicators of production of steel or cement, use of tractors, telephones, radios, television, consumption of paper, protein, sugar, or cereals (Janossy, 1963; Ehrlich, 1971). Others following a political scientist's perspective see modernization chiefly in terms of the development of political institutions concentrating on such things as the disappearance of tribalism, the concentration of political power, the emergence of nationalism, the development of an articulate public opinion and even citizen participation. (Cf., Eisenstadt, 1966a; Lerner, 1958) If the latter two qualities seem to have a western flavor, such appears to be the reality; as pointed out by Nettl (1968: 45-50), much writing on the subject does implicitly follow the assumption that modernization is the imitation of western democratic nations. A common sociological perspective gives emphasis to institutional differentiation calling attention not only to the increasing separation of the major social institutions from each other—familial, economic, political and religious—but also elaboration, specialization and differentiation within each institutional area as well (Cf. Etzioni, 1964; Coughenour, 1969). Others see modernization as mainly a change in attitudes and values (Waisanen, 1968) and this leads to attitude surveys and psychological tests as measures of it (Inkeles & Smith, 1970; Barndt, 1969; Armer & Schnaiberg, 1972; Stephenson, 1968).

Perhaps the most eclectic treatment of the concept is that of Eisenstadt (1966a). While he stresses institutional differentiation, he is careful to incorporate all institutional areas including such peculiarly modern ones as education, science, and leisure. He also encompasses the psychological and cultural aspects of the process including changes of values. The work is quite eclectic and comprehensive, but one will search in vain for a concise, usable definition.

A somewhat less detailed and more meaningfully focused treatment of the subject is that of Lerner. In his discussion in the *International Encyclopedia of the Social Sciences* (1968), he falls into the tautological trap: "Modernization is the current term for an old process—the process of social change whereby less developed societies acquire characteristics common to more developed societies," but elsewhere he calls it ". . . the infusion of 'a rationalist and positivist spirit'" (1958:45). However, his main thesis has stressed the four interrelated processes: urbanization, literacy, mass media, and political participation. Urbanization comes first and gives rise to literacy which in turn leads to the demand for and the use of mass media; rising levels of education elicit informed opinions on public afffairs and the demand for participation.

Weiner (1966), like Eisenstadt, catalogs an extensive range of aspects of modernization without giving a definition.

Having failed in the attempt to find a ready-made definition and in the search having gained a fuller appreciation of the vast all-encompassing nature of the process which has led many to avoid the attempt and others to fall short, I am probably foolhardy to assay the task myself. However, I want to be as explicit as possible in what follows and that requires definition of terms.

Modernization is the transformation of a total society from a relatively rural way of life based on animate power, limited technology, relatively undifferentiated institutions, parochial and traditional outlook and values, toward a predominantly urban way of life based on inanimate sources of power, highly developed scientific technology, highly differentiated institutions matched by segmented individual roles, and a cosmopolitan outlook which emphasizes efficiency and progress. There are two fundamental aspects to this definition: (1) It is the transformation of a *total* society; no part of the society is left untouched. (2) The change is *unidirectional;* it always moves away from the rural traditional form in the direction of the urban, highly differentiated form. This is not to assert that the process is uniform; on the contrary, as Nettl (1968:42-57) has pointed out, just as each society is unique in specific content at the start of the process, so it will be uniquely selective as the process goes on and certainly none should expect a uniform, standard outcome.

For Parsons (1964) the unidimensional nature of this change takes on the quality of a functional imperative when he calls it an "evolutionary universal." And the same idea is contained in Levy's (1966:744) characterization of modernization as a universal social "solvent." He asserts that whenever there are contacts between the members of a traditional society and those of a modern society, the structures of the traditional society begin to dissolve and to change in the direction of the modern society. Eisenstadt (1966a:1) appears to have the same quality of compulsive inevitability in mind in the opening sentences of his book:

> Modernization and aspirations to modernity are probably the most overwhelming and the most permeating features of the contemporary scene. Most nations are nowadays caught in its web. . . ."

This statement also calls attention to another quality of the process, namely, that it is international in scope. Indeed, Eisen-

stadt (1966a:15-19) goes on to note that while in any given
society one aspect of modernization is the eclipse of tribalism
and the emergence of "mass-consensual orientation" in the form
of nation-states, it is not confined within any set of political
boundaries, its thrust and impact are truly international.

One point on which there appears to be consensus is that
while modernization began in a limited number of western
countries who are still leaders in the process and within these
societies it was a self-generating autochthonous process, for the
late-comers in the rest of the world it has now become largely
a matter of imitation (Cf. Eisenstadt, 1966a:67; Nettl, 1968:42-
57; Levy, 1966:744; Coughenour, 1969; Dore, 1969; Bendix,
1968).

The acknowledgement that modernization is the transformation of a total society carries with it some problems of utility.
How can one discuss the relationship of modernization to some
particular phenomenon without treating the total society, an
enterprise which becomes prohibitive in terms of time and space?
Obviously there is need for selectivity and abstraction in any
such undertaking. In the current case we shall need to abstract
from the total range of societal changes those which are salient
to the subject of aging. We shall also attempt to differentiate
among societal changes which are major and minor, on the
one hand, and those which are relatively independent and
relatively dependent, on the other.

At the outset we shall affirm that the major independent, and
most salient societal changes which are subsidiary aspects of
modernization—salient to the conditions of older people are: (1)
scientific technology as applied in economic production and distribution, (2) urbanization, (3) literacy and mass education,
and (4) health technology (the application of scientific technology in the range of environmental control, nutrition, and
curative medicine). In many respects it is difficult to differentiate between the effects of scientific technology as applied
in economic production and distribution, on the one hand, and
its effects in the areas of public health and medicine, but we
believe that with respect to aging, this is an important distinction.

MODERNIZATION AND AGING

The general thesis of the book was that modernization results in, *inter alia,* a relatively lower status of older people in society. Each of the major salient aspects of modernization appears to conduce to this effect and the following discussion seeks to analyze the causal sequences.

It is ironical that one of the most salient aspects of modernization with reference to aging is the development of health technology. Within this area we include all public health technology arising in consequence of the germ theory of disease, all aspects of modern knowledge of nutrition, and all aspects of curative and surgical medicine. The ironical aspect of this is that in none of the treatises on modernization is this aspect given more than passing notice. Yet, certainly in all contemporary development plans, health technology is given high prominence, backed up by significant budgetary allocations, and health programs are among the earliest and most liberally supported programs of assistance offered by the most modernized to so-called developing nations.

The most immediate, and sometimes dramatic, effect of such programs is the prolongation of life in these societies. In the initial instance the saving of life is most effective in infancy and childhood, consequently the most immediate impact when these measures are applied rapidly, as they have been in developing countries since World War II, has been not only a population explosion but also a "younging" of the population, i.e. a rapid increase of the child population. Theoretically this could have major significance for inter-generational relations but, so far as I know, this phenomenon has not been subjected to empirical study.

However, in the long-run the application of modern health technology results in an aging of population, since it not only results in a prolongation of life of the young, but also (and perhaps this is an integral aspect of modernization) eventually a reduction of the birth rate which in turn reduces the ratio of children in the population. The combination of increased longevity followed by decreased fertility eventually results in the aging of the population (i.e. the increase in the proportion of the population in the upper age brackets).

Just how and when and to what degree this results in an increase in intergenerational competition for jobs (roles) is certainly unclear from present research, but that such competition eventually develops does seem clear and it is also clear that out of such conflict of interest, within the setting of an impersonal, highly-differentiated society with the emphasis on youth and new occupations, older people are eventually pushed out of the labor market. In the modern world this has led to the phenomenon which we know as retirement.

In a society which values the work role above all others and metes out its rewards on the basis of this role, retirement from it is likely to be prejudicial to the perpetuation of those rewards both material and non-material. Thus monetary income is drastically reduced (Riley & Foner, 1968) and whatever prestige and honor (psychic income) was ascribed to the position fades. The loss of income is probably a fairly accurate index of the decline of status, but in a society which tends to use consumption patterns as status symbols, the loss of income itself contributes to the decrement in status.

Therefore it appears that the introduction and application of modern health technology tends ultimately to contribute to the undermining of the status of older people in society. Figure 6-1 shows the analytical sequence in simplified form. However, the reader should note that the Work Ethic appears as an extraneous variable, important for the result, but not an intrinsic part of the sequence.

There will be further discussion of this exogenous variable later.

A second salient aspect of modernization is economic modernization, more commonly called "development." This includes a

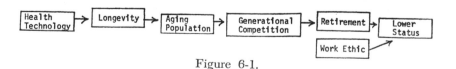

Figure 6-1.

broad range of economic changes which can be dissociated from other aspects only by intellectual abstraction. These are so profound that some see modernization as consisting entirely of them, while others, adopting a Marxian view, see them as the precipitating causes of modernization.

I can only illustrate the elements included in this aspect of modernization. It would certainly include: the increasing application of inanimate sources of power, the extensive application of new inventions in agricultural production, industrial production, transportation, communication, and distribution. These obviously led to and were intertwined with profound changes in the work world including factory organization and the separation of work from the home; they included the creation of new occupations and increasing specialization and professionalization; they included the increasing scale of operations in all spheres and consequent bureaucratization of organization, the proliferation of special interest associations, the impersonalization of relationships, including employer-employee relationships, and increasing interdependence withal (Cf. Eisenstadt, 1966a; Levy, 1966).

Out of this melange of developments, one which appears highly salient in its ultimate consequences for older people is the emergence of many new specialized occupations. It is highly significant that most of these new occupations emerge in cities and remain fundamentally urban in context. One of the most firmly established principles of demography is that the most mobile members of a society are its youth. It is they who are attracted by new frontiers including the job frontiers of the city. It is they who take the new jobs and acquire the training to fill them, leaving their parents behind both geographically and socially. Generally speaking the new occupations carry greater rewards in both money and status. Consequently there is an inversion of status, with children achieving higher status than their parents instead of merely moving up to the status of their parents as in most pre-modern societies. This not only leaves the parents in older, less prestigeous, perhaps static and sometimes obsolete positions, it also deprives them of one of the most traditional roles for older people—that of providing vocational guidance and instruction to their children.

Some of the pressure toward early retirement occurs because of shifting patterns of vocational application resulting in static conditions or even declines in the demand for some types of workers. Usually these are the very lines of work in which older workers are concentrated. And again, retirement within this social and cultural setting is fraught with insecurity, is usually accompanied by loss of income and its attendant lower status. And again, the Work Ethic is a persistently conditioning, perhaps extraneous, factor.

Furthermore, the work role is only one of the roles which is lost in modernizing societies; other familial and community roles also tend to be eroded and with the decline of useful, prestigeous roles the status of older people declines (Rosow, 1967; Cowgill & Holmes, 1972:11).

A greatly over-simplified sequence of influences flowing from changes in technology is shown in Figure 6-2.

The third major aspect of modernization with respect to aging is urbanization. Although this clearly is a process which is closely interrelated with economic development, it is at least partially independent and has significance for aging which extends to facets which were not discussed in connection with economic development.

We did call attention to the separation of work from home and to the geographical separation of youthful urban migrants from their parental homes. This puts a heavy strain upon bonds of the extended family which has been so prevalent in so many traditional societies. I am not contending that the extended family completely disappears in modern societies nor that relations with kin are unimportant; I am asserting that urbanization

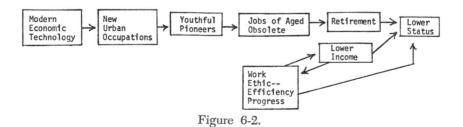

Figure 6-2.

does tend to break up the extended family as a household unit, to increase the spatial separation between generations and to establish neolocal marriage and the nuclear family as the norm. Recent findings of moderately frequent contacts between adult children and aged parents do not warrant the conclusion that nothing has changed. Weekly visits across town are profoundly different from constant association within the same household. The current mode of calling the occasional contacts between selected remnants of kin networks the "modified extended family" (Litwak, 1959-64; Sussman, 1965; Shanas, *et al.* 1968) must not blind us to the profound impact of urbanization upon the family.

It does produce residential segregation of the generations and, while this is certainly not synonymous with isolation, it most assuredly reduces the frequency and intimacy of contact; it militates against immediate availability of help in time of crisis; it decreases not only the extent of interaction but also the amount of interdependence in daily activities. This makes aged parents peripheral to the nuclear families of their adult children (Williams, 1970), it fosters independence of the generations from each other and this ecological reality is moved to a moral obligation when, as in Western society, it is undergirded by the Protestant Ethic which makes individual independence and self-reliance a moral virtue. The prevalence of such an ethic is attested by much research in Western industrialized societies (Cf. Streib & Thompson, 1960; Shanas, *et al.* 1968).

Urbanization not only induces geographic mobility, it also accelerates social mobility (Smelser & Lipset, 1966). One aspect of this is the emergence of new social classes and a restructuring of the status system (Cf. Coleman, 1968) tending toward a much more fluid situation and a blurring of class lines. Another aspect which is more relevant to the present discussion is the inter-generational mobility whereby children move up through the system (upward mobility is much more frequent than its opposite in a modernizing society) with the inevitable consequence that they ultimately achieve a status which is superior to the maximal achievement of their parents. To the extent that they internalize the values of the society, and the more successful ones are very likely to espouse those values, the children consciously or unconsciously feel superior to their parents.

The inversion of status is accentuated by geographic separation as the youths move to the cities and the old folks stay behind because, at least in the early stages of modernization, urban comes to mean "modern" and rural means "traditional" or "backward" (de Briey, 1966).

When to this inversion of status based on active work roles is added the humiliation of retirement, the contrast and debasement of the older generation is exaggerated. If to this combination of factors is added the further insult of enforced dependency, severe mental conflicts tend to occur (Clark, 1967).

Recapitulating the chain of forces stemming from urbanization bearing on the status of the aged, we have Figure 6-3.

A fourth salient aspect of modernization with respect to aging is education (Cf. Smelser & Lipset, 1966:29-42). In pre-modern societies most of the population is illiterate and thus their knowledge of the world is severely limited. Their knowledge of the past beyond their own personal experience was confined to verbal recitations of other living persons whose experience transcended their own or who were repositories of oral tradition. This tended to provide an important role for older people and to reinforce their status in that type of society.

Early in the process of modernization one always finds measures being undertaken to promote literacy and to advance education. In fact, Lerner (1958:60-65) suggests that after the initial impact of urbanization, the second significant aspect of modernization is the spread of literacy and, as a matter of fact, literacy is sometimes used as an index of modernization especially during its early stages (Cowgill & Holmes, 1972:306). Closely

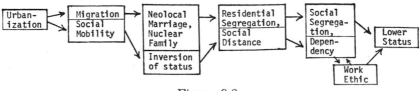

Figure 6-3.

interrelated with efforts to promote literacy are programs to extend the educational level of the populace, sooner or later taking the form of public mass education of the child population to a prescribed minimal level. Paralleling these developments are training programs conducted either by employers or by technical schools designed to develop skills in particular jobs.

The main targets of such programs are always the young; in the case of mass public education, children; in the case of technical education, teenagers or young adults. The major consequence of this is that once a society is launched into the process of modernization, no matter what its stage of development, adult children are always more highly educated than their parents. In the early stages this may manifest itself in a situation in which most of the younger generation are able to read while their parents are not and the parents have to rely on the expertise of their children to keep them informed about current events as well as communicating with their own kin who have moved away to the city. At another stage we may find that most of the children have had an elementary school education while their parents are barely literate. At a still later stage we may find that most of the children have completed secondary school while their parents only completed primary school. In the United States of America, probably in an advanced stage of modernization today, it is fairly accurate to say that the average older person (65 and over) has about an elementary school education (the last illiterate generation has already passed from the scene); their children, currently in middle age, are on the average high school graduates; their grandchildren, just now completing their formal education, will have the advantage of several years college.

The continuation of a condition in which the children always have greater skill than their parents and know more than their parents, including more about their own past history, cannot avoid fostering a different relationship between generations and different roles in the society as compared with a traditional society in which the situation is reversed. The obvious tendency will be for the child generation to be in a superior status *vis-a-vis* their parents, and for the child generation to occupy positions according them higher status in the community than had been achieved by their parents.

Furthermore it appears that once launched into the process of modernization, the rate of social change continually accelerates. This implies that the generation gap continually becomes wider and places the older generation at a greater and greater disadvantage tending further to depress its relative status in society (Moore, 1966; Cowgill & Holmes, 1972:9).

When, as in the most highly modernized societies, we approach a stage of development in which not only are past forms of education and socialization inappropriate but the young must be socialized for a future which is unknown (Cogswell, 1970) it is evident that the older generation is deprived of much of its earlier socializing role and is incapable of sharing the experiences and problems of the younger generation. The generation gap becomes a nearly unbridgeable chasm.

This generalization speaks to the situation while both generations are still active participants. When we add to this discrepant status some actual deterioration of the status of the older generation with retirement and/or dependency the generation gap may become rather wide indeed. Certainly under these circumstances there can be no mystique of old age. There can be no reverence deriving from superior knowledge and no awe based on recognition of superior power.

This generation gap produces a real intellectual and moral segregation of the aged in modern societies. The sequence in simplified form is shown in Figure 6-4.

In this instance the extraneous factor is labeled "Cult of Youth" but it is a companion of and partially derivative from the Work Ethic with its emphasis on efficiency and progress. But it extends beyond the usual dimensions of that concept to include

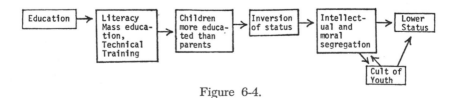

Figure 6-4.

not only an emphasis on vigor and athletic prowess but a dominating value on youth itself. Youth becomes the symbol of and means to progress. When choices between generations are forced, youth is given priority. We have already seen this in two contexts: in applying modern medical technology the early thrust is toward the reduction of infant and child mortality, and in the application of modern education the main targets are children and youth. We could add that in the spending of local community resources through such devices as community chests and united funds there is further conclusive evidence of the prevalence of this value system. And, be it noted, this is not something created by the pressures of youth; these are values which are prevalent throughout modern societies, concurred in by all generations and implemented by the power structures of the societies. This is what is called here the Cult of Youth. It is a conditioning factor which operates interactively within the total system to accentuate the decline of the status of the aged (Havighurst & Albrecht, 1953).

However, there is a related but quite different phenomenon which is often called Youth Culture. This is an indigenous intra-generational development in which a particular youthful generation creates to a recognizable degree its own culture—its own idiom, its own standards of dress and behavior, and its own organizations. Some of this is in rebellion against what is perceived as the archaic standards and values of old-fashioned and "ignorant" parents. It occurs within the context of a mass urbanized society where the generation gap has become very wide, where tradition has been debunked, and where each generation to a considerable extent evolves its own culture and is guided by the standards of its peers (Riesman, 1950). Smelser and Lipset (1966:42) see a functional relationship between their "other-directedness" and economic development. The term "youth culture" is probably a misnomer because it connotes that the current generation of youth are behaving as they do because they are young and that there is likely to be some continuity to these patterns, that oncoming contingents will adopt the culture and behave the same way because they have now become a part of youth society. This is a static and dated view of what is really a very dynamic, ever-changing condition. Since the term "youth culture" first came into vogue its content has made several drastic shifts; we have already had several generations of different youth cultures. It is temporally myopic to see the culture of any particular generation as "youth culture;" to the extent that there is any permanence to it, it will be carried forward by that generation into adulthood, becoming in succeeding years the young adult culture, then the culture of middle age, then of later middle age and finally of old age. A more realistic appraisal of this stage of modernizing society indicates a succession of increasingly segregated generations (segregated from each other physically, socially, psychologically, intellectually and morally) each in turn inventing and evolving to a significant degree its own culture. Given the pressures toward segregation of the generations surely such an eventuality is predictable.

Those who are speculating about the incipient emergence of a "sub-culture of aging" (Cf. Rose, 1965) are subject to the same myopia while looking in the opposite direction. The cultural characteristics of the current generation of older people are attributes of a generation; they are not attributes of old people. Those who have hopefully or fearfully looked for emerging self-consciousness and mutual peer loyalty among the aged have so far had little evidence on which to base their hopes or fears. As a matter of fact, there is much evidence that many people born before the turn of the century still refuse to classify themselves as old or aged. However, I doubt whether many of these would reject being classified with their generation.

It may be that future older generations will develop more self-consciousness of generational identity and perhaps more loyalty to their peers. Such a development would appear not unlikely in the context of increasing numbers and proportions of older people and increasing segregation.

Throughout the previous discussion the Work Ethic has been treated as an extraneous variable, perhaps not inherent in or essential to the process of modernization. This is of course a moot point. Weber (1958) gave a different interpretation many years ago. According to that view Western capitalism arose on the foundation provided by the prior emergence of Protestantism whose leaders espoused and promulgated an ethic of individual salvation demonstrated by hard work, frugality and self-reliance. One does not have much difficulty in defending the proposition that the rise of Western capitalism signaled the beginning of modernization. One can also agree with Weber, as Eisenstadt (1966b, 1968) does, that in the particular historical setting in European society where both developments were initiated Protestantism did play a significant role. But these two propositions do not force us to the conclusion that either Protestantism or capitalism are essential to the continuing process of modernization. It would be tenuous indeed to argue that the modernization of Japan should be attributed to Protestantism and by the same token the extensive modernization Russia can scarcely be identified with capitalism. Indeed these and other illustrations of modernization appear to demonstrate that neither Protestantism nor capitalism is an essential ingredient in the process. However, it does appear that all societies which have advanced very far in the process have by diffusion or independent invention acquired a value system which incorporates the motivating forces analogous with those provided by Protestantism in Europe. Parsons (1960:162) asserts that one of the most crucial non-economic factors underlying the industrial type of economy is "drive" and Bendix (1966) finds the analogue in Japan in the reactions of samurai after the Meiji restoration. Certainly industriousness, frugality, accumulation of savings (capital), rational organization of work, efficiency, time-consciousness, a secular outlook, orientation toward this world and hope of individual achievement in it, rising expectations and standards of living are a part of the value system associated with economic development and modernization.

I have sought to capture the most salient aspects of this "new cultural outlook" (Eisenstadt, 1966a:5) in the term "Work Ethic." The concept is obviously derived from the Protestant Ethic but these values can no longer be attributed to any single religious orientation or event.

This still does not resolve the issue of its role in the process— whether as a major, primary variable or as a facilitator and conditioning agent. Myrdal (1968) assumes a Weberian stance when he holds that South Asia will not succeed in its economic development without a fundamental change of values. Weiner (1966:5-12) acknowledges the Weberian view but points out that the opposite view, supported by considerable research on cognitive dissonance, is that attitudes change when they get out of consonance with behavior, i.e., they tend to follow rather than lead.

The present treatment is a compromise between these views. It holds that while the Work Ethic is a significant factor in the process and while it does have an important role in motivation, it is not the primary nor even one of the major salient aspects of modernization. Nevertheless it is a very important conditioning factor and because of its pervasive cultural nature it has impact and modifying effect upon the operation of each of the major salient aspects of modernization as they affect the status of older people.

In summary, the thesis is that modernization does tend to diminish the relative status of older people in their society and that this relationship is not a mere statistical correlation, it is a functional relationship which can be analyzed. Selecting the four most salient aspects of modernization, we have sought to delineate the causal chain linking each with the ultimate outcome —diminished status for the aged. Figure 6-5 integrates the four chains into a single system. This shows parallel influences through and between the four chains converging in a single direction and tendency. Thus the introduction of modern health technology, modern economic technology, urbanization and rising levels of education, all operating within a climate which incorporates the Work Ethic and a Cult of Youth, tend to have a depressing effect on the status of the aged in society.

THE FUTURE TREND

Until very recently the evidence for the general proposition that modernization tends to diminish the status of the aged was largely anecdotal and impressionistic. Palmore and Whittington (1971) recently found for the United States that not only was the status of the aged lower than the younger population in terms

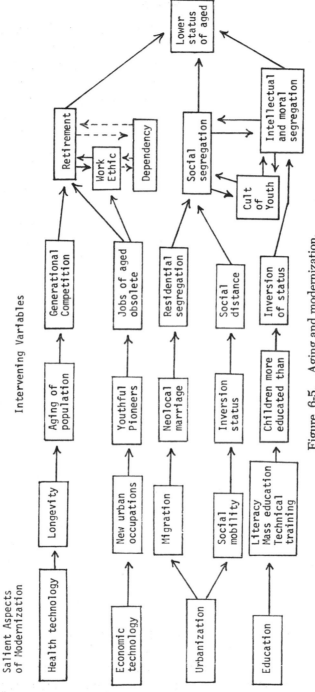

Figure 6-5. Aging and modernization.

of several socio-economic indicators but it had also declined significantly between 1940 and 1969. The theorem is still more convincingly demonstrated by Palmore and Manton (1973) in a study just completed which correlates indicators of modernization with indicators of status in thirty-one countries. As indicators of modernization they used gross national product per capita, percent of the labor force in agriculture, change in the percent of the labor force in agriculture, percent illiterate, percent of youths in school, and percent of population in higher education. It may be noted that these indicators include measures of three of the four salient aspects of modernization treated above—economic technology, urbanization and education; again health technology was slighted. The relative status of the aged was measured by indexes which measured the difference in employment, occupation and education of the older population (65 and over) as compared with the general adult population (25-64). The correlations gave rather decisive indication that the relative status of older people was lower in the more modernized countries.

However, Palmore and Manton found on more intensive analysis that for two of the indicators of status—occupation and education—the relationship was curvilinear. The relative status of the aged declined through most of the range of modernization represented by the thirty-one countries, but at the most advanced stages the relationship turned positive. This suggests that while modernization is detrimental to the status and interests of the aged in is early stages this trend may "bottom out" in later stages of modernization and from then on there is some comparative improvement in the status and condition of older people.

These are encouraging symptoms fostering some hope that modernization does not inevitably and unendingly sacrifice the interests of the aged on the altar of progress. Perhaps there comes a time when they begin to share in the fruits of that progress.

In the light of the theory presented in this paper it is interesting to speculate about the possible bases for this reversal of the trend and to search for further symptoms of it. One possibility for which there is some impressionistic support is that there is a softening of the Work Ethic; that work is no longer such a high virtue and that not working does not connote such disgrace. With declining work hours and increasing leisure, even during the prime working years, it is reasonable to believe that increased leisure in old age in the form of retirement would be less destructive to one's status. A second possibility is that only after a society reaches a certain stage of affluence is it able or willing to provide adequate incomes to non-productive members such as the aged retired and this occurs long after the extended family has lost its capability for adequately fulfilling this function. Another possibility is that illiteracy may be the most serious handicap of an aged generation vis-a-vis younger literate generations and when illiteracy disappears even among the aged the degree of their handicap is decreased. A similar possibility which pertains also to the education variable is that societies in advanced stages of modernization may approach a point of diminishing returns in terms of further increases in the amount of education to be provided to the oncoming generations. Beyond this point the differential in the levels of education of the generations begins to decline. This is strongly indicated in the data of Palmore and Manton (1973). A final possibility which will be mentioned here, though this certainly does not exhaust the possibilities, is that with increased numbers and proportions of the aged and with increased segregation there may be an increasing self-awareness in the older generation and increasing group pressure on behalf of their interests. Cutler (1973) finds that increased awareness of status decline is associated with increased demands for governmental assistance and increased support for organized political actiivty. These various possibilities are obviously not mutually exclusive and certainly most if not all of them could occur concurrently.

SUMMARY

This chapter has sought to extend and develop a theory of aging which was stated elsewhere in elemental form (Cowgill & Holmes, 1972). It has sought to abstract the most salient aspects of the general process of modernization and analyze the ways in which these aspects taken severally and in concert contribute to the general tendency for the relative status of the aged to decline with modernization. The salient aspects which were examined were the introduction of modern health technology, the introduction of modern economic technology, the increase of education and urbanization. Each of these prime factors was found to initiate a chain reaction which tended to diminish the status of the aged. The effects were amplified by the presence of the Work Ethic and the Cult of Youth. However, new evidence indicates that this trend may "bottom out" in advanced stages of modernization and from that point on the relative status of the aged may begin to improve. The evidence suggests that this may be happening in the most modernized nations today.

REFERENCES

Armer, Michael, and Schnaiberg, Allan: Measuring individual modernity: a mere myth. *American Sociological Review,* 37:301-16, 1972.

Barndt, Deborah: Changing time conceptions. *Summation,* 1:17-28, 1969.

Bendix, Reinhard: A case study in cultural and educational mobility: Japan and the Protestant Ethnic. In Neil J. Smelser and Seymour Martin Lipset (eds.). *Social Structure and Mobility in Economic Development,* Chicago, Aldine Publishing Company, 1966.

Bendix, Reinhard: Proba definicji modernizacji (Towards a Definition of Modernization). *Studia Socjolgiszno Polityczne,* 25:31-43, 1968.

Clark, Margaret, and Anderson, Barbara Gallatin: *Culture and Aging.* Springfield, Illinois, Charles C Thomas, 1967.

Cogswell, Betty E.: Socialization and modernization. Paper at International Congress of Sociology, Varna, Bulgaria, September 14-19, 1970.

Coleman, James S.: Modernization: political aspects. In David L. Sills (ed.), *International Encyclopedia of the Social Sciences,* 10, The MacMillan Company and The Free Press, 1968.

Coughenour, C. M.: Modernization, modern man and social change. Paper at Rural Sociological Society, 1969.

Cowgill, Donald O., and Holmes, Lowell D. (eds.): *Aging and Modernization.* New York, Appleton-Century-Crofts, 1972.

Cutler, Stephen J.: Perceived prestige loss and political attitudes among the aged. *The Gerontologist,* 13:69-75, 1973.

de Briey, Pierre: Les agglomerations urbaines et la modernisation des etats du tiers monde. *Civilisations,* 15:454-70, 1966.

Dore, R. P.: The modernizer as a special case: Japanese factory legislation, 1882-1911. *Comparative Studies in Society and History*, 11:433-50, 1969.

Ehrlich, E.: Comparisons internationales de developpement economique. *Analyse et Prevision*, 11:81-107, 1971.

Eisenstadt, S. N.: *Modernization: Protest and Change.* Englewood Cliffs, Prentice-Hall, 1966.

Eisenstadt, S. N.: Problems in the comparative analysis of total societies. Transactions of the Sixth World Congress of Sociology 1:187-202. Published by International Sociological Association. Louvain, Belgium: Impriemerie Nauwelaerts, 1966.

Eisenstadt, S. N.: *The Protestant Ethic and Modernization.* New York, Basic Books, 1968.

Etzioni, Amitai, and Etzioni, Eva (eds.): *Social Change.* New York, Basic Books, 1964.

Havighurst, Robert J., and Albrecht, Ruth: *Older People.* New York, Longmans, Green, 1953.

Inkeles, Alex, and Smith, David H.: The fate of personal adjustment in the process of modernization. *International Journal of Comparative Sociology,* 11:81-114, 1970.

Janossy, F.: The problem of measuring the level of economic development: a new method of estimation, Budapest, 1963.

Lerner, Daniel: *The Passing of Traditional Society: Modernizing the Middle East.* New York, The Free Press, 1958.

Lerner, Daniel: Modernization: social aspects. In David L. Sills (ed.), *International Encyclopedia of the Social Sciences*, 10, The MacMillan Company and the Free Press, 1968.

Levy, Marion J.: *Modernization and the Structure of Societies.* Princeton, Princeton University Press, 1966.

Litwak, Eugene: The use of extended family groups in the achievement of social goals. *Social Problems,* 7:177-87, 1959-60.

Moore, Wilbert E.: Aging and the social system. In John C. McKinney and Frank T. de Vyver (eds.), *Aging and Social Policy.* New York, Appleton-Century-Crofts, 1966.

Myrdal, Gunnar: *Asian Drama.* New York, Pantheon, 1968.

Nettl, J. P.: *International Systems and the Modernization of Societies.* New York, Basic Books, 1968.

Nettl, J. P., and Robertson, R.: *International Systems and the Formation of National Goals and Attitudes.* New York, Basic Books, 1968.

Palmore, Erdman, and Whittington, F.: Trends in the relative status of the aged. *Social Forces,* 50:84-91, 1971.

Palmore, Erdman, and Manton, Kenneth: Modernization and status of the aged: international correlations. *Journal of Gerontology* (forthcoming).

Parsons, Talcott: *Structure and Process in Modern Societies.* Glencoe, The Free Press, 1960.

Parsons, Talcott: Evolutionary universals in society. *American Sociological Review*, 29:339-57, 1964.

Riesman, David: *The Lonely Crowd*. New Haven, Yale University Press, 1950.

Riley, Matilda W., and Foner, Anne: *Aging and Society: An Inventory of Research Findings*. New York, Russell Sage Foundation, 1968.

Rose, Arnold M.: The subculture of the aging: a framework for research in social gerontology. In Arnold M. Rose and Warren A. Peterson (eds.), *Older People and Their Social World*. Philadelphia, F. A. Davis Company, 1965.

Rosow, Irving: And then we were old. *Transaction*, 2:20-26, 1965.

Rostow, Walt W.: *The Economics of Take-off into Sustained Growth*. New York, St. Martin's Press, 1963.

Shanas, Ethel; Townsend, Peter; Wedderburn, Dorothy; Friis, Henning; Milhøj, Poul, and Jan Stehouwer: *Old People in Three Industrial Societies*. New York, Atherton Press, 1968.

Smelser, Neil J., and Lipset, Seymour Martin: *Social Structure and Mobility in Economic Development*. Chicago, Aldine Publishing Company, 1966.

Stephenson, John B.: Is everyone going modern? a critique and a suggestion for measuring modernism. *American Journal of Sociology*, 74:265-75, 1968.

Streib, Gordon F., and Thompson, Wayne E.: The older person in a family context. In Clark Tibbitts (ed.), *Handbook of Social Gerontology*. Chicago, The University of Chicago Press, 1960.

Sussman, Marvin B.: Relationship of adult children with their parents in the United States. In Ethel Shanas and Gordon F. Streib (eds.), *Social Structure and the Family: Generational Relations*. Englewood Cliffs, Prentice-Hall, 1965.

Waisanen, Frederick B.: Actors, social systems, and the modernization process. Paper presented at Carnegie Seminar, Indiana University, April, 1968.

Weber, Max: *The Protestant Ethic and the Spirit of Capitalism*. New York, Charles Scribner's Sons, 1958.

Weiner, Myron (ed.): *Modernization: The Dynamics of Growth*. New York, Basic Books, 1966.

Williams, Robin M., Jr.: *American Society*. New York, Alfred A. Knopf, Publisher, 1970.

Chapter 7

OLD AGE AMONG THE BAGANDA: CONTINUITY AND CHANGE[1]

NINA NAHEMOW AND BERT N. ADAMS

T HE STATUS OF the aged in pre-industrial societies around the world has been characterized often in the literature as both dominant and multifaceted. It has been seen as involving the following types of functions: (1) Official community leader, power and authority (chief, etc.). (2) Repository of knowledge and teacher of oral traditions to the community; bearer of culture and link to the past including ancestor worship and the supernatural. (3) Object of respect and source of affection for grandchildren and other kin, in extended families which tie generations together both emotionally and economically (Simmons, 1960).

A further assumption concerns the changing status of the aged in such societies. It is argued that the thrust toward urban life has called the legitimacy of several aspects of this traditional role into question. Specifically, the roles of official authority and economic head have been weakened, as has the value of the elderly as advisers and storytellers. These changes have been widespread enough that they have sometimes been viewed as virtually universal phenomena in the modernization process. The problems encountered today by the aged are placed within this historical context and the tendency to idealize the role and status of the aged in the past continues.

Harlan has demonstrated how these myths have been per-

[1] This research was supported by funds from National Institute of Child Health and Human Development Training Grant HD-00160, granted to the senior author.

petuated to the point where "they have become firmly rooted in current gerontological thought" (Harlan, 1968). This thesis, that the traditionally high social status of the aged was undermined as a concomitant of modernization has been expressed by Davis and Coombs, Epstein, Frank, Dunham, Moore, Smith, Simmons, and the White House Conference (Davis and Coombs, 1950; Epstein, 1931; Frank, 1943; Dunham, 1945; Moore, 1950; Smith, 1950; Simmons, 1960; White House Conference, 1961). Harlan states that these views "are reiterated frequently, but rarely questioned" (Harlan, 1968).

More recently Cowgill has attempted to alter the "universal" view of pre-industrial aged by enumerating a series of generalizations about the status of the aged which treats it as variable, not universal (Cowgill and Holmes, 1972).

> Cowgill sees the status of the aged as higher where: 1. accumulation of knowledge is important; 2. the aged can maintain property rights; 3. the aged may continue to perform useful functions; 4. the aged operate within an extended family structure; 5. there are fewer role shifts through maturation and thus, where the aged are less likely to become obsolete; and 6. there is less emphasis upon individual ego development (Press and McKool, 1972).

Working among peasants in Mexico and Guatemala, Press and McKool found that "almost point for point, our independently derived determinants coincided with Cowgill's (Press and McKool, 1972).

In keeping with this variable approach, evidence is emerging which suggests that there was considerable variation in pre-industrial societies in terms of the position of the aged. It is becoming apparent that there were societies among which, in the past, the elderly did *not* necessarily enjoy great official authority and high status as a function of their age.

Harlan, for example, looked at the status of old people in three pre-industrial Indian agricultural villages little affected by urbanization and industrialization and found that traditional family norms were, in fact, not observed in practice. He states: "The common view of gerontologists and others as to the high status of the aged within the family of pre-industrial society is not valid with reference to a majority of these men" (Harlan, 1968).

Arth studied the Ibo people of southeastern Nigeria and found that:

> There is little doubt that the Ibo demand respect for the elderly, and that the elders play important roles in the society. In one of the few sources dealing with the role of the aged among the Ibo, Shelton (1965) expresses this clearly. Lineage elders have important ritual functions to perform. Compound elders are required to make daily sacrifices to household shrines. It is the old who often control the knowledge of midwifery, of curing, and of divining the future. Respect is seen in the fact that the funerals of the aged are the most elaborate; the list could be extended. In the village studied, all these functions of the aged persist, though modern medical practices and the introduction of Christianity have lessened their exclusiveness.
>
> Still, one does not find among the Ibo the intense respect pattern reported in some cultures, for example, village Thailand (Cowgill, 1965). Among tribal peoples, the degree of respect-deference varies enormously, an important fact for gerontologists to note. Too often one finds reference in the literature to respect patterns in non-Western cultures as if all such patterns were the same. There is a broad range of attitudes and behaviors on this dimension in non-Western societies, too. The author's own observations suggest that though the ideal of respect holds in Ibo culture, behavior often indicates a highly ambivalent attitude. Furthermore, the acculturation process seems to be contributing to increasing the stress and conflict between generations (Arth, 1972).

Rebellion and resentment, it appears, constitute an integral part of intergenerational relations. LeVine, in his discussion of intergenerational tensions in extended families in Sub-Saharan Africa, also points out such strains as inherent in the father-son relationship in particular, raising some interesting questions about the dysfunctional aspects of the extended family structure (LeVine, 1965).

Even in ancient times Haynes reports, in a study of literary concepts of old age in Ancient Greece, that "the conclusion may be drawn with certainty that there was not a golden age for aged men and women in ancient Greece" (Haynes, 1962).

There are pre-industrial societies, in short, in which the aged have been undervalued *qua* aged, with their functions restricted to the general community role of adviser-storyteller and to the two foci of grandparenthood, i.e. teacher and source of affection. In the modern world, the aged in such societies continue to play the affective grandparent role, to have minimal authority and to be undervalued, with the major change being the lessening importance of their role as adviser and repository of oral traditions. It is one of these societies, the Baganda, that we are concerned with in the present paper.

METHODOLOGY

We are looking over time to discover patterns of continuity and change. In order to describe the position of the aged in traditional Baganda society, and rather than depending on idealized and perhaps distorted perceptions of the past on the part of present respondents, we have relied on ethnographic materials from a variety of sources. It was necessary to glean information from references to age sets or the age-grade system in order to get at the position of the aged *vis-a-vis* other age groups. Unfortunately, the bulk of the literature emphasizes the earlier stages of life, focusing largely on the birth and initiation ceremonies and the surrounding rituals. This, of course, can be taken as an unobtrusive measure of the insignificant place of the aged, but it may also result in over-stating the position of the aged in those ethnographies where they are discussed at greater length. By using a number of different ethnographies there is an "averaging" or "equalizing" effect, and we are thereby likely to increase the extent to which the total picture that emerges will approximate reality.

Much of the ethnographic material is not the work of trained anthropologists using rigorous field methods. Rather, we are confronted with reports from travellers who supply little more than patchwork descriptions and observations made, oftentimes, under unusual circumstances and for generally short periods of time. Secondly, there are accounts of missionaries whose observations were often distorted by the moralistic perspective they brought to the field. This is especially a problem in their discussions of home life and family practices, which are crucial to the present analysis. Finally, there are studies done by anthropologists which are of varying quality though, with the increasing sophistication of the discipline, the more recent ones tend to be more rigorous. Taken together, we are left with a less than systematic conglomerate of reports, anecdotes and tales which suffer somewhat from a lack of comparability arising in part out of different foci of the investigators. Credence, then, is lent to those points on which the various writers reinforce each other.

To address the question of the saliency of traditional roles for modern life and the position of the aged today, data will be presented from two social surveys carried out in 1971 as part of a larger Ugandan study. The data consist of a questionnaire study of secondary school students and intensive interviews with 115 Baganda between the ages of 60 and 90.

All government secondary schools are conducted in English and the questionnaires were administered to all of the students in fifteen schools in central, southern, and western Uganda. Since the majority are boarding schools and draw on a broad population base, the student bodies tend to be heterogeneous with regard to tribe though geographic proximity fosters tribal predominance in different regions. The sub-sample dealt with in the present analysis comprised the 1699 Baganda secondary school students between the ages of twelve through twenty-one. The questionnaire took an average of one and a quarter hours to complete, although this ranged from forty-five minutes to two and a half hours, and varied inversely with age and level of English proficiency.

The Baganda respondents consists of 1015 males and 684 females. Each was asked to recall when he or she was in the fifth grade (P5), and to discuss relations with one grandmother and one grandfather who was living at that time. The rationale is that since we were dealing with students of different ages— the majority of whom were currently enrolled in boarding, as opposed to day, schools—it was necessary to establish some common baseline to which they would all refer. Consequently, recall data were used to define their relationships with grandparents, or if their grandparents were not living, with another old person whom they knew well or was like a grandparent to them.

According to Radcliffe-Brown, ". . . it is not the children who replace their parents but those of the grandparent generation are replaced by those of the grandchildren's generation. . . . This relation of the two generations is recognized by some African peoples. In East Africa, where age-sets are arranged in cycles, the cycles are such that a son's son may frequently belong to the same one as his father's father" (Radcliffe-Brown, 1967). Although 57 percent of our respondents were not named for anyone, 35 percent were named after a grandparent, with the remaining 8 percent named for other assorted kin. Of those named for a grandparent, 84 percent were named for a paternal grandparent. Since this is a patrilineal tribe and the belief is that one is immortalized through one's heirs this is not unexpected. In fact, among the Baganda it is the father's mother who is called upon to give the baby his personal name (Mair, 1969).

Uganda follows the British educational system. Admission to secondary school is highly competitive and requires the payment of fees during Senior 1 through Senior 4, thereby eliminating many. At the end of four years of secondary school, students take 0-level ("ordinary" level) examinations and those few who distinguish themselves are eligible for two years of senior secondary school—at government expense—which is a college preparatory program. This sample, then, is somewhat better off than the general Ugandan population both because the Baganda are privileged among Uganda's peoples and because it involves secondary school students.

The major problem in the secondary school study was communication failure. This failure took four forms: (1) use of an American word when the students were familiar with a different British word; (2) use of a word which meant something quite different in "British English" (for example—the word "spoil" which the British do not define as "to make one selfish or self-centered" but rather as "to ruin or destroy"); (3) use of a word which the students simply didn't know; (4) use of a word with a vague or inaccurate local cultural referent (Adams, 1974).

Recognizing the possibility of such communication difficulties we employed a pre-test of the instrument with several non-sample secondary school students ranging from Senior 1 (eighth grade) through Senior 6 (thirteenth grade). This pre-test was a great help in reducing all four forms of communication failure, and in fact, most questions concerning the role of the aged, division of tasks, residential patterns, and interaction patterns caused no great problems to the secondary school respondents.

The second portion of our data collection involved interviews with elderly Baganda themselves. This introduces several additional problems to the research task. We had to begin by developing a common definition of who to include in the study. Our definition evolved into a composite of age (on which most were quite vague), being a grandparent, and certain physical manifestations, used only when the prospective respondent did not know his age and was omitted as "looking too young."

Few of these elderly are located in Ugandan urban centers, and the interviewers were thus left to find them in the rural areas through "snowball" sampling techniques.

One problem involved language. Few of the respondents know English and the questions were therefore asked in Luganda. This necessitated translating the original schedule from English into Luganda and then translating the old peoples' responses into English. Such translations were checked for accuracy and equivalence by two University students who know both languages well.

Thus, methodologically we are working with three data sources: ethnographic reports, questionnaires from students, and interviews with the elderly. Where they diverge we cannot be sure that the results are not a function of differing techniques of collection. However, where they are consistent our confidence in the results is heightened by the very diversity of sources.

BACKGROUND

Uganda is a landlocked agricultural country, bordered on the south by Lake Victoria, and was a British Protectorate until independence in 1962. It is the least urbanized of the three East

African countries; of its 9½ million people only 5 percent, according to the 1969 census, live in urban centers. Approximately six per cent of the population are over sixty years old, with aged males slightly outnumbering females. The ratio of aged in rural areas is two to three times that of major towns. There are over forty tribal or ethnic groups in Uganda and English is the language of education and government.

The Baganda comprise 25 percent of the population and have traditionally been the dominant tribe. The word *Banamawange* means outsider or foreigner and is used by the Baganda to refer to everyone who is not of their ethnic group. Their ethnocentrism and political dominance prior to independence have made them unpopular with other groups, while recent political pressures have made their position precarious. The Baganda live in the fertile south central region of Uganda and enjoy both an ideal climate and a dependable food supply. This has especially important implications for the status of the aged because it means that as long as they are physically able to care for themselves they can remain independent. Since land is fertile and plentiful, young people are not as dependent on their fathers as they are in societies where a son is dependent on jointly-held parental property.

The Baganda are a Bantu-speaking people with a loose patrilineal social structure and, traditionally, a sophisticated hierarchically organized political system. They are an eclectic people who for centuries have adapted their way of life to changing conditions. Thus, while they have a patrilineal kinship system in which the father-son relationship is emphasized, they are nuclear in their households and the generations are often residentially segregated by considerable distance. This neolocal residence pattern reduces the power a parent exercises over his son. Equally important, it reduces the frequency of their interaction in adulthood.

According to Audrey Richards, a man acquired rights over land through his political affiliations rather than through kinship ties.

> Thus, the Muganda was apparently as anxious to live with his relatives as are members of societies with villages based on corporate

patrilineages but his life cycle was different. . . . In brief, the traditional system was one in which political ties were more important to a young man's career than his links to a local patrilineage. By the middle of the 19th century, hereditary rights to land or office had been so far eliminated that a father had few assets with which to advance his sons, except the political links he or his lineage had made with different chiefs, ministers, or court functionaries or with the king or other royals (Richards, 1970).

At the beginning of this century a free-hold tenure system and the introduction of cash crops made for many changes in Buganda according to Richards. "It is often assumed that modern economic developments break down kinship and family groupings in African society and that they produce a new kind of individualism. It is my thesis that the changes which took place in Buganda in the early part of this century actually strengthened the ties of the individual family and the minor lineage rather than weakening them" (Richards, 1970). This is also a contention of the present analysis.

The traditional Baganda value system emphasizes individualism above familism and they have a positive orientation toward achievement and change. Individualism, as opposed to the corporate or collective notion, is in accord with the traditional patterns of Ganda life. The dominant features of their social organization, therefore, are (1) a weak patrilinealism; (2) individualism; (3) achievement orientation; (4) neolocality; and (5) political hierarchy. Gibbs notes that "Ganda agriculture does not require the cooperation of people outside the single household" (Gibbs, 1965), and as cash crops become increasingly more important, the Baganda tend to hire tenants rather than relying on kin. Fallers reports that, in the modern world, the Baganda continue to be on the "cutting edge" of achievement and change. "Baganda," he says, "do, of course, participate in a money economy to a degree which is relatively unusual for East Africans and they generally value the goods and services which this participation provides. But the incentive for most is the 'carrot' of the essentially luxury goods which the proceeds from their cotton and coffee will buy, not the 'goad' of actual privation or landlessness . . ." (L. Fallers, 1964).

Since Kampala, the major urban area and capital of Uganda

is in Buganda those who enter the wage labor force are able, if they so desire, to maintain ties with their rural roots either by commuting daily or more often through visiting. "Thus, for the Ganda, there is not, even under modern conditions, the sharp discontinuity between urban and rural life that there tends to be for many African peoples. On the one hand, there are few Ganda who do not have rural roots in a bit of agricultural land; on the other, there are also few who have not, at one time or another, spent time in the metropolis. Baganda society and culture thus have a unity which embraces both urban and rural people" (M. Fallers, 1960).

Traditionally, the division of labor has been on the basis of sex and to a lesser extent on age. With regard to the sexual division of labor, Gibbs reports that:

> In the old days men took little part in agriculture, since their only task was the clearing of new land, not frequently required; men built houses, made bark clothes, hunted and in some places fished, but much of their time was spent in attendance on the chief and waiting for the call to go to war, or to labor on public works. Today men are considered responsible for earning cash, usually by cultivating cash crops, so that they can pay taxes for their children's education, and provide their families with clothes, meat, sugar, tea, kerosene, and all the other minor necessities and luxuries of modern life. Men, unless in employment, are perforce cultivators now, at least in the cotton and coffee gardens—though their wives also help with these. Most men put in an average of about four hours' work a day, and spend much of their free time in drinking banana beer, or even brewing it. Women, with their domestic duties as well as their work in the food gardens, have less free time (Gibbs, 1965).

In terms of the division of labor based on age, the pattern is not nearly as clear-cut. According to all the ethnographic reports, old people played many of the ceremonial roles, especially those associated with birth and to a lesser extent marriage. Their daily activities, like those of the Ibo, can best be described as continuity from the past at a reduced level (Arth, 1972; Nahemow and Adams, 1972).

Ethnographic reports on the status of the aged emphasize the obedience and respect aspects of intergenerational relationships. Fallers notes that children used to owe their father a deference that would be reckoned extreme according to modern European standards. Children knelt when they spoke to their father, crouching on the floor at the door of his room. This is still done in most village homes and most chidren kneel to meet older guests, putting their clasped hands in those of the visitor and speaking in a high-pitched squeaky voice which is thought to be especially respectful, though educated parents discourage excessive humility in a girl, calling it *bukopikopi* (very peasant-like). In the more traditional households young, and even grown, men still sometimes crouch at the threshold of their father's house when they greet him after an absence and they address him kneeling. This custom is more common if the man is a prince or a man of note (L. Fallers, 1964).

This is typical of the tenor of the ethnographic material, which, it is being suggested here, must be combined with those accounts of the elderly as having little official authority role in the Buganda community. They have had family respect traditionally, but little political or economic influence *qua* aged. Let us, therefore, look at our data.

RESULTS

Our first question sought to discover whether our student and elderly respondents thought the aged have a specific role to play. "Do old people have any special position or do different things JUST BECAUSE THEY ARE OLD?" Looking at Table

TABLE 7-I

OLD PEOPLE HOLD ANY SPECIAL POSITION?

	Students		Aged	
	N	%	N	%
No	791	50.8	60	55.5
Clan Head	26	1.7	—	—
Officiates at Ceremonies	12	.8	3	2.7
Family Head	19	1.2	—	—
Respect, obeyed	124	7.9	20	27.2
Adviser	106	6.8	9	8.2
Storyteller	6	.4	—	—
Light Work	72	4.7	1	—
Behavioral Changes	97	6.2	—	—
Miscellaneous: smokes, drinks, sits around	302	19.4	7	6.4
TOTAL	1555	99.9%	110	100%

7-I we can see that even those special positions that were proposed seldom involved power or authority. An interesting aspect
of Table 7-I is the fact that the students, when they see the aged
as playing a specific role, more often see it as a weak position.
That is, more students speak of the old as doing only light work,
sitting around smoking or drinking, or behaviorally manifesting
senility, than acting in a positive way as adviser, storyteller,
official, or object for respect. Further, it should be recalled
that this sample is not representative in that we have over-
sampled for both age groups the more elite segments of society.
Thus, if anything the position of the aged in our sample should
be *higher* than for the populace as a whole. Among our respondents, then, it seems that expectations with regard to the position
of the aged are consistent across the generations, the majority
seeing them as having no special position at all. A large minority
view the aged negatively—a function of responsibilities forfeited
and abiilties lost. Only a few see the aged as either officials
or advisers.

This does not, of course, suggest that old people are altogether
estranged from the larger community. However, given their
infrequent official involvement as clan leaders in the past, and
the growing devaluation or inappropriateness of their advising
and storytelling or tradition-passing skills for the challenges of
contemporary life and the demands of the cash economy, the
position of aged Baganda *vis-à-vis* other groups in society appears
to be becoming increasingly confined to the familial role of
grandparent. Formerly, this role within the family sphere functioned in tandem with the adviser-storyteller role in the community as a source of meaning and gratification for the aged.
Today, as the latter loses its significance, the former—which never
contained a large element of authority—remains to give meaning
to the life of the elderly, much as we find in many European
nations (Shanas *et al.*, 1968). Much of our data, then, will focus
on the role of grandparenthood among the Baganda. We will
look at how both old and young define the role, as well as the
life experiences of each in terms of their joint interaction patterns.

Who is a good grandparent? Elderly men and women agree
that a good grandparent is defined as one who teaches, loves,

and cares for his or her grandchildren, in that order. An ideal grandparent-grandchild relationship emphasizes love, and teaching about life, manners, morality, and work roles (see Table 7-II). A typical response, from a seventy-six year old man with "many, many" grandchildren is that it is important" not to show too much love—although this is very difficult. (One should) train them to work and above all send them to school." Of less significance is the role of providing assistance, gifts or care—at least in the idealized conception of the relationship.

While teaching is the principle "ingredient" of the relationship, it seems somewhat more important to the grandmother role. This is a function of the existing division of labor in the larger society, where females are concerned with activities centered around the household, while males are more involved in economic or leisure affairs. Since young children are expected to do tasks around the house, this serves to strengthen ties with grandmothers or at least increase the frequency of interaction between them, although residential distance is a limiting factor. The Baganda, it must be remembered, are neolocal, which restricts

TABLE 7-II

IDEAL GRANDPARENT-GRANDCHILD RELATIONSHIP

	Aged Males N	Aged Males %	Aged Females N	Aged Females %
One who loves grandchildren	11	25.0	6	18.8
One who teaches them	18	40.9	17	53.1
Loves and teaches	3	6.8	4	12.5
Gives things/cares for them	9	20.4	5	15.6
Other	3	6.8	—	—
TOTAL	44	99.9%	32	100%

interaction between many grandparents and their grandchildren (see Table 7-III). Many grandfathers explained that, presumably for the types of skill and activities they are interested in and/or feel competent to impart, their grandchildren are too young. Part of the sex difference, then, may be a function of the age distribution of our sample of old people.

Since there is neither a pattern of joint residence, nor extensive interaction between generations within most families, as reported

TABLE 7-III

ACTIVITIES DONE WITH GRANDCHILDREN

	Males		Females	
	N	%	N	%
Nothing	11	25.0	8	27.6
Digging and Tasks	13	29.5	10	34.5
Too young	11	25.0	1	3.4
Too far away	6	13.6	7	24.1
Other	3	6.8	3	10.3
TOTAL	44	99.9%	29	99.9%

by our respondents, it is of interest to ask to what extent grandparents think they share in the responsibility for how their grandchildren turn out. That is, do they perceive their role as integral, complementary, or extraneous to that of parents?

A theme repeatedly expressed is that grandparents, even if they have no money (and few have very much), still place a high value on education and want their grandchildren to go to school. While few are in a position to absorb the cost of school fees, they nevertheless seek to teach their grandchildren what they think will be useful in society, and this generally takes the form of teaching appropriate behavior.

While about a quarter of the sample say that the parents must take full responsibility for their children, it is nevertheless clear that to the majority of these old people to be a good grandparent one must meet the criteria of the ideal relationship. That is, a good grandparent is responsible for teaching traditions as well as right and proper behavior. To the extent that a grandparent fulfills these role demands he perceives himself as sharing with parents in a complementary fashion in the process of molding future generations (see Table 7-IV).

Both the old people and the students were asked a series of attitude questions regarding intergenerational relations and definitions of family obligations. Interestingly, there is general consensus between them on a wide variety of issues. Thus, for the entire sample, there is agreement that it is legitimate to criticize parents and grandparents; that grandparents should not "spoil" grandchildren, and that each individual has a responsibility to both descending and ascending generations in terms of

TABLE 7-IV

DO GRANDPARENTS HAVE SOME RESPONSIBILITY FOR
HOW THEIR GRANDCHILDREN TURN OUT?

	Males		Females	
	N	%	N	%
To teach them traditions and proper behavior	24	51.0	19	57.6
It's major responsibility of parents	12	25.5	8	24.2
Should send them to school	6	12.8	1	3.0
Care for them	3	6.4	1	3.0
Other	2	4.3	4	12.1
TOTAL	47	100%	33	99.9%

providing for them; particularly if they are helpless, but not just limited to this. This does not, however, extend to joint residence, which is a violation of traditional living arrangements and is resorted to only in dire circumstances.

Despite general consensus on these expectations there are marked differences between the generations on the extent of agreement as well as variations within the student groupings. Among the students, for whom sex differences on these variables are minimal, the most interesting differences are a function of year attained in school. Senior Secondary students—5th and 6th year students—are consistently in greater agreement with the old people than they are with their fellow students. For example, in terms of whether it is a child's responsibility to care for his aged parents, 96 percent of the old people agree that it is, compared with 79 percent of the students. However, among the students, 92 percent of the S6's agree that a child is responsible for his aging parents, compared to 69 percent of the S1's (see Table 7-V). It is this pattern which essentially characterized each of the attitudes investigated.

The acculturation hypothesis would have led us to expect that with increasing exposure to education and modern life styles there would be greater discontinuity between the traditional values of the aged and the forward looking individualism of the more educated young. This, however, is not borne out by our data. One reason for this is that among the Baganda traditional and "modern" values are not that different. Therefore, the older students' attitude toward the aged converge with the

TABLE 7-V

IT IS A CHILD'S RESPONSIBILITY TO TAKE CARE
OF HIS AGED PARENTS

Year in School

	S1		S2		S3		S4		S5 & S6	
	N	%	N	%	N	%	N	%	N	%
Agree	194	68.8	195	80.9	180	76.6	163	85.3	106	92.2
Disagree	88	31.2	46	19.1	55	23.4	28	14.7	9	7.8
TOTAL	282	100%	241	100%	235	100%	191	100%	115	100%

attitudes of the elderly themselves, instead of diverging. This pattern can be seen most clearly from responses to the statement: "When adults move to the city, they should make room for their aged parents to come and live with them" (see Table 7-VI).

Eighty-nine percent of the old people disagree with this statement as compared with 46 percent of the students. But interestingly, over half of the younger students chose this over traditionally preferential residence separation. It is possible that older students, having had greater experience and exposure to city life, have a realistic conception of the urban conditions. The old people and the advanced students, therefore, agree that city life is not good for the aged, and thus their urban-oriented children should not bring them to the city to live. Traditional neolocality is reinforced, then, by the educated and the elderly agreeing that the former's place is in the modern urban milieu, and the latter's is in the rural environment. Whether this will, that the skills of today must be imparted. Grandparents feel that there is a contribution they can make first in manifesting love, and also in directly teaching and encouraging appropriate

TABLE 7-VI

WHEN ADULTS MOVE TO THE CITY THEY SHOULD MAKE ROOM FOR
THEIR AGED PARENTS TO COME AND LIVE WITH THEM

Year in School

	S1		S2		S3		S4		S5 & S6	
	N	%	N	%	N	%	N	%	N	%
Agree	151	57.9	125	53.4	87	41.8	67	38.1	26	24.5
Disagree	110	42.1	109	46.6	121	58.2	109	61.9	80	75.5
TOTAL	261	100%	234	100%	208	100%	176	100%	106	100%

in the years ahead, further weaken the social-emotional role of grandparents remains to be seen.

Perceived freedom to criticize older people was used as a gross measure of respect attributable directly to age. Slightly more than half (53%) of the students feel that it is wrong to criticize their grandparents even if they make a mistake. This compares with 20 percent of the old people. That is, 80 percent of the aged say that grandchildren should feel free to criticize them if the situation warrants it. Again, older students were more likely to share this view (see Tables 7-VIIa and 7-VIIb).

TABLE 7-VIIa

IT IS WRONG FOR GRANDCHILDREN TO CRITICIZE THEIR GRANDPARENTS EVEN IF THEY MAKE A MISTAKE

Year in School

	S1 N	S1 %	S2 N	S2 %	S3 N	S3 %	S4 N	S4 %	S5 & S6 N	S5 & S6 %
Agree	160	56.3	148	58.7	127	54.0	101	52.3	35	31.8
Disagree	124	43.7	104	41.3	108	46.0	92	47.7	75	68.2
TOTAL	284	100%	252	100%	235	100%	193	100%	110	100%

TABLE 7-VIIb

IT IS ALL RIGHT FOR YOUNG PEOPLE TO CRITICIZE THEIR PARENTS

Year in School

	S1 N	S1 %	S2 N	S2 %	S3 N	S3 %	S4 N	S4 %	S5 & S6 N	S5 & S6 %
Agree	135	50.8	79	34.6	64	28.4	74	39.6	72	66.8
Disagree	131	49.2	149	65.4	161	71.6	113	60.4	36	32.2
TOTAL	266	100%	228	100%	225	100%	187	100%	108	100%

With regard to criticizing parents, over 95 percent of the aged say that this is all right as compared with 42 percent of the students. In other words, the vast majority of old people affirm that it is legitimate to criticize parents and, somewhat less so, to criticize grandparents, if they are wrong. Roughly half of of the students share this definition of legitimacy. Either older students come to realize the license they have to question adults while the younger ones have not yet tested this, or else older generations, though they pay lip service to such openness, have demonstrated that they actually feel otherwise, making the younger students more cautious in the criticisms. The data do not resolve this question, but the value system of the Baganda—with its emphasis on individual freedom—would support the view that the individual is rewarded for speaking out.

CONCLUSIONS

What emerges from the foregoing analysis is a picture of the Baganda as a people among whom the aged have no tradition of societal leadership, but only of advice, storytelling and trying to be "good" grandparents. The change that has occurred has been in the weakening of the advisory role. What remains is the grandparent role, limited in its expression by neolocality and the lessening of the adviser-storyteller roles, due to the awareness on the part of all concerned that it is primarily through formal education—not through the oral traditions of the aged—behavior by their grandchildren. The elderly have assumed a small but complementary share of the responsibility in the child-rearing process and perceive their contribution as important, though bounded by both traditional and modern limitations on the role of aged in Baganda society.

There is marked agreement across generations on overall patterns of interaction, and definitions of responsibility toward family members and appropriate role behavior. It appears that the highly individualistic value system of the Baganda complements and encourages this, and rather than fostering conflict there is a sense of intergenerational understanding and solidarity, as well as independence.

Finally, then, our data are consistent with the picture of old age among the Baganda gleaned from the ethnographic literature. Baganda values and norms "fit" fairly easily into the modern world. Baganda society has *not* traditionally accorded official economic or political authority to the aged, and this is still true today. The grandparent role among the Baganda today is likewise quite consistent with and similar to that of the past. The major change appears to occur as modern education weakens

the position of the aged as advisors and storytellers— as repositories of the oral traditions and wisdom of the past.

REFERENCES

Adams, Bert N.: Doing Cross-Cultural Research—Some Approaches and Problems. *Journal of Marriage and the Family,* August, 1974.

Arth, Malcolm: A Cross-Cultural Perspective. In *Research Planning and Action for the Elderly,* Kent, Kastenbaum, and Sherwood (eds.). New York, Behavioral, 1972.

Cowgill, Donald, and Holmes, Lowell D.: *Aging and Modernization.* New York, Appleton, 1972.

Davis, Kingsley, and Coombs, J. W.: The Sociology of an Aged Population. In *The Social and Biological Challenges of Our Aging Population,* I. Gladstone (ed.). New York, Columbia Press, 1950.

Dunham, H. W.: Social Aspects of Mental Disorders in Later Life. In *Mental Disorders in Later Life,* O. J. Kaplan (ed.). Stanford Press, 1945.

Epstein, A.: Facing Old Age. In *The Care of the Aged,* I. M. Rubinow (ed.). Chicago Press, 1931.

Fallers, Lloyd: *The King's Men.* London, Oxford Press, 1964.

Fallers, Margaret Chave: *Eastern Lacustrine Bantu.* International African Institute, 1960.

Frank, L. K.: The Older Person in the Changing Social Scene. In *New Goals for Old Age,* G. Lawton (ed.). New York, Columbia Press, 1943.

Gibbs, James L., Jr.: *Peoples of Africa.* New York, Holt, 1965.

Harlan, William H.: Social Status of the Aged in Three Indian Villages. In *Middle Age and Aging,* Bernice Neugarten (ed.). Chicago Press, 1968.

Haynes, Maria S.: The Supposedly Golden Age for the Aged in Ancient Greece (A Study of Literary Concepts of Old Age). *The Gerontologist,* 2:93-98, 1962.

Kalibala, E. B.: *Social Structure of the Baganda Tribe of East Africa.* (unpublished Ph.D. Thesis), Harvard University, 1946.

LeVine, Robert A.: Intergenerational Tensions and Extended Family Structures in Africa. In *Social Structure and the Family,* Ethel Shanas and Gordon Streib (eds.). Englewood Cliffs, N. J., Prentice-Hall, 1965.

Mair, Lucy: *An African People in the 20th Century.* London, Routledge, 1934.

Mair, Lucy: *African Marriage and Social Change.* London, Cass, 1969.

Moore, Wilbert E.: The Aged in Industrial Societies. In *The Aged and Society,* M. Derber (ed.). Industrial Relations Research Association, 1950.

Nahemow, Nina, and Adams, Bert: Grandparenthood in a Changing Society. Paper presented at the 25th Annual Meeting of the Gerontological Society, San Juan, Puerto Rico, 1972.

Press, Irwin, and McKool, Mike, Jr.: Social Structure and Status of the Aged—Toward Some Valid Cross-Cultural Generalizations. *Aging and Human Development,* 3:297-306, 1972.

Radcliffe-Brown, A. R.: *African Systems of Kinship and Marriage.* London, Oxford Press, 1967.

Richards, Audrey I.: *The Changing Structure of a Ganda Village.* East African Studies, 1970.

Roscoe, John: *The Baganda.* London, Frank Cass, 1911.

Shanas, Ethel, *et al.: Old People in Three Industrial Societies.* New York, Atherton, 1968.

Simmons, Leo: Aging in Preindustrial Societies. In *Handbook of Social Gerontology,* Clark Tibbets (ed.). Chicago Press, 1960.

Smith, T. L.: The Aged in Rural Society. In *The Aged and Society,* M. Derber (ed.). Industrial Relations Research Association, 1950.

White House Conference on Aging—The Nation and Its Older People. Washington, D. C., Dept. of Health, Education and Welfare, 1961.

CHAPTER 8

LESSONS FROM THE ISSEI[1]

CHRISTIE W. KIEFER

HAVING HAD VERY little training in the field of aging, but quite a lot in the speaking of Japanese, I was recruited in 1968 by Margaret Clark to work on a cross-cultural study of aging which was already underway at the Langley Porter Neuropsychiatric Institute in San Francisco. I was to interview aging Japanese immigrants—or *issei*, as they call themselves—and their children and grandchildren, while Professor Clark worked with Mexican Americans. In the folowing five years, I got to know about twenty issei, and the community they lived in, quite well. My assistant, Doug Sparks, and I interviewed most of our issei informants in their homes several times each, averaging about ten or twelve hours per person altogether. We gathered information about them from their children and grandchildren, their pastors, their friends, and their ethnic news media. We concentrated mainly on the problems of old age in their culture and their ways of handling these problems. This turned out to be more than an academic job for me.

There are about 12,000 Japanese Americans living in San Francisco, of whom some seven or eight hundred are issei. The issei we saw were probably among the healthiest members of their culture in America. Many had survived to a ripe old age under hard circumstances, or they wouldn't have been around to interview. All were volunteers living in the community. We did not see the seriously sick, nor those who might have been

---

[1] The research on which this paper is based was supported by a grant from the National Institute of Child Health and Human Development, U.S. Department of Health, Education, and Welfare.

too ashamed of their condition to talk with us. However though several of our issei did have distinct problems of health, morale, and even livelihood, my impression is that the vast majority of the issei belong to the healthy end of the scale, and that what follows is a reasonably accurate portrayal of the culture of aging among Japanese-American immigrants.

THE HOME CULTURE

Japan at the time our issei left it (about 1900 to 1920) was a complex, closely stratified society in a storm of social change that would deliver the country from several hundred years of agrarian feudalism. Although urban life was highly developed, the moral standards of Japanese society were still very much based on the agrarian traditions of the family and the small, stable, face-to-face community. In order to understand the adaptation of the issei to their American environment, we must look briefly at the working assumptions about self, society, and nature which they brought with them . Here I must of course be overly brief and general because of space, with apologies to the complexity and subtlety of Japanese culture.

Traditional Japanese society favored social relationships which were stable and closely cooperative. Every normal individual was integrated into a household, a lineage, and a village or urban ward which functioned for many purposes as a corporate group, by means of a rather elaborate system of mutual rights and obligations, including the exchange of services and goods.

As part of the pattern, tremendous emphasis was placed on the maintenance of equanimity and harmony. Values were *eco*-centric as opposed to *ego*-centric, and situational as opposed to universalistic. By eco-centric, I mean that the individual was seen as co-extensive with his nature and social environment. Struggle against the environment under normal conditions was seen as the height of foolishness, as was the deliberate disruption of natural or group processes. The individual's well-being was intimately tied up with that of the various groups and natural settings to which he belonged, and his groups shared in his prosperity as well as his hardship. By situationality, I mean that values were held to be specific to the social situation at hand, not transcendant and applicable to all situations. Little or no contradiction was felt when a fanatic anti-Western studied European etiquette, or when a person offered Shinto prayers at a wedding and Buddhist prayers at a funeral on the same day. What was inappropriate was also immoral, under ordinary circumstances. Such a moral attitude can and does produce many ethical dilemmas when contexts overlap, but the tendency was to solve such dilemmas on an *ad hoc* basis, without agonizing about universal principles.

Harmony and situationality were reinforced by the functional diffuseness of social groups. Since the individual's loyalties were to other people, more than to ideals, the fewer integrated groups he belonged to, the less conflict he was likely to get into, and the more intense his group loyalty was likely to be. As a result, groups tended to be "paternalistic;" that is, they performed a very wide variety of services for their members, thereby limiting the need for numerous groups. A boss was often called upon to float a loan or arrange a marriage, a teacher was consulted on many issues outside of the academic realm, and so on.

The ideal type of personality under these circumstances was one with a disinclination to express direct hostility, or to assert an unpopular opinion or a disruptive emotion (intense affection included).

An internally balanced and conflict-free personality was emphasized. A partial list of widely valued attitudes might include the following:

Kansha (gratitude): A sense of the great dependence of the self on the human, natural, and supernatural world around one—including the ancestors—and a feeling of gratefulness for whatever comes one's way.

Gaman (forbearance, patience): The ability to keep calm and carry out one's duties in the face of frustrating circumstances, without nurturing grudges. Also emotional stability or stoicism.

Makoto (sincerity): Making inner feelings and external acts coincide, mainly by controlling (but not suppressing altogether) the feelings and conforming to role demands.

Giri (duty): Knowing what is expected of one, and fulfilling such obligations to the best of one's ability.

Indirect and non-verbal means of communication were often used to convey emotion which might threaten the serenity of social interaction or the continuity of relationships. Great attention was paid to facial expressions and to innuendos in the speech of others—in an atmosphere of strict politeness—in order to avoid the disruption of social processes. Under the circumstances, individuals were typically very sensitive to criticism, and shaming was an effective means of social control.

These were some of the broad cultural norms which tended to distinguish the Japanese immigrant from his American contemporary, and later to a lesser extent, from his American-born children and grandchildren. In order to understand the adjustment of the issei to old age, however, we have to look at still another set of traditional Japanese norms—those normal features of the aging process which set up *expectations* about what the later years of one's life ought to be like. Here again I am aiming at a high level of abstraction and overlooking the great variety in aging patterns which fell within the normal range in traditional Japan. I am simply suggesting that culture places certain broad limits on the individual's perceptions of what is normal and expectable in the social characteristics of his later years. By observing his elders, a person builds up some sense of what the next stage of his own life will be like. His culture, we can say, provides him with some sort of map of the developmental territory ahead.

The ideal type of family in traditional Japan was the patrilineal, patrilocal extended family based on primogeniture. According to this ideal, every old person would live in the same household with his or her oldest son, and the son's wife and children. Of course this pattern was by no means always followed even in olden times, and has declined steadily with urbanization,[2] but it did guide people's expectations about old age. The position of elder, both in the household and in the local community, was ideally a respected one. Women were expected to dominate

---

[2] Koyama (1962) reports a decline in the percentage of extended families as one moves from rural areas (35.3% of all families in 1960) to large urban centers (19.9% of all families in 1960).

(benignly, one hopes) their daughters-in-law with the help of loyal sons. Men retained the headship of the household until formal retirement (*inkyo*) at the age of about sixty, after which they were still to be sought out for guidance. In rural areas, most communal rituals and religious activities were under the supervision of the retired men, or "elders." There is some indication that longevity itself was considered only partly a matter of luck, and partly a reflection of wisdom. A person's eighty-eighth birthday was an occasion for great ceremony and rejoicing, as was a couple's fiftieth wedding anniversary.

Old people were ideally indulged by their juniors. They were allowed greater freedom in dress, speech, and comportment, and were encouraged to enjoy themselves within their means. Food, drink, song, bathing, conversation, and sightseeing were among the most popular indulgences of ordinary old people. Truly filial children and children-in-law would "spoil" their old parents with such indulgences. However, old age was much more than a blissful "second childhood," as some have suggested. Artists, craftsmen, politicians, and holy men were expected to gain skill with advancing age, and grew steadily in veneration after their middle years. Among humbler folk, Morioka has shown (1966) that the labor of the elderly was often badly needed, suggesting that they were rewarded with gratitude for such tasks as baby-sitting, caring for animals, tending fires and floodgates, mending tools, sewing, cooking, providing home medicine, and dispensing their store of knowledge concerning nature and human affairs. Interviews I conducted with old people living in an apartment complex in Osaka in 1966 support the observation that the sense of being needed was indeed an important part of aging in traditional Japan.

Perhaps the most striking period of the traditional Japanese life cycle, to a Westerner, was that following physical death. In Japan, a person did not cease to function as a member of a family when he died:

> As a corporation, the Japanese household includes both living and dead members, and both are essential to its existence. All members are responsible for the welfare and continuity of the

corporation, and all should be mutually concerned for their co-members. The dead provide a spiritual charter guaranteeing the right of their household line to a separate existence. The living provide the material stuff, both productive and reproductive, that keeps the line in motion. The living carry out household business. The dead remain passive except episodically; they serve mainly as moral arbiters and sources of emotional security. (Plath, 1964a: 307)

The presence of the dead was symbolized by the Buddhist memorial tablets (*o-ihai*), each inscribed with an ancestor's death-name, which were kept in the house. Offerings and prayers were regularly made to the ancestors through the *o-ihai*, and many people were in the habit of holding silent conversations with them on matters of personal and family importance. Grave visiting also often had the purpose of communicating with—or simply feeling emotionally close to—the dead.

This attitude is also ritualized in the Buddhist practice of memorial services for the dead, called *hōji* ("invoking the [Buddhist] Law"), or *senzo kuyo* ("offering sustenance to the ancestors"). These services used to consist of the reading of prayers and Sutras at the household Buddhist alter by priests called in for the purpose, accompanied by the offering of incense to the departed by relatives and neighbors, and followed by a communal feast and *sake* drinking. Ideally, these services were held on the seventh, fourteenth, twenty-first, twenty-eighth, thirty-fifth, forty-second, forty-ninth, and one-hundredth days after death, and thereafter on the first, second, seventh, thirteenth, seventeenth, twenty-fifth, thirty-third, fiftieth, sixty-first, and one-hundredth anniversaries. The ceremonies themselves varied a good deal in length and elaborateness—lasting usually a day or so, and employing anywhere from one to ten priests.

Prior to our research, we thought it might be very important to the elderly to feel confident that their children would carry out these duties after their own death; but this did not seem to be the case. The issei would simply shrug when asked about this, saying "Who knows?" in an unconcerned way. This puzzled me until I had conversation with a local Buddhist minister about the meaning of the ceremonies. He explained that the real benefit of the ceremonies is to the *living;* through the *senzo kuyo* they learn the connectedness of all lives, and the humility and patience which, in the Buddhist view of things, give joy to life.

These ideas partake of a vast and subtle difference between the two cultures—a difference in the whole perception of self and time. The traditional Japanese view sees the individual life as a single segment of a continuous cord. Life and its circumstances are gifts from countless prior generations, whose repayment flows on to the generations of the indefinite future. Ruth Benedict (1946) grasped this principle in Japanese thought, but took the one-sided view that it produced a wearying sense of ceaseless obligation in the individual. It often produces an uplifting sense of gratitude for life, and an equanimity in the face of death as well. It is of a piece with the overall Japanese pattern of personal development: human life is group life; the changes experienced by a person throughout his time on earth are also experienced by the groups of which he is a member. Those groups share intimately the credit for his achievements and the responsibility for his difficulties, as he shares theirs. These influences extend outward, both in space and in time, from his biological presence.

HISTORIC FACTORS

The issei departed radically from the expectable Japanese lifecycle in a number of ways when they crossed the Pacific to California. Sojourning abroad was at that time extremely alien to the Japanese way of doing things, the only notable exception being those who had gone to Hawaii two decades earlier. For that majority of the issei who expected to return to some semblance of the normal lifecycle at a later time, leaving was viewed as an unknown adventure, and as "time out" from life as usual.

Perceiving that life at home went on as usual without them, the issei felt that their borrowed days in America were precious and not to be wasted. The conservation of time (and other commodities) was a very familiar feature of their native culture, but in America it had a new urgency. One of the disparaging epithets most frequently heard on the lips of the issei was, "wastetime," applied to anything trivial or inefficient. Life was to be devoted to the acquisition and saving of things that would be of use when the mainstream of life was rejoined. Money was not the only thing that escaped the "wastetime" category, or even the main thing, necessarily. Education in things both Japanese and American was of major importance, as was the cultivation of spiritual values. Churches and study groups made a strong early beginning in the issei culture.

With this sojourner's view of their American experience in mind, we can better understand the reaction of the issei to the severe discriimnation they suffered on the West Coast from their arrival until after World War II. Their reaction was to grit their teeth and make the best of it. Although they were willing to learn from Americans, few made any concerted effort to assimilate, or to "sell" themselves in their host country. They were barred from citizenship, property ownership, intermarriage, and a host of other potential ties to American culture anyway, either by law or by custom or both. For the most part, they banded together and were thrown together by discriminatory housing practices into tight-knit cooperative rural hamlets and urban ghettos.

The dissatisfactions and anxieties of living "time out" must have been considerable. We can speculate that many issei sojourners soon began to weary of the sense of urgency I described, and to discover aspects of their dissected lives which were satisfying *in themselves,* as the newly necessary aspects of their lives gradually took on the familiarity of custom. If they did not get used to life in the United States, they at least got used to not getting used to it. Time out from some developmental processes could be softened by taking time-in again with some others.

Marriage was for most issei men such a partial time-in; but it had to be adapted to the time-out situation. For one thing, most men had already postponed their marriage well past the normal age by the time they made the decision, and in their mid-thirties took wives ten or more years younger than themselves. In order to save the expense of going home to select a bride, many married girls who were familiar to them only through letters and photographs, and often both parties to such matches were disappointed at first.

Men who followed this pattern soon found themselves middle aged with young wives and children. This fact further bolstered a cultural pattern which assigned authority on the basis of sex and age, by giving the issei father and husband a tremendous amount of responsibility. Although the home was for many purposes the wife's domain, the community was run with a strong hand by the issei men. The community was something like an out-post in a hostile wilderness, and it needed strong leadership. In the absence of a long-established hierarchy among the immigrant families, these men tended to be jealous of their equality, and demagoguery was discouraged. If a man made his living honestly and looked after his reputation and that of his family, he felt he had as much right as anyone else to take part in decisions that affected the group.

On this austere democracy of issei men, World War II descended like a crippling disease. A few months after Pearl Harbor the issei and their families were rounded up and packed off to concentration camps as potentially dangerous aliens. The authority of the men was largely replaced by that of the War Relocation Authority, who favored the American-born children of the issei in their dealings with the prisoners. The men lost their jobs and their businesses, and with these the economic basis of their authority within the family. Even the communal rituals which had functioned to dramatize the values and authority patterns of the prewar communities became all but impossible in the camps. To many an aging issei male, the War must have been an unimaginably upsetting experience.

Following the War, the issei found themselves faced with two new problems: First, they had to reconstruct their lives in America. Most of them had children who were still too young to look after them, and had to take menial jobs, being now too old themselves to start over economically. Second, the country of their birth and their fancied old age had been levelled by the War. With their relatives scattered or dead, their ancestral homes shattered, and their homeland hungry, most felt that returning was now out of the question. On the positive side, prejudice against the Japanese in America was largely undone by the War. The issei now found a measure of acceptance in America. As the men grew into advanced old age, most of those who had been lucky enough to marry at all now had vigorous wives and children in their economic prime. There appear to be few widowers and few men with chronically ill wives among the issei today. Moreover, it is my impression that this pattern is—as one would expect—highly desirable from the man's point of view. Both of the issei men we interviewed who had been widowed earlier in life had remarried, and both seemed to be satisfied with this decision. A healthy wife can be expected to provide more than the necessities in the way of comfort and companionship to an old man, even if she may often undermine his dignity by "babying" him. Wives of our elderly subjects tended to take an active part in the interviews, offering help and advice—often when it was not solicited.

The effects of the age gap on the issei women is another matter. Mostly very young and inexperienced when they reached America, they were greeted by much older husbands, who had already acquired some understanding of the United States culture. The Japanese norm of deference to one's husband was reinforced, then, not only by the seniority and experience factor, but by the tight-knit cooperativeness of the issei male community, which could make life very difficult for a reluctant bride. Going home to mama[3] was practically out of the question, since it amounted almost to divorce under the circumstances. Wives tended to remain quite ignorant of the world beyond their families and neighborhoods. This factor has increased the dependency of the aged issei woman on her ethnic community and on her children, and undermined seriously her function as socializer of grown children and grandchildren. On the positive side, putting an ocean between herself and her mother-in-law gave the issei mother greater autonomy in her own arena—the home. The

---

[3] According to some informants, this was a very forceful threat in the hands of rural Japanese brides of the time.

mother-child alliance is traditionally formidable anyway, and father's age could be used to his disadvantage if he found himself afoul of that alliance.

The age differential of course meant the greater likelihood of a rather prolonged widowhood for issei women. We did not systematically study the effects of widowhood,[4] and perhaps we could not have, given the reluctance of issei widows to discuss their deceased husbands in any terms other than ideal stereotypes. The loss of a husband is sure to be met with great ambivalence when the years preceding the event have been devoted to nursing him in his advanced senescence. Japanese widows are not constrained to a long period of formal melancholy, being generally forgiven if they enjoy their new freedom a little. Then too, widowed issei women have little trouble finding companionship of their own kind. The homogeneous age structure of the community and the frequency of widowhood result in a variety of associations made up mostly of women in the same developmental stage. One way of describing the situation is to say that a relatively early and prolonged widowhood is a "normal" pattern of aging for this subculture, and the new widow these days is likely to find plenty of acceptable models to help her in her adjustment to the role.

Perhaps the most important historical factor in the issei aging process—and the most difficult to absorb into a tidy description of that process—is the fact that their children, the *nisei*, were born and raised in America. The nisei are truly bicultural and bilingual, at home in many (not all) contexts of American life. For most of their lives, most nisei have felt a certain embarrassment about their parents' "Japaneseyness," even while they took their responsibilities toward those parents seriously. While they do not openly oppose many of the issei's ideas and customs, they are prone to ignore them when it is expedient to do so. Considerations of responsibility and family reputation generally bring material support from the nisei to the issei, but there is relatively

---

[4] We sampled for vertical, not horizontal family structure. All but one of our issei women were widows, as it happened. The non-widowed woman's husband was incapacitated with a stroke.

little of the deep moral harmony between the generations which Japanese culture holds up as ideal.

Turning to the issei's grandchildren—the *sansei*—the picture is both better and worse. It is better in the sense that many sansei look to their grandparents' generation as a kind of model of their ancestral culture, and attribute to the old folks the Japanese equivalent of "soul." There are a number of volunteer organizations in the Japanese community staffed mainly by sansei, which are performing valuable services for the issei, and even trying to promote intergenerational understanding. On the negative side, few sansei can speak Japanese, or have any deep understanding of the Japanese way of looking at the world. They cannot talk to their grandparents, and the view they have of them often lacks the ring of real empathy, however genuine are the sansei's good intentions.

Although one might expect that the loss of the Japanese language by the third generation would have a great effect on the issei pattern of development, this is not borne out. The inability of the generations to converse greatly limits the kind of knowledge and emotion which they can exchange, but has surprisingly little effect on the exchange of moral outlook. Japanese culture makes greater use of innuendo and of gestures and facial expressions as channels of communication than does American culture, and anyway, close relationships in any culture often seem to get on well to the extent that words are left out of them. The issei are aware of the fact that examples speak louder than commands, and consciously strive to influence their children and grandchildren in a silent way. The most serious limitation on their influence, then, may not be the lack of English, but the lack of experience with the problems of mainstream American life.

However, one of the serious developmental problems faced by the issei today is that of maintaining a sense of the wholeness and "rightness" of their way of life in the face of generational differences. This is perhaps one important reason for the strength of tradition among them, and also for the importance of friendship groups which exclude members of other cultures and other generations.

ADJUSTMENT TO AGING

I now turn to the important psychological problems faced by the issei today. Although our intention was to be as inductive as possible in searching for such problems, we obviously could not study everything. Implicit both in our interviews, and in our analytic procedures, then, was a set of developmental issues of typical importance to the aged, derived from the pan-cultural study of personality, and limited by the practical problem of getting the best possible information with the time and means at hand. It is very possible that the issei are more concerned with problems of sexuality, deviance, and aggression than we perceived them. The best I can do is to show how the issei handled the great issues of aging around which we implicitly formed our study, and which can be conveniently reduced to five categories of personality needs: a) companionship; b) authority; c) autonomy; d) productivity; e) acceptance of death. Many other classifications of the same data would of course be possible (such as "morale," "self-esteem," "social involvement," etc.). Another caution I must raise in offering this analysis is that there is much overlapping of behavior and need category in any such scheme. For instance, the desire to keep working might in some sense be aimed at the satisfaction of *all* these needs; and conversely, the need for autonomy might be reflected in ideas about religion, family, leisure use, health, and so on. I have chosen this particular analytic outline because I think it corresponds fairly closely to those points on which our data are richest, and because I think it is relatively (not completely) free of culture-bound associations.[5]

Companionship

The local Japanese-American community offers many opportunities for companionship to the healthy issei. First, it is our impression that the great majority of the issei living in this area

---

[5] Students of Henry Murray, Erik Erikson, George DeVos, and other personality theorists will see that I have been influenced by psychoanalytic ego psychology to a great extent. I have touched on my reasons for leaving out sexuality and aggression. The inclusion of productivity derives partly from the works of C. G. Jung and Erik Erikson.

have a spouse or other kind either in the same house or close-by.
Of the twenty-one issei who answered a questionnaire distributed
at a senior center (a group composed mostly of widows), only
two said that they were living "alone." Three were living "with
spouse," and the other sixteen indicated that they were living
"with relatives." Families as a rule include the elderly in many
of their leisure activities, and make some efforts to see that the
elders can see their friends regularly. Observation of church
groups, hobby classes, and senior center meetings shows a striking
contrast with similar urban Caucasian groups. Among the issei,
the level of noise and activity is high, many activities are shared,
and personal space is minimal (i.e. there is a good deal of close
face-to-face interaction and touching). The issei we interviewed
might have been more socially active than the average, since
many were contacted through social groups; however, only three
of our issei subjects did not have regular social activities outside
their home and family more than once a week. Two of these
were quite physically weak.

This brings up the very serious relationship of health and
companionship. Most issei who are healthy enough to live at
home, but too weak to get out often, can and do receive visitors
and talk with their friends daily by telephone, even though they
are much more restricted in their social activities than the more
healthy. However, there are two conditions which impose severe
social isolation on an unknown number of issei: ambulatory
mental illness and long-term hospitalization.

Any prolonged emotional distress that does not have an immediate and identifiable cause is likely to be labelled "mental
illness" in the Japanese-American culture, and mental illness
always carries intense stigma. Emotionally disturbed issei tend
to shut themselves off from family, church, and friends, and
suffer in isolation.[6] Japanese-speaking ministers and mental health
professionals have had very little success so far in finding and
helping these people. One important source of help seems to be
the more messianic variety of ethnic churches; but because of
the sensitivity of this problem and limitations on our time, we
were unable to study the role of these churches adequately.

The possibility of severe physical disability tends to be

regarded by our healthy issei subjects with horror, mostly because of its social consequences. They know that some issei's children place their disabled parents in nursing homes and leave them there to languish in relative isolation. Oddly enough, this problem is dynamically related to the isolation of the mentally disturbed. The issei's children (nisei) typically react with intense shame and guilt to a situation where the presence of a dependent old person in the home has led to severe emotional strain within the family. Rather than let the problem be known, many prefer to cover it up as carefully as possible for as long as possible. At some point or other, the family's tolerance of the burden gives out and the decision is made to move the grandparent elsewhere. By this time, family relationships may have deteriorated to the point where the thought of the old one can scarcely be tolerated by the others; a condition which is further infected by the guilt surrounding institutionalization itself.

This situation is perceived by the issei as the result of a certain decline in filial piety, but I think I can offer a more precise explanation. First, most nisei have a highly instrumental perception of their parents' generation which may be out of keeping with many of the issei's emotional needs. That is, they tend to describe their parents in terms of health, capacity for work, intellectual clarity, or sense of duty; rather than in emotional terms. This might be partly a result of the fact that most nisei never knew their own grandparents, who stayed in Japan. In Japanese culture, it is the grandparent who gives unconditional affection to children who have reached the age of understanding, and teaches them the warm, spontaneous side of grown-up personality. Second, women of all ages (but especially nisei) are generally more involved in day-to-day interaction with the elderly than men are, but the burden of responsibility for major decisions regarding dependent grandparents falls on the shoulders of the nisei men. This sex role difference is reflected in

---

[6] In addition to a number of personal observations of this phenomenon, there are the data on mental hospitalization, which show that Japanese have a low rate of admission, but tend to remain in hospital comparatively longer. This suggests that those who do reach hospitals may be severely deteriorated by the time help is sought (cf. Kitano, 1968).

attitudes. When we asked our subjects, "How do young people feel about the elderly?" we got the following results: a) Nisei and sansei (children of nisei) women are almost four times as likely as men to give an opinion on this question; and b) in all three generations, all those who said the young feel supportive toward the elderly were women, and all those who said otherwise were men. Thematic Apperception Test results are also interesting. In response to the "mother-son" card (6BM), themes of conflict and filial guilt are prevalent (twenty-five out of forty) throughout the study sample. Such themes are virtually absent (two out of forty-three) in response to the scene which shows both sexes in two adult generations (the Kansas City Card). A possible interpretation of this finding is that the role of Judas often falls on nisei men *vis-à-vis* their mothers.

So far I have been discussing some of the social structural features of the problem of companionship for the issei. The issei live in a social world which offers many opportunities for rewarding human contact. It is a small world, and a fairly homogeneous one in a cultural sense, when compared with urban industrial society on the whole. Concern for the emotional well-being of the elderly is a strong value holding the generations together. I now turn to the very difficult question of cultural patterns bearing on the conduct of interpersonal relations in general, and how these affect issei "management" of the companionship problem.

Japanese culture might be considered in many ways a system which disciplines, trains, and pre-adapts the young for the tasks of late life. A wide complex of values and beliefs aims at the maintenance of continuous, reliable relationships within small groups at close quarters. The dreadful boredom which this complex often imposes on the young person (and which might have motivated many a sanguine issei's flight from his homeland) is compensated, ideally, by the development of habits and skills well suited to the circumstances of his later life; that is, to the husbanding of a few quietly genial and unshakable relationships. I have mentioned the main features of this complex above, namely, the values of *duty* (*giri*), *patience* (*gaman*), *gratitude* (*kansha*), and *harmony*.

This style of interaction of course has its costs. For one thing, issei are extremely self-conscious among strangers, and easily hurt by those who fail to understand their deliberate and indirect style of communication. A young nisei Buddhist minister told me how the local issei treated him with steely politeness for many agonizing months after his transfer to their temple. "Then, gradually," he said, "they began to open up; and I found them to be just like the issei back home—the warmest people you could hope to meet."

In the most thorough psychological study of the issei prior to this, Caudill found a high level of anxiety in response to certain projective tests, which he interpreted as evidence of a "vulnerable, inflexible ego," (1952:57) resulting from the rigid formalism of Japanese culture which I have been discussing. My own interpretation of Caudill's findings is somewhat different. First of all, the issei whom Caudill studied had come out of relocation camps only a few years before, and had settled in an unfamiliar city. They were probably still reeling from the shock of this experience, scared, and desperately anxious to convince the Caucasian researchers of their sanity. Secondly, they were unfamiliar with psychological tests. And thirdly, they were culturally unprepared for dealing confidently with new relationships under unfamiliar rules. Under the circumstances anyone's ego would appear vulnerable and inflexible.

On the other hand, I do not want to understate the very serious effect of social isolation on the issei. Typically, they find making new friends extremely difficult, and are apt to suffer severe loneliness and depression at the loss of familiar social supports. There is also the possibility that the loss of such supports can become associated in an issei's mind with the trauma of the wartime experience.

Another possible cost of the issei style of interaction is the bottling-up of aggression, and its consequent availability as a source of energy for neurotic behavior. On this subject I have very little information. However, the general healthiness of most issei seen in this study leads me to speculate that they must have access to adequate ways of sublimating or displacing aggression. Recent experimental studies with other groups even show that aggressive behavior increases *following* periods of aggressive license (Berkowitz, 1973), suggesting that the presence of pervasive and clear-cut cultural controls can actually restrict the intensity of the general aggressive impulse (if indeed the concept of a "general impulse" is useful at all).

Authority and Autonomy

I have described the authority and respect due the elderly in traditional Japan, and I have mentioned how the relocation experience undermined the authority of the issei, both men and women, over their children's generation. Whereas it was customary in Japan for the elderly to willingly relinquish their control of family matters to their mature sons, and their leadership in government and enterprise to their loyal successors, the issei had these things wrested from them prematurely. This was not only a personally painful situation for many, it was a morally disappointing process: The demonstration of due respect to one's superiors is a fundamental Confucian principle, and disregard of that principle is a sign of moral weakness. The ritual of bowing, and the bewildering hierarchy of deferent and demeaning forms of speech in Japanese language, are concrete expressions of this principle. Ruth Benedict (1946) devoted a whole chapter to it, under the heading, "Knowing One's Proper Place."

For the issei, the problem of authority and that of autonomy are closely linked. The granting of favors is frequently an expression of dominance in the traditional culture, and places the recipient in a subordinate position, at least until he is in a position to return each favor with one of equal value. One who is repeatedly or continually in debt to another becomes a social subordinate in his own eyes, whether or not his benefactor treats him as such. Under the traditional value system, dependent elders are not seen as subordinates because whatever they receive from society (especially from their descendants) is classified as *repayment* for their life's work. In order for this system to work, it must be recognized implicitly by the parties involved; and this is the condition that is not clearly met in the present-day Japanese-American culture. The issei face a double problem, then; the premature loss of considerable authority, and a certain sense of their dependency as demeaning.

Needless to say, the problem varies in extent from individual to individual and family to family. In six of the families we interviewed—and several others we saw casually—issei grandparents refused various kinds of important help proffered by their children. In several cases, the issei refused to live with their children's families. In other cases, they refused assistance with necessary chores, or offers of financial help. These issei were usually not very articulate about their reasons for this behavior, merely saying that human relations are smoother if they are reciprocal. Their feeling was not that they had no right to depend on their children, but that "the children do not understand their obligation." Under the circumstances, a difficult and restricted autonomy is preferred to an unwanted dependency.

This struggle for autonomy is also found in intergenerational perceptions about personality. We asked, for instance, "What makes it possible for an old person to live happily?" Seven out of the eight issei who had an opinion on this subject listed personal qualities of the old person. In contrast, eight out of fifteen nisei answered either some form of support from others, or health—things over which the elderly have no control. Apparently, the issei perceive themselves as more autonomous than their children see them.

This pattern is not so different from one frequently found among aging Euro-Americans, of course. What makes it interesting is that the help-rejecting issei are part of a culture in which lifelong interdependency among members of intimate groups is the *normal* pattern, and the one which these issei's children outwardly support. Moreover, they seem perfectly willing to accept limited help when it is *willingly* offered by friends, community organizations, or anthropologists who are not constrained by custom to help them. I believe the great sensitivity of the issei to the feelings of others in general is augmented here by a certain anxiety touched off by their early loss of authority. Some issei are extremely susceptible to the idea that they are perceived as helpless by others.

Doi (1973) thinks that the need for indulgent nurturance from others is a cornerstone of Japanese personality, and that the satisfaction of this need is taken for granted normally in the parent-child relationship. There is much to support Doi's view of Japan—I believe the exception in the case of the issei is a very important acculturative change. It may be that needs for nurturance, or *amae* (Doi, op. cit.) have been transferred to a very large extent from the family to the issei peer-group. As I mention elsewhere, a great deal of nurturance is shared among members of issei groups, in the forms of sympathy, food, and even physical care of dependent members.

In most cultures, fatherhood is an ambiguous status. It implies authority on one hand, but it also implies love on the other hand. The affectionate dimension is strongly developed in Japanese culture, and may be emphasized by the aging male himself, as a compensation for the loss of authority. In response to the "father-son card" (7BM) or the TAT, a strong contrast emerged between the generations. The nisei men saw the father figure in a solid position of authority over the son. The sansei men tended to see the son as rebelling against or escaping from the authority of the father; and the issei men tended to see the relationship as one of mutual affection and concern. This is somewhat contrary to Caudill's (1952) finding that the issei use intellectualization as a defense. The discrepancy might be explained by the fact that the issei (and the nisei) have gotten a lot older since Caudill's study. I also take this finding to be supplementary to Gutman's (1969) conclusions from the study of aging men in three cultures. Gutman found that among the Highland Maya, the Navajo, and the Kansas Cityans, men's attitude toward the mastery of their environment tends to change from "active" to "passive" to "magical" as they age.

Productivity

The problem of autonomy is also closely related to the problem of productivity for the issei. All but two of our seven formally interviewed issei men had income-producing work at the time, and both of these retired men were active in their community. Three of the working men—aged eighty-one, eighty-two, and eighty-five—still held jobs consisting mainly of manual labor, and each expressed his pride and gratitude in being able to work hard at his age. Three of the ten issei women interviewed —ages sixty-five, sixty-nine, and seventy-four—also had regular, income-producing work, all of it involving physical labor. While the women weighted family support more heavily than ability to work as sources of morale, they too seemed to be grateful for the opportunity to contribute to their own economic maintenance.

The worth of the individual to his group in Japanese culture is measured to a fair extent by what he contributes concretely toward its goals (See Plath, 1964b); and as I have repeatedly said, self-worth and group-worth tend toward an explicit unity. The issei's children and grandchildren often describe the old folks as "hard working." This perception derives from a general task-orientedness on the issei's part, often with group goals in mind. When anything needs doing, an issei is likely to set about it quietly but intensely, without being asked and without agonizing about whose responsibility it is. Work builds social harmony, and harmony builds happiness. A major part of the issei perception of "productivity," then, has nothing to do with any permanent or material effect on the world: Productivity is often the simple building of human bonds. For this reason, the issei seem to derive an unusual sense of satisfaction from the performance of simple routine work of the sort that gadget-happy America has come to refer to as "drudgery." A spotless house, a well-ironed dress, a bountiful garden are not only aesthetically pleasing and morally instructive, they are statements of the owner's concern for the sensibilities of others, and his or her willingness to work tirelessly in a basically social cause.

An important part of practically any social gathering involving issei (or at least issei women) is the sharing of food. Issei women seem to be at their very happiest when watching something they have prepared disappear amid sounds of gusto. The culinary consumer might be a husband, another issei at a pot-luck, a grandchild and his friends at a picnic, or an anthropologist taking a coffee break in her parlour. When I invited one of my issei informants to dinner at my house, she showed up with a pailfull of her own cooking big enough to feed six hungry people.

This is not the type of giving for which the issei expect to be reimbursed. It is another form of productivity which they find satisfying in its own right. I will return to the symbolic import-ance of food and feeding presently.

Recreation, too, often has a similar productive component for the issei. Many issei devote a good deal of time to the study of art, flower-arranging, poetry reciting, music, needlework, tea ceremony and other domestic arts (*okeikogoto*); which can be said to have a kind of social productivity as their goal. Some issei have taken up the serious study of English in their old age with the same motivation.

However, part of the issei's concern with the culturally tradi-tional has to do with that form of productivity which Erikson (1963:266-269) calls "generativity;" namely, the passing-on of the important meanings and values of one's own life to the next generation. We have seen that the traditional Japanese concept of time portrays individual life as a segment of a continuous filament. If there is little passing-on of value, the filament of time is weak. Being able to die peacefully requires a sense of having been a strong segment—of having given back at least what one received of life. Says Mr. Uchida (age 81):

—As I told you, the War made a fundamental change [in our lives]. And after that, our younger generation—going to work anywhere—any direction—and we see we can establish our finer foundations in this country. Since the War, we have a strong founda-tion to live in America, for our younger generation. The nisei and sansei have the same hope and desire—to be good American citizens —as their Japanese ancestors had. That way, we see that they are enjoying life and working very diligently to establish the family and teach their children as the issei did.

The issei have found it hard to preserve some of the old traditions, not just for the sake of maintaining their authority, or for the aesthetic satisfaction which they themselves derive from those traditions, but because the preservation and carrying-forward of those traditions was an important part of the issei's life work—their product and their legacy, as well as their responsi-bility as parents.

With a few exceptions the issei seem to have long since

relinquished their role as primary socializers of their children. Although they see themselves as a moral restraining force and example, they rarely try to manage their children's careers or social lives, and do not seem very disturbed about major filial decisions with which they themselves disagree. In cases where the issei still take an active part in the management of family business, they are usually genuinely needed in their leadership role. I believe the issei differ from many aging Caucasian Americans in this respect. Professor Lowenthal's (1972) current work indicates that many American women suffer considerable anxiety regarding the careers of grown children, over whom they no longer have any control. These women are haunted by the fear that they have somehow failed to complete the tasks of motherhood, and are unwilling to relinquish this role.

I believe this results partly from the relative lack of criteria for judging parental success in the American culture. There is no clear-cut notion of what a successful mother does, nor what she achieves by it; nor is there much feedback from peers on the subjects of whether and when she has succeeded. Japanese criteria are simpler, I believe, and information about one's performance of the parental role is more available from peers in the community. Most issei appear to have done quite well in the terms of their own culture. Family reputation in the tight-knit community is a good indicator of parental performance—and we did not turn up any families whose reputation was bad enough to raise questions of issei failure in the parental role.

While some kinds of productivity derive from autonomy and authority, others involve the relinquishing of these—a relaxing and giving-in to primitive impulses. Cultivation of the traditional arts can be a returning to the bosom of the mother culture, as cultivation of the soil is to mother earth. Jung (1931) speaks of the creative process as a natural force against which Man struggles only at his peril. Religious and philosophical ideas, also products of this type, are highly cultivated among issei men (a more masculine role in Japanese culture). They quickly warm to questions about the meaning of life and death; the development of character; the secret of happiness. They freely offer speculations showing an appreciation for life as-it-is; a contemplative, aesthetic understanding:

> (Interviewer): What sort of thing makes you angry with people?
> (Mr. Fujii): Well, in people's relations with each other, they are sometimes unreasonable. That's because human beings are emotional animals.
> (Interviewer): Do you feel sorry afterwards?
> (Mr. Fujii): It such times, I feel as though I'm talking to myself —as though I'm talking to a mirror.
> (Mr. Ono) [In response to TAT Card 6BM]: I think a mother has a very great influence on her children, whether they are young or old. I watch my wife around the kids, and I watch my daughter-in-law. There is a very pure and beautiful love between a mother and a child. . . .
>
> ✿   ✿   ✿   ✿   ✿   ✿   ✿   ✿
>
> (Mr. Uchida): I like to understand things about the places I travel. Such as in South America, the way the native people live, and what their history is . . . especially what kind of government do they have, and thirdly the economic condition. For instance, we saw a nice capitol in Argentina, but the guide told us the capitol building was for rent because some general did away with the congress. Because of that sort of thing, some are very rich and some are very poor. . . .

If it is possible to draw together these various forms of issei productivity—work, art, heritage, and philosophic insight—and name the goal toward which they all strive, I would say that goal is neither abundance nor novelty, but rather *harmony*. As the traditional arts, such as flower arranging and tea ceremony, seek to nourish a feeling of inner poise through the balancing of natural forms, materials, and movements, so work harmonizes human relations. As the leaving of a legacy balances the pendulum of life and death, so philosophic creativity settles a personally satisfying order—a floating bridge—on the ceaseless flux of experience.

This is a sense of productivity based on the principles of social organization and ethics which I have described as typical of Japanese culture. It is a conservative rather than a generative productivity. Like a *bonsai* artist who by patient attention both limits the growth of his trees and bends them toward ever-greater perfection, the proper work of the issei is to order the resources at his disposal into an ever more harmonious microcosm.

In reality, of course, the work often goes awry and the sense of harmony eludes the aging issei. However, as Margaret Clark and Barbara Anderson concluded in their study of aging (1967), the chances of high morale are best for the aging person who has productive goals, but whose goals do not involve the maintenance of a youthful capacity for bringing the world to heel.

Acceptance of Death

(Mr. Daigen): I feel life fading away. Fading . . . and I can't stop it.
(Interviewer): Do you worry about growing older?
(Mr. Daigen): No. If you get over eighty . . . I'm ready to kick the bucket. (Chuckles) I'm over eighty-one. I'm ready. Dying is not at all a worry.

It would be a sign of morale weakness for an issei to show much fear of dying, so we cannot place great credit in such interview responses alone. They are typical of issei expressions on the subject. However, the words just quoted take on deep meaning in view of what followed. A few months after the interview, Mr. Daigen died quietly.

Independent support for the idea that the issei have little fear of death comes from ministers of various Christian and Buddhist churches in the community. These ministers also agree that acceptance of death is not typical of Japanese Americans in general; only of the issei generation. The nisei are said to have much more difficulty discussing death, or handling the deaths of others, than the issei.

Explaining this issei equanimity is of course a complicated and inconclusive business. When I discussed the question of an afterlife with a group of four issei ladies, they showed little anxiety but were also sceptical of afterlife theories. Other individuals showed a firm conviction in the idea of eternal life, and seemed to draw great strength from this conviction. Filial care of the spirit after death, as I mentioned earlier, did not seem to be an important concern for any issei. I see three related attitudes about death which are strongly developed in Japanese culture, and which seem to help those issei who are developmentally "successful" to face death.

First, Japanese culture shows a deep reverence for nature. From the use of natural materials in architecture to the worship of natural phenomena in popular Shinto faith, Japanese people demonstrate in their everyday lives a sense of satisfaction at the appropriateness of things in their original, unprocessed state. This is more than a romantic philosophy, as visitors to rural Japan often remark even today. Living close to nature in the way valued by the traditional culture involves shivering in winter, sweating in summer, ignoring the bites of insects and the stinks that attend life in the ripe. The Japanese are often critical of the intellect's artificiality, and use approvingly such terms as *mushin* (mindlessness), and "knowing *mono-no-aware*" (the "pity of things") and *yugen* (the "is-ness" of things). Buddhism teaches that all life is suffused with an unifying force—the "Buddha nature."

According to this view, death is natural and the fear of death amounts to the fear of nature—a sad error of perception. This is probably one reason why suicide was traditionally considered an acceptable solution to a wide variety of personal difficulties, and why the fear of either the bodies or the souls of the dead is not strongly developed in the culture (although it is not altogether absent either). In short, it is considered incorrect and gauche to struggle against nature's inevitabilities. One who lives long is lucky, and one who dies young unlucky, but the prolongation of life at great expense lacks dignity. When the physical powers have waned and the business of life has been set in order, death is "appropriate." It is almost as though one who knows his "proper place," dies at a reasonable age.[7]

Secondly, the relatively clear sense of one's responsibiilties and obligations to the world mentioned earlier, together with the conservative attitude toward productivity, seem to help the healthy issei achieve a sense of the completeness and wholeness

---

[7] Plath (1972) cites a popular Japanese folktale in which a particularly robust old woman becomes so ashamed of her abnormal vitality that she resorts to knocking out her teeth with a stone.

of their lives. On the subject of death they are likely to say, "I have finished up my work in this world. I am ready any time."

The third and most important feature of Japanese culture leading toward the acceptance of death is of course the perception of time. Meyerhoff (1955) reminds us that it is the consciousness of aging and death which, more than anything else, gives human psychological time its irreversible quality, and that this quality is fundamental to our whole perception of the world, including the self. The meaning of death is in turn conditioned to a great extent by whether we perceive time as continuous and supra-personal or as discontinuous and personal. Just as the Western tendency to perceive time as personal leads toward our Grim Reaper symbolism and our preoccupation with the destructiveness of time in philosophy and literature (Meyerhoff, op. cit.), so the supra-personal tendency in Japanese thought leads toward a relatively sentimental portrayal of time and its effects. A common metaphor for death in Japanese literature is the falling of cherry blossoms. The metaphor comes from nature, and carries a reference to renewal.

These attitudes toward death, however, make sense only when they are supported by other cultural norms. A person who sees himself as a deviant or a failure will probably find in the approach of death a threatening or a mocking element out of keeping with the naturalistic ethos, and his deviant perception may well deepen his isolation and self disgust. An old person without the support and gratitude of family or disciples may have great difficulty seeing time in supra-personal terms, and consequently feel overwhelmed by the significance of time's personal end. For these reasons, social isolation in old age is particularly tragic in the issei's case.

A NOTE ON DISENGAGEMENT

Much attention in American social gerontology has been devoted to the "disengagement theory" of aging developed by Cumming and Henry (1961). In essence the theory was put forward to explain research findings which did not fit with the common American notion that old people continue to *want* the same level of social involvement that characterized their middle age. Cumming and Henry found that, among older people living in Kansas City, the withdrawal of psychological energy and affect from social relations often accompanies the gradual decline in social activity and loss of social roles found among the elderly. They hypothesized that perhaps a *mutual* disengagement of individual and society in old age is normal, and even desirable. Later work (e.g. Havighurst, Neugarten, & Tobin, 1968) has questioned whether disengagement is the best way for people to grow old, or simply an aberration of our era and culture to which many people are subjected willy-nilly.

The large literature on the subject of disengagement indicates that it is an interesting theory, and I would like to comment on its relevance to the issei without actually reviewing all the arguments that have been mustered for and against it. First, neither the level of social activity nor that of psychological involvement found among the physically healthy issei shows a process of disengagement. Most issei spend a great deal of time in interaction with a variety of other people, and are extremely interested in this activity. The fact that they see the same dozen or so people day after day, or that the range of cultural background represented by their consociates may be quite narrow, is probably a life-long characteristic of their social life.

Second, it seems to me that the psychological process of disengagement requires a perception of one's self as something fundamentally distinct from one's social roles—a perception which is alien to the issei. Behind the Westerner's perception of himself as purposefully "engaged" in, and potentially "disengaged" from, his intimate social relations lies a long history of philosophic individualism and a personal biography which includes early independence training and the self-conscious development and dismantling of many relationships. What is continuous about his self-feelings is the stream of sensations, moods, and ideas which he feels originate inside his own skin. The issei, on the other hand, cannot "disengage" from his social roles, because he *is* those roles. His stream of consciousness is felt as a product of the quality (harmony vs. disharmony) of his relations with the social and natural world. As I have written elsewhere

(Kiefer, 1971), I think the issei resemble a very large sector of humanity in this respect.

LESSONS

Before I began this study, it was not hard for me to see how the fear surrounding old age and death in American culture is related to our individualism, our pragmatism, and our aspiritual rationalism. I saw that our moral aloofness from untidy human needs was first a means of getting closer to God, and later a bitterly lonely proclamation of our personal might in a godless world. I saw how our glorification of human progress makes nature an enemy, wielding the terrible weapon of decline and death, against which youth is our only shield. What I could not see was how it looks and feels in a culture with a vastly different set of ideals.

The most important lesson from the issei, then, is a very old one, but one that bears repeating anyhow. Life is lived in society, and for ordinary folk society exacts a heavy price in self denial in return for the conditions of a humane and peaceful old age. It is analogous to the mastery of a satisfying craft: the habit of self-discipline generally seems to improve both the craftsman and his art. Like craftsmanship, successful aging depends on the careful mastery of communicative skills; a learning process itself arduous, but once completed, an avenue of self expansion.

A second lesson is that culture is not a stamping die, turning out a narrow range of personalities that fit nicely into the jigsaw structures of society. Culture allows many strategies of aging, and many possible meanings for the private conditions and events from which we construct our biographies. In any culture there are those whose appreciation of their lives leads to an anxious and forlorn old age, and those whom we might call successful agers. It helps greatly, I think, to know this fact thoroughly. The struggle to wrest meaning from life is never final until our last breath, and this very endlessness may be (as Kafka would have it) the meaning we seek.

A third lesson is that history stands as a gigantic obstacle to an applied gerontology. If the issei's children had grown up Japanese, as their parents often wished, perhaps they would still be scraping out a sour living in ethnic ghettos. If the War had not happened the way it did, when it did, most issei would probably be growing old in Japan, where a dramatic upsurge in the lifespan has created a new "problem population" of old people who are idle, lonely and poor. If Japan had not re-emerged as a world super-power in the last decade, pride in their national culture would not be nearly so easy for the issei. If immigration had not been cut off when it was, the issei might have melted into the ethnic landscape and lost their identity as a generation. The adaptive skills we now see in issei personality might be very badly suited to a different historical niche.

A fourth lesson is that minorityship itself might hold certain large benefits for the aged. The issei are few in number. In any given West Coast city most issei are likely to know each other at least by reputation, if not by sight. They are a little community unto themselves, tightly bound by the sharing of a unique identity. To be a member of this group may not guarantee the friendship of other members, but to some extent it guarantees their understanding. It means the sharing of a set of beliefs and practices which has now largely vanished from the earth. It means the sharing of a series of unforgettable memories, again unique. Between issei, a world or a gesture can convey meanings that volumes could not convey to anyone else—even to most nisei. Perhaps there have been times in human history—before the medical propagation of old age—when gray heads were rare enough that their meeting signified mutual recognition and support. Almost certainly, the technology which creates a vast class of elderly and keeps them supplied with evidence of their anonymity does not make aging any easier.

REFERENCES

Benedict, R.: *The Chrysanthemum and the Sword.* Boston, Houghton Mifflin, 1946.
Berkowitz, Leonard: The case for bottling up rage. *Psychology Today,* 7:2, 1973, pp. 24-31.

Caudill, William A.: Japanese American personality and acculturation. *Genetic Psychology Monographs*, 45, 1952, pp. 3-102.

Clark, Margaret, and Anderson, Barbara G.: *Culture and Aging: An Anthropological Study of Older Americans*. Springfield, Thomas, 1967.

Cumming, Elaine, and Henry, William: *Growing Old: The Process of Disengagement*. New York, Basic Books, 1961.

Doi, Takeo: *The Anatomy of Dependence*. Tokyo, Kodansha, 1973.

Erikson, Erik H.: *Childhood and Society*. New York, W. W. Norton, 1963, (rev. ed.).

Gutman, David L.: The country of old men: cross-cultural studies in the psychology of later life. *Occasional Papers in Gerontology*, No. 5, Institute of Gerontology, University of Michigan—Wayne State University, April 1969.

Havighurst, Robert J.; Neugarten, B. L., and Tobin, S. S.: Disengagement and patterns of aging. In *Middle Age and Aging*. Chicago, University of Chicago Press, 1968, pp. 161-72.

Jung, C. G.: *Seelenprobleme der Gegenwart*. Zurich, Rascher, 1931.

Kiefer, Christie W.: Notes on anthropology and the minority elderly. *The Gerontologist*, 11:1, Part 2, 1971, pp. 94-98.

Kitano, Harry H. L.: *Japanese Americans: The Evolution of a Subculture*. Englewood Cliffs, N. J., Prentice-Hall, 1968.

Koyama, Takashi: Changing family structure in Japan. In Smith and Beardsley (Eds.), *Japanese Culture: Its Development and Characteristics*. Chicago, Aldine, 1962.

Lowenthal, Marjorie F., and David A. Chiriboga: Transition to the empty nest: crisis, challenge, or relief? *Archives of General Psychiatry*, 26, 1972, pp. 8-14.

Meyerhoff, Hans: *Time in Literature*. Berkeley and Los Angeles, University of California Press, 1955.

Morioka. Kiyomi: Life cycle patterns in Japan, China, and the United States. Presented at *Sixth World Congress of Sociology*, Tokyo, 1966.

Plath, David W.: Where the family of God is the family: the role of the dead in Japanese households. *American Anthropologist*, 66:2, 1964a, pp. 300-317.

————: *The After Hours*. Berkeley, University of California Press, 1964b.

————: Japan: The after years. In Cowgill, Donald O., and Holmes, Lowell D. (Eds.), *Aging and Modernization*. New York, Appleton-Century-Crofts, 1972, pp. 133-150.

ENVIRONMENTAL

POLICY

CHAPTER 9

MATCHING ENVIRONMENTS TO NEEDS OF THE AGED: A CONCEPTUAL SCHEME

EVA KAHANA

T HE MOST GENERAL goal of applied research in social gerontology may be seen as the specification of "the conditions of both person and environment under which the mutual need satisfactions of individual and society are maximized" (Lawton, 1968). However systematic guidelines have largely been absent for providing the optimal environmental input to meet needs of the aging individual.

Although the importance of a fit between environmental characteristics and individual needs is explicitly or implicitly expected to contribute to adjustment (Goffman, 1961; Kleemeier, 1961; Hunt, 1961), the relationship between such congruence or dissonance and adjustment has not been systematically evaluated. In social gerontological practice and research, the approach of searching for an optimal environment for all aged is still prevalent. Yet apparently helpful environmental characteristics may be harmful to some elderly people while apparently undesirable features may benefit others.

The aim of this paper is to present a conceptual scheme for matching environments to needs of the aged. This scheme has been put to test in a recently completed empirical investigation (Kahana, 1973). An attempt is made in that study to specify dimensions of congruence between individual and environment which are necessary to promote adjustment of the older person. While the conceptual model presented here was developed for institutional or protective residential settings where the problem of a mismatch between the environment and needs of the person may be especially acute, it is seen as applicable to living arrangements in community settings as well.

During the last few years, social aspects of the aging process and problems of the aged have become important areas of scientific inquiry. The two major analytic approaches to research in these areas have been the well-known activity and disengagement theories. The former pointed to a universal need for maintaining high levels of activity with advancing years. The latter suggested an intrinsic need of elderly individuals to withdraw from interpersonal relationships and to decrease activity (Cumming and Henry, 1961). In their original forms these theories were presented as optimal theories of aging, posing activity or withdrawal respectively as preconditions for a sense of well-being or adjustment.

Based on subsequent studies, however, it appeared that the relationship between amounts of activity and psychological well-being for the aged is not a simple one (Havighurst, Neugarten, and Tobin, 1963). Some elderly individuals showed patterns of high activity along with high life satisfaction whereas others showed equally high life satisfaction with low levels of activity. It became clear that, among other things, characteristics of the individual intervene between levels of activity and adjustment (Reichard, Livson, and Peterson, 1962; Neugarten, Crotty and Tobin, 1964). Thus, several different patterns of adjustment were found to exist which depended to a great extent on individual differences in modes of coping with the environment and in personality and cognitive characteristics. It is now understood that providing environments which foster either activity or disengagement cannot meet the needs of most elderly individuals. When considering programs for the elderly, their individual needs along the dimension of activity-disengagement must be considered along with other factors.

The maintenance of earlier life patterns has been seen as especially important for the aged group. Rosow (1967) sug-gested that "the greater the disruption of previous life styles, activities and relationships, the greater the risk of personal demoralization since a major readaptation is required from them at an age when their adaptive capacities are diminished." In a recent study Bultena (1969) found support for the hypothesis that "the greater the discontinuity in life problems between pre and post-retirement periods, the greater will be the impact on his ability to function successfully relative to the attainment of culturally valued goals and thereby the greater the probability of his being demoralized."

The disadvantages of the older years in terms of reduced income, frequently impaired health and loss of social roles reduce the options and choices available to the older person in maintaining or finding an environmnet in keeping with his preferences. It is usually due to these very losses that the aged enter into care settings. Based on the above considerations, it is hypothesized here that a close fit between environmental characteristics and individual preference and needs should result in a sense of well-being and adequate functioning of the elderly individual. It is suggested that the individual's profile of personal needs and preferences must always be considered in conjunction with the profile of the environment in evaluating residential settings.

PREVIOUS WORK ON THE ENVIRONMENTAL CONTEXT OF RESIDENTIAL ENVIRONMENTS FOR THE AGED

Goffman's (1961) characterization of the total institution has provided a major point of departure for sociological investigations of various residential care settings. Working in a sociological tradition Goffman (1961) viewed the environment as consisting of parallel cultural and operational worlds of staff and of inmates each in turn impinging upon the individual. He focused on general and all pervasive aspects of the environment and the commonality of its depersonalizing features.

Kleemeier (1961), dealing specifically with the aged, proposed three dimensions which permit more accurate description of the impact of settings for the elderly upon their life-styles. These are the segregate, congregate, and institutional control dimensions. They form a basis for later conceptual models of environment for the aged including the one presented here.

Institutions which are high on the segregate, congregate, and institutional dimensions of Kleemeier's scheme may also be seen as having strong totalistic features in Goffman's sense.

Based to a great extent on Kleemeier's and Goffman's notions, Pincus (1968) has developed a conceptual framework for the evaluation of the social—psychological milieu in institutions for the aged. He studied institutional environments using a multi-dimensional model considering physical characteristics of the environment, rules and regulations, and staff behavior. The four major dimensions of settings for the aged for which Pincus (1968) found empiricial support as well as theoretical basis are the public—private, structured—unstructured, resource sparse—resource rich, and integrated—isolated dimensions. While Pincus implicitly acknowledges the differential appropriateness of given environments for elderly with diverse needs, the model is restricted to conceptualizing the environment.

Another important approach to the measurement and con-ceptualization of behavior settings is Barker's (1970) classic work in the area of ecological psychology. While not explicitly aimed at studying institutional living arrangements, Barker pro-vides a useful approach for the study of person-environment interaction which takes into account the complex spatial-temporal context of human behavior.

The congruence model of environment-individual interaction which is here proposed has its roots in Lewin's (1935) notion that behavior is a function of the relationship between a person and his environment and in Murray's (1938) need-press model of human behavior. According to this model individuals with certain types of needs are most likely to seek and be found in environments which are congruent with their needs. Dissonance between press and need is seen as leading to a modification of the press or the individual's leaving the field in a free choice situation. When such choice is unavailable and the individual must function in a dissonant milieu, stress and discomfort follow (Stern, 1970).

This model is especially suited for the study of behavior and functioning within social organizations. A model similar to the one to be presented here has been applied by Stern (1970) to the study of college environments and needs of students, although the focus of that study was on the distribution of various need configurations in diverse settings rather than on congruence *per se*. Diverse aspects of the environment may contribute to the environmental press along given dimensions including the physical environment, the social environment and what Lawton (1968) termed the supra-personal environment.

It must also be recognized however that the impact of the larger environment is mitigated by the personal life space of the individual. Thus it is possible that even residents whose needs are not met by the larger environment of the home may find a "nook" (physical or social) which may shelter them from a generally incongruent environment. Conversely it is possible that even if programs and general characteristics of a setting are ideally suited to a resident, presence of a significant figure, e.g. roommate who is not congenial to the resident, may have deleterious influences.

The personal environment of an elderly resident in a residential setting may be defined in terms of a) physical environment (resident's room), (b) social environment (extensity and intensity of interaction with people), and (c) activities.

DIMENSIONS OF CONGRUENCE

Based on theoretical considerations, two broad areas of congruence between environment and individual characteristics appear to be especially important. These are dimensions based on differences in settings and dimensions based on individual differences.

Dimensions Based on Environmental Differences

The first set of variables are the dimensions along which settings for the aged may be characterized. The segregate, congregate and institutional control division used by Kleemeier and the elaborations presented by Pincus provide a comprehensive method of classifying "the impact of the setting on the lifestyle of the residents."

To the extent that most institutions, residential and behavior settings for the aged, may be characterized along the above dimensions, it may be of special interest to study the effects of the extent of congruence between the setting and resident characteristics along these dimensions. These dimensions appear useful both in characterizing institutions as a whole and in specific activities.

    a. *The Segregate Dimension* was originally used by Kleemeier (1961) to refer to "the condition under which older persons may live exclusively among their age peers having little contact with other age groups." In broader terms, however, the concept may refer to the heterogeneity or homogeneity of the setting in terms of the sex, health status, and level of functioning of the participants. It may thus contrast living or participating with a group of persons much like one's self and living with persons who are different.

    b. *The Congregate Dimension* refers to "the closeness of individuals to each other and to the degree of privacy possible to attain in the settings." (Kleemeier, 1961).

    c. *The Institutional-Control Dimension* refers to the extent of staff control of residents, the use and importance of rules and the degrees of resident autonomy which are tolerated.

In absolute terms, environments which are highly controlling, homogeneous and restrict privacy (i.e. are institutionally controlled, segregate, and congregate), may often disregard individual needs and have little therapeutic value. The majority of settings for the aged do not represent such an extreme. It is here proposed that settings without extreme totalistic features may more fruitfully be viewed in terms of their degree of congruence with the needs of the individual.

Some elderly individuals have especially strong needs for privacy while others may enjoy being with others and participating in group activities much of the time. Thus the feeling of some aged that "I am afraid to be alone" has long been familiar to clinicians. Similarly, some elderly persons have great needs for autonomy or independence and a controlling institutional environment with many rules and regulations would be inconsistent with their self-image, previous life-styles and present needs. Others, however, have a great need for structured situations, clearcut rules as to what is expected of them and may have entered the institution expecting that the burden of making decisions will be taken from them. It may therefore be expected that congruence of individual needs and characteristics of the setting along these dimensions should lead to a sense of well-being, satisfaction and lead to adequate functioning in the institution.

Dimensions of Congruence Based on Characteristics of the Aged Individual

Age related changes have been established in previous studies along several dimensions of cognitive functioning and of personality organization (Neugarten, *et al.* 1964; Reichard, *et al.* 1962; Korchin, 1956; Burgess, 1960). These changes are frequently in the form of decrement in the ability to cope with the environment. Thus, inability to tolerate ambiguity, inability to delay gratification, flattened affect and avoidance of stimuli have been observed among the elderly in the above studies.

One may expect then, the lack of congruence between environmental expectations and the needs and characteristics of the aging individual may be especially difficult to cope with in these areas. The very existence of psychological changes may present the aging person with a lack of congruence between his needs and his environment placing stress on his weakened coping abilities. Utilization of a residential or institutional living situation may often be precipitated or hastened by these changes.

It is an important role of the environment, then, to accommodate as much as possible to areas of changed needs of the aging individual. To the extent that the environment succeeds in recognizing the needs of the new resident and provides a setting which can accommodate his needs, stress is reduced and the pace of decline may be checked.

An elderly individual who is becoming increasingly intolerant of ambiguity and shows need for structure may experience considerable discomfort in the role of a retired person living in the community. It has been well documented that there are few clearcut social expectations and norms for the post-retirement period (Burgess, 1960; Neugarten, 1964). If the aging person who reacts adversely to the lack of clarity in his social situation enters a residential setting for the aged, he is in need of fairly clearcut expectations and directives for behavior and for activities providing him with structured tasks. If the environment has few norms for behavior and the role of the new resident is very ambiguous, one may expect further difficulties in coping with the situation and in adjustment.

Similarly, placing an older person with weakened impulse control in an environment or, in activities which require a great deal of control may lead to decreased coping ability and a reduced sense of well-being (Kahana and Kahana, 1966).

Some elderly individuals may continue or even increase their need for activity, affect, or stimulation and thrive in environments which tolerate and encourage expressions of affect and which provide a great deal of stimulation, while others may be adversely affected in such milieus.

Thus, congruence along personality and cognitive dimensions which are characterized by age-related changes should be considered with special care. Based on a review of previous studies, the following dimensions appear to be especially important:

Environmental Characteristics:
1. amount of stimulation
2. affective milieu (tolerance for expressing feelings)
3. amount of structure
4. indulgence of needs

Individual Characteristics:
1. need for activity vs. passivity
2. affective expression and needs
3. tolerance of ambiguity
4. impulse control

Age-related changes in the ability to tolerate ambiguity and in delay of gratification (impulse control) have been shown in numerous studies (Korchin and Basowitz, 1956; Peck, 1959; Neugarten, 1964; Cumming and Henry, 1961; Kastenbaum and Pollack, 1964; Kahana and Kahana, 1966). Decline in affect and activity level with aging have been shown in the Kansas City Studies (Cumming and Henry, 1961; Neugarten, *et al.* 1964). The above dimensions are also important in differentiating institutional environments and activities.

Table 9-I summarizes the seven dimensions of necessary congruence between environmental settings and individual preferences. Each of these dimensions is further subdivided into its component aspects.

TABLE 9-I

DIMENSIONS OF CONGRUENCE

1. SEGREGATE DIMENSION

Environment	*Individual*
A. Homogeneity of composition of environment. Segregation based on similarity of resident characteristics (sex, age, functioning physical and mental status).	A. Preference for homogeneity, i.e., for associating with like individuals. Being with people similar to yourself.
B. Change vs. sameness. Presence of daily and other routines, frequency of changes in staff and other environmental characteristics.	B. Preference for change vs. sameness in daily routines, activities.
C. Continuity or similarity with previous environment of resident.	C. Need for continuity with the past.

2. CONGREGATE DIMENSION

Environment	*Individual*
A. Extent to which privacy is available in setting.	A. Need for privacy.
B. Collective vs. individual treatment. The extent to which residents are treated alike. Availability of choices in food, clothing, etc. Opportunity to express unique individual characteristics.	B. Need for individual expression and idiosyncracy. Choosing individualized treatment whether that treatment is socially defined as "good" treatment or not.
C. The extent to which residents do things alone or with others.	C. Preference for doing things alone vs. with others.

3. INSTITUTIONAL CONTROL

Environment	*Individual*
A. Control over behavior and resources. The extent to which staff exercise control over resources.	A. Preference for (individual) autonomy vs. for being controlled.
B. Amount of deviance tolerated. Sanctions for deviance.	B. Need to conform.
C. Degree to which dependency is encouraged and dependency needs are met.	C. Dependence on others. Seek-support, nurturance vs. feeling self-sufficient.

4. STRUCTURE

Environment	*Individual*
A. Ambiguity vs. specification of expectations. Role ambiguity or role clarity, e.g., rules learned from other residents.	A. Tolerance of ambiguity vs. need for structure.
B. Order vs. Disorder.	B. Need for order and organization.

5. STIMULATION—ACTIVITY

Environment

A. Environment input (stimulus properties of physical and social environment); (Not only availability of stimulation, but that which is directed to resident).

B. The extent to which resident is actually stimulated and encouraged to be active.

Individual

A. Actual energy level of individual activity and participation.

B. Preference for activities vs. disengagement.

6. AFFECT

Environment

A. Tolerance for or encouragement of affective expression. Provision of ritualized show of emotion (e.g., funerals).

B. Amount of affective stimulation. Excitement vs. peacefulness in environment.

Individual

A. Need for emotional expression-display of feelings, whether positive or negative.

B. Intensity of affect, e.g., need for vs. avoidance of conflict and excitement (shallow affect).

7. IMPULSE CONTROL

Environment

A. Acceptance of impulse life vs. sanctions against it. The extent to which the environment gratifies needs immediately vs. postponed need gratification. Gratification/deprivation ratio.

B. Tolerance of motor expression—restlessness, walking around in activities or at night.

C. Premium placed by environment on level headedness and deliberation.

Individual

A. Ability to delay need gratification. Preference for immediate vs. delayed reward. Degree of impulse need.

B. Motor control; psychomotor inhibition.

C. Impulsive closure vs. deliberate closure.

Empirically the congruence hypothesis may be tested at several different levels. One may consider congruence between various aspects of the environment and measures of individual preferences, or characteristics, or inferred intrapsychic need dispositions. While the model is applicable in comparative studies of environments it may be equally valuable when dealing with only one environmental setting. A congruence model may be also helpful in providing answers to questions raised by practitioners. It may be used in various settings in order to predict which residents are most likely to make an easy adjustment upon entering. As such, a consideration of residents' expressed preferences may be used by practitioners to aid them in the placement of residents in appropriate settings. In addition, this model also may be used to guide practitioners' efforts in channeling residents to available activities, programs, and facilities within a given setting.

TESTING THE MODEL

The conceptual model presented here has been utilized in an empirical study of three nursing homes. The design of the study was one of replication, examining the relative importance of congruence for predicting adjustment in each of three homes serving diverse populations. The relative saliency of seven dimensions of congruence for the elderly individual was also studied.

The sites selected included one traditional nonprofit home for the aged, one home for the aged with a professional orientation, and a proprietory nursing home catering to well-to-do customers who pay for their own care.

The homes thus selected represent different types of ownership and sponsorship patterns, different environmental features and resident populations with diverse cultural and ethnic backgrounds. In spite of these differences, however, the homes were selected to represent high quality care. The major reason for the exclusion of homes where adequate physical comfort and care were not available was that such environments would by definition be noncongruent with basic resident needs and therefore testing of the congruence hypotheses would be for all practical purposes impossible.

Residents in the three homes represented a cross-section of individuals with diverse backgrounds and characteristics, simply by virtue of residing in the different homes. Nevertheless only "well" residents, i.e. those without incapacitating physical or mental impairment, were included in the sample. Exclusion of ill residents insured that subjects were able to respond to a rather extensive interview. In addition, severe illness might have diminished the potential importance of congruence along the proposed dimensions, and thereby invalidate the test of our hypotheses.

The selection of relatively intact residents was generally a simple matter since all three homes housed residents on different floors according to their levels of physical and mental functioning.

Thirty interviews were completed at the commercial nursing home, forty-three at the nonprofit Jewish home, and fifty at the Protestant church-related home—a total of 124 completed interviews.

Assessment of congruence between environmental and individual characteristics necessitated developing two parallel sets of measures—one for the individual and one for the home environment. In addition, individual assessments had to include measurement of the outcome variables of adjustment or well-being and coping ability.

Additional data were obtained on a number of potentially important background variables which may intervene between congruence and adjustment. Additional variables considered included demographic data, data about cognitive functioning, and personality disposition.

The environment of the residents was conceptualized and studied on two levels—on the one hand the term referred to the total institutional environment along specified dimensions; on the other, it was used to describe the personal life space (physical and social environment) of each individual resident.

In two out of three homes, congruence between individual needs and the environment emerged as important and significant determinants of adjustment, when related in a stepwise regression analysis to the Lawton Morale Scale as shown in Table 9-II.

TABLE 9-II

MULTIPLE CORRELATION COEFFICIENTS AND FRACTIONS OF
EXPLAINED VARIANCE FOR STEPWISE REGRESSION
ANALYSES OF THE CONGRUENCE CONSTRUCT

| | Lawton Morale Scale | | Self-Rated Life Satisfaction | |
	Multiple R	Multiple R²	Multiple R	Multiple R²
Professional Home	.677	45.8%	.711	50.5%
Church related home	.540	29.1%	.634	40.2%
Commercial home	.913	83.3%	.715	51.1%

Further, the congruence construct explained about half of the variance in the two adjustment indices in two of the three homes. In the professional home, 45.8 percent of the variance in morale and 50.5 percent of the variance in self-rated life satisfaction was explained by the congruence sub-dimensions. In the commercial home, the congruence items explained 83.3 percent of the variance in morale and 51.1 percent of the variance in self-rated satisfaction. The congruence construct explained a smaller proportion of the variance in adjustment in the church related home: 29.1 percent for morale and 40.2 percent for self-rated life satisfaction.

Dimensions of congruence related to adjustment differed from home to home. The sub-dimensions of privacy, motor control, and stimulation proved to be important predictors of morale in the two homes in which the congruence construct seemed to have most explanatory power. The privacy sub-dimension was also among the best predictors of morale in the third home. Continuity with the past was an important predictor in both the church related and the professional home, and change vs. sameness proved to be among the best predictors of morale in both the commercial and church related home.

Thus, five sub-dimensions of congruence were shown to have an important role in explaining morale in at least two of the three homes. Privacy was among the best predictors of morale in all three homes, and motor control, stimulation, continuity with the past, and change vs. sameness appeared as best predictors in two out of three homes. The emergence of these five sub-dimensions as important predictors in at least two homes provides fairly firm grounds for attesting the salience of these congruence sub-dimensions in predicting morale. It is noteworthy that in the third home where congruence was least important in predicting morale more options were open to residents. This home had fewer total institutional features.

These results indicate that the concept of congruence has considerable explanatory power with respect to adjustment. A closer examination of the conditions under which this hypothesis received most—or least—support may provide further clues to understanding the nature of congruence and its operation.

REFERENCES

Barker, R. G.: *Ecological Psychology, Concepts and Methods for Studying the Environment of Human Behavior.* Stanford, Stanford University Press, 1968.

Burgess, E. W.: *Aging in Western Societies.* Chicago, The University of Chicago Press, 1960.

Bultena, G.: Life continuity and morale in old age. *The Gerontologist,* 9:4, 1969.

Cumming, E., and Henry, W. E.: *Growing Old.* New York, Basic Books, 1961.

Goffman, E.: *Asylums.* Chicago, Aldine Publishing Company, 1961.

Havighurst, R.; Neugarten, B., and Tobin, S.: Disengagement and patterns of aging. In Neugarten, B. (Ed.), *Middle Age and Aging.* Chicago, The University of Chicago Press, 1968.

Hunt, J.: *Intelligence and Experience.* New York, Ronald Press, 1961.

Kahana, Eva: *Matching Environments to Needs of the Aged.* Final Progress Report submitted to NICHD, Fall, 1973.

Kahana, B., and Kahana, E.: Age changes in impulsivity among chronic schizophrenics. Proceedings of the *7th International Congress in Gerontology,* Vienna, 1966.

Kleemier, R. W.: *Aging and Leisure.* New York, Oxford Press, 1961.

Korchin, S. J., and Bosowitz, H.: The judgment of ambiguous stimuli as an index of cognitive functioning in aging. *Journal of Personality,* 25:81-95, 1956.

Lawton, M. P.: Ecology and aging. Unpublished mimeographed paper, 1968.

Lewin, K.: *A Dynamic Theory of Personality.* New York, McGraw-Hill, 1935.

Murray, H. A.: *Explorations in Personality.* New York, Oxford University Press, 1938.

Neugarten, B.: A developmental view of adult personality. In J. E. Birren (Ed.): *Relations of Development and Aging,* Springfield, Illinois, Charles C Thomas, 1964.

Peck, R. F.: Psychological developments in the second half of life. In Neugarten, B. (Ed.): *Middle Age and Aging,* Chicago, The University of Chicago Press, 1968.

Pincus, A.: The definition of measurement of the institutional environment in homes for the aged. Paper presented at the 20th Annual Meeting of the Gerontological Society, St. Petersburg, 1967.

Pollack, K.. and Kastenbaum, R.: Delay of gratification in later life: an experimental analogy. In Kastenbaum, R. (Ed.): *New Thoughts on Old Age,* New York, Springer Publishing Company, Inc., 1964.

Reichard, S.; Livson, F., and Petersen, P. G.: *Aging and Personality.* New York, John Wiley & Sons, Inc., 1962.

Rosow, I.: *Social Integration of the Aged.* The Free Press, 1967.

Stern, G.: *People in Context.* New York, John Wiley & Sons, Inc., 1970.

CHAPTER 10

RELOCATION RESEARCH AND SOCIAL POLICY[1, 2]

MORTON A. LIEBERMAN

$\mathbf{D}$OES THE EVER-BURGEONING research on relocation of the elderly and on the nature of institutional life offer us any collective wisdom that can lead to a rational and humane strategy of care for the aged in distress? How should we, on the basis of the empirical evidence that now exists in our field, construct a public policy that would cope with the plight of the very aged, especially those who have diminished capacities and increased need for service? Such service has all too often been construed as being possible only within the walls of institutional structures. Clearly there are theoretical alternatives to institutionalization, and ample demonstrations exist that portray the practical consequences of such theoretical alternatives. However, for many of the elderly, some form of congregate living becomes a practical necessity. What then? Here, the accumulation of empirical data over the

[1] The present chapter is based on a paper given at Symposium on Long-Term Care, Gerontological Society, November 7, 1973, Miami Beach, Florida.

[2] The empirical research described in this chapter is based upon four studies of relocation. The Old Age Home Transfer Study (Wilmington-Quincy), Morton A. Lieberman, principal investigator; the Institutionalization Study, Morton A. Lieberman, principal investigator; Sheldon Tobin, project director. Both were supported by a Public Health Service Research Grant #HD-00364 from the National Institute of Child Health and Human Development. The Therapeutic Transfer Study (Manteno State Hospital), Morton A. Lieberman, principal investigator, Sheldon Tobin, co-principal investigator, and Darrell Slover, project director, was supported by a Department of Mental Health, State of Illinois grant, project #17-328. The Mass Relocation Study (Modesto State Hospital), Morton A. Lieberman and Roberta Marlowe, co-principal investigators, was supported by a grant from Department of Mental Hygiene, State of California.

years provides some important clues as well as some annoying inconsistencies. The absence of a clarion ring to this empirical accumulation is in large part a consequence of method problems. Most of the studies in this area are small-scale; their populations are not comparable, and they lack the elegance of random design and the power of quasi-experimental methods. Methods and measures do not overlap. Methodological elegance has all too frequently been called for to burden the reader with a detailed account of the various sins that have been committed. However, there are a few points relevant to method that vitiate much of this research when the purpose is better planning for human services.

Foremost on my list of near idiocies has been the over preoccupation with death rates. All too often investigators have been involved in what may appear to be a bizarre numbers game. If we manage to provide service to the very elderly by relocating them into institutional structures, and find we have not statistically increased the probability of death, our subjective experience is a sense of relief, nay, almost a sense of victory and a feeling that we have done our job well. To be sure, such data do prove that we have not been dramatically destructive, but to construct a rational policy of planning for the care of the elderly solely on the basis of minimizing the risk of mortality is narrow from a humanitarian perspective and also, I believe, scientifically suspect. Let me illustrate with an analogue from psychotherapy research. Psychotherapeutic literature is replete with studies which examine the consequences of particular arrangements of psychotherapy on drop-out rates, as if determining what factors minimize such behavior will increase knowledge about what aids the psychotherapeutic process. Simply keeping people in therapy, or keeping the elderly alive, when our goal is to enhance service and the state of human beings in both therapy and service for the elderly, does not provide a meaningful approach to either problem.

A more useful orientation for studying the effects of relocation would be to ask the question whether the individual departs subsequent to being moved in major ways from his prior physiological, behavioral and psychological status. Is his level of competence reduced? Such studies can perhaps more precisely assess the negative impact of moving the elderly into caretaking facilities. Yet again, while these studies tell us more about the reasons for negative effects, they still resemble the simple assessment of mortality rates as they are also open to the criticism that preventing failure does not necessarily insure success. Most of my work on the effects of environmental change in the elderly, and that of my colleagues, has involved assessments of behavioral, psychological, and physical departures from homeostasis. Taken together with the findings on mortality rates, these studies point the direction towards how to minimize risk, but unfortunately do not answer the question how to facilitate the well-being of the elderly. In general, examination of the literature suggests that with few exceptions, empirical studies of relocation have done a much better job of assessing and quantifying destructiveness. There is a rough correlation between studies demonstrating destructiveness with methodological sophistication and studies suggesting more positive outcomes with impressionistic data.

Does the work on relocation in any way suggest that resources be reorganized to maintain the elderly in their original environments? Four studies my colleagues and I have conducted over the past years covering 640 individuals (including 175 controls) —some on healthy elderly moving into affluent, high-care, sophisticated institutions; others involving sick, highly-debilitated human beings moving into circumstances that would delight a muckraker—have yielded roughly comparable findings. Namely, no matter what the condition of the individual, the nature of the environment, or the degree of sophisticated preparation, relocation entails a higher than acceptable risk to the large majority of those being moved.

The number of aged showing marked decline, behaviorally, physically (including death), socially or psychologically range from a low of 48 percent to a high of 56 percent. Death rates showed a much higher variation, from a low of 2 percent to a high of 18 percent. Table 10-I shows the one year outcomes for the four studies. In all cases, outcome or effects are defined in terms of ratings and test behaviors from each individual's own baseline prior to relocation.

Late Life

TABLE 10-I

COMPARISONS—LONG-RANGE EFFECTS OF RELOCATION

	N	Stable	Marked Decline (Including Deaths)	Number of Deaths
Transfer	45	22 (48%)	23 (52%)	4 (09%)
Institutionalization	85	52 (52%)	41 (48%)	13 (15%)
Therapeutic Discharge	82	42 (53%)	40 (47%)	2 (02%)
Mass Transfer	427	190 (44%)	237 (56%)	78 (18%)

In each of the four studies marked decline was defined as changes from the individual's own pre-location baseline behaviorally, psychiatrically, socially or physically. Intercorrelations among the four realms of outcome suggest considerable overlap, with most individuals who are classified as marked decline showing multiple signs of such decline. Stability was defined in terms of lack of negative change. In fact for some of the studies, a certain percentage of those shown as stable in Table 10-I did manifest signs of positive change. The number and percentages for each of the four studies was as follows: For the transfer study, one out of the 45 residents showed definite improvement (.02%); in the Institutional study, five of the 85 (.06%) showed definite improvement; in the therapeutic transfer study, 17 of the 84 showed improvement (20%), and finally for the mass transfer population 87 of the 427 (20%) showed improvement.

Although there is variation in death rates and in number improving, an examination of Table 10-I indicates that the elderly rated as having shown marked decline subsequent to relocation is rather constant. This despite the wide variation in the populations studied and the conditions under which individuals were relocated. In two of the four studies, we examined aged who are mentally and physically comparable to the elderly living in the community (the Transfer study and the Institutionalization study); two involved populations of aged who were or had been mentally ill. The range of psychological and physical resources in the four-population study is considerable as are the conditions under which relocation occurred. In the initial study (Transfer study), physically healthy and psychologically robust elderly were studied in a forced relocation from a small hotel-like institution to a larger quasi-military institution for the aged. In the second study (Institutionalization study), community-dwelling aged were studied who voluntarily entered homes for the aged, in part for physical and in part for social needs. The third study (Therapeutic Relocation) examined a highly selected group of geriatric mental hospital patients who were discharged to a variety of community-based institutional and semi-institutional settings. The final study (Mass Transfer) examined a population of geriatric mental hospital patients who were relocated en masse from a state mental hospital to a variety of other institutional studies. The two latter studies differed in that although they both involved mental hospital patients, the former were highly selected, physically healthy "therapeutic discharges," while the latter study involved the total population of a state mental hospital, including individuals who were both physically and mentally deteriorated as well as patients who could have been discharged for therapeutic purposes to community residency.

But this assertion of an empirical reality sheds little light on the problem of how to care for those aged, and suggests even less about the options available. It simply supports the position that relocation not be taken lightly as a social policy and that resources be organized to minimize the amount of institutionalization required for the elderly.

Having accepted that relocation is a major stress that radically affects many elderly, distinctions among the elderly and the conditions that surround relocation must be made that can guide development of a strategy for minimizing risk. What steps can and should be taken to minimize the risk in entering congregrate living situations? Let me again draw an analogue from the field of psychotherapy that perhaps illustrates one aspect of the state of our knowledge more poignantly than bald statistics. The best advice one can give to a beginning psychotherapist who asks the question, "What can I do to enhance my therapeutic potential?," is to tell him to select his patients carefully. The patient's characteristics are the single most powerful predictor of successful outcome in psychotherapy. A similar finding is echoed in much of the research on relocation; that is, choose the right person to be relocated. Over and over again studies on relocation report findings that indicate that physical status, cognitive ability, and certain other characteristics of personality are powerful predictors of the outcome of relocation. Combinations of such personal traits entered into multivariate statistical models frequently yield predictive equations that could substantially reduce the risk factor in relocation. Even if we abandon as unrealistic an intensive application of selection criteria based on physical status, some of the principles implied can help mitigate the risk of relocation.

Our own studies are illustrative of this general finding. The Transfer study examined physically healthy and psychologically intact individuals with little inter individual variation in physical status and cognitive ability. For such a population personality traits play a crucial role in outcome prediction; we found that the personality variable of hopelessness or despair was the single most powerful predictor of outcome. However for a sub-group of individuals who did have signs of cognitive malfunctioning (six out of the sample were so defined) four showed marked decline subsequent to relocation. In the second study, Institutionalization, where again the physical status of the population was relatively homogeneous, personality traits, cognitive functioning, despair, the ability to maintain and defend a consistent self-image, and the absence of primitive defense mechanisms such as denial were all significant predictors of outcome. A combination of these five factors produced a linear discriminate analysis which correctly placed 79 percent of the sample. In the third study (Therapeutic Transfer) characteristics of the person that indicated subsequent adaptation included cognitive ability, level of physical health and personality variables—particularly an aggressive versus passive stance to the world; a similar personality trait to those described in the previous study. In the Mass Transfer study initial person characteristics discriminated between those who died from those who remained alive (the previous studies could not make such fine distinctions but combined marked decline or deterioration and deaths). In this last study three central factors account for the majority of outcome variance (with regard to survival)—initial physical condition, cognitive ability, and level of responsiveness to the environment. Using a linear discriminate model, 73 percent of the variance was accounted for by initial physical condition.

It seems eminently clear that the characteristics of the person prior to relocation, particularly his functional adequacy in terms of physical condition and cognitive ability, play a crucial role in accounting for those who react negatively to relocation. Under conditions where the populations of elderly relocated are in better physical and mental condition, certain personality characteristics become the salient qualities to account for differences in adaptation.

However, while the isolation of personal characteristics relevant to stress adaptation is not a matter of idle inquiry, increased precision in this area will not contribute significantly to the development of social policy on congregate care facilities. For it is often the *very people who require supportive services that can empirically be shown to entail the greatest risk*. This is another illustration, for an audience that probably does not need it, that empirical research often fails to help us with the nitty-gritty of policy issues.

Emphasis on selection criteria has never been a popular policy among those who must deal with the everyday realities of caring for the elderly. There is no question, given both the accumulation of research findings and practitioner experience, that the transition from community to institution living is a major upheaval involving loss and requiring a redefinition of self. Long before research began to accumulate, the cost in human misery of entering institutions was evident to practitioners, who developed a wide variety of ameliorative strategies. Psychological preparations such as helping the elderly make decisions about their needs, permitting them some influence on the outcome of their service requests, working with the family, developing programs of trial visits and the like, are among the many strategies practiced by enlightened social agencies. Such a policy is correct not only in its estimation of the human misery involved in this transitional stage, but also with regard to the best available evidence on strategies for coping with threat. Appropriate cognitive appraisal of an impending threat has been shown in a wide variety of research contexts to be the crucial element for dealing adequately with stress (Lazarus, 1966). Yet despite the good sense of psychological preparation, and its firm footing in empirical research on threat, evidence from our research on relocation suggests that it is not a powerful tool in minimizing relocation risk. The reason is not poor practice, but rather incorrect strategy. Relocation is a risk to the individual not because of the symbolic meaning that such transitions imply, but because it entails radical changes in the life space of an individual that require new learning for adaptive purposes. In other words, the cure has been addressed to the wrong problem.

Evidence we can bring to bear on this issue is only indirect— well-controlled studies which compare preparation with no preparation are not available. Our own four relocation studies involve a large range of conditions from relocations which could be described as voluntary, and perhaps even desired, to those in which decision making was totally outside the control of the elderly, and the moves were decidedly unwelcome. Applying the same measurement devices to a variety of variables concerned with and directly related to the substance of preparation— appraisal working through, the nature of the positive and negative expectation, voluntary/involuntary, degree of control exercised by the individual, aspects of realistic appraisal, and so forth—has suggested that there were scant differences among the vastly different circumstances with regard to negative effects on the individuals involved in relocation. Furthermore, within any one study, such parameters did not substantially differentiate those who weathered the relocation successfully and those who showed decrements in behavioral, psychological, and physical functioning.

Specific data is available on three of the four studies (the Mass Transfer study involved primarily observational rather than interview data). Table 10-II shows the mean scores for each of the three samples for which data was available. Examining first the locus of control we find that the model response for the Institutionalization sample was that the aged feels that he has a major responsibility in his decision to relocate, although he may have been advised by others or feel that he has had to listen to

TABLE 10-II

COMPARISON AMONG STUDIES
ATTITUDES AND EXPECTATIONS TOWARD RELOCATION

	Transfer	Institutionalization	Therapeutic Transfer
Amount of Perceived Control[1,2,3] (Scale 1 to 6)	2.02 (0.15)[*]	4.57 (1.20)	2.40 (0.97)
Anticipatory Reactions:			
Positive Feelings Toward Leaving (Scale —2 to +2)[1,3]	—1.00 (1.28)	1.29 (1.12)	1.21 (1.14)
Expected Loss[1,3] (Scale 1 to 5)	2.87 (104)	1.76 (0.99)	1.97 (0.93)
Anticipated Satisfaction[1,2,3] (Scale —2 to +2)	—0.11 (1.26)	1.31 (1.08)	0.44 (1.16)
Congruence of Actual Site with Description of Preferred Site[1,2,3] (Scale 1 to 5)	2.73 (1.36)	4.58 (1.23)	3.42 (1.16)
Objective Evaluation:			
Degree of Realism[2,3] (Scale 1 to 5)	2.67 (0.60)	3.42 (0.68)	2.84 (0.79)
Amount of Information[1,2,3] (Scale 1 to 4)	2.91 (0.63)	3.20 (0.56)	1.81 (0.76)

[*] (Standard Deviation)
[1] $p \leqslant .05$ significance level, Therapeutic Transfer and Transfer Sample
[2] $p \leqslant 0.05$ significance level, Therapeutic Transfer and Institutionalization Sample
[3] $p \leqslant 0.05$ significance level, Transfer and Institutionalization Sample

the needs and opinions of others in making a decision. In contrast, for the Transfer sample the model response was the person feels he has neither control nor influence over the decision to be relocated. He may feel either helpless (just have to do whatever they decide), or passive-accepting (I'll do whatever they think best). The Therapeutic Discharge sample model position is that the person feels he has influenced the decision in some small way; that they consulted with him or took him into account in making the decision. Similar wide differences shown in terms of the person's perceived control over his own fate *vis-à-vis* relocation can be found among the studies with regard to the person's feelings about leaving, anticipated loss and satisfaction as well as the type of information the individual possessed about the forthcoming location. Thus there were large differences among the three samples of relocated aged with the Institutionalization sample perceiving themselves as having been instrumental in making the decision to relocate and having much more positive expectations about the relocation than any of the other groups. Despite the differences among the samples, as was shown in Table 10-I, the degree to which the outcomes or effects of relocation differ among the samples is much less than would have been expected in examining the anticipation and expectational data. In other words despite these large differences in expectations and anticipations, the negative effects of relocation are within a much smaller range than one could anticipate if expectations and anticipations had a major impact in minimizing the risk of relocation.

Research where investigators have suggested different outcomes for voluntary compared to involuntary relocations can be reinterpreted as yielding differences due to population characteristics rather than degree of voluntarism. Involuntary relocations most often involve individuals who are poor risks on the basis of person characteristics—health, cognitive status, and the like. In one of our studies closer examination of the voluntary/involuntary concept suggested some interesting findings. Voluntary commitment and participation in decision making is a myth shared by the social agency, the older person himself, and by his family. Being able to maintain a sense of personal integrity and control is essential to the maintenance of an adequate self-image, particularly for the older person. However, when elderly supposedly voluntarily relocated are studied through devices such as projective techniques, or are re-examined after relocation, their feelings about the positive nature of the step and the degree of control they exercised in the decision are considerably altered (Lieberman and Lakin, 1965). Our evidence suggests that the voluntary/involuntary variable is, at best, a crude and nonalytic concept for looking closely at what happens in the transition from community to institutional living. (One cautionary note here: our findings around the expectations, attitudes, and anticipations with regard to impending institutionalization are not powerful outcome predictors except at one extreme—the *practice of primitive defense mechanisms* such as blatant denial portends future trouble.) All this does not mean, however, the total abandonment of preparing the elderly as they move from independent community living to institutions, for such procedures can and do alleviate the human misery inherent in the transition process. What they cannot do is to radically alter the toll so frequently observed in relocation.

Although anticipations and expectations are relatively low in power of predicting outcome associated with relocation, it can be shown that differences among the sample with regard to expectation and individual differences within any one sample affect the short-term reaction to relocation, the degree of dysphoric affect. Negative affective reactions were found in 55 percent of the Transfer sample, 13 percent of the Institutionalization sample, and 18 percent of the Therapeutic discharge sample (x^2 difference significant as $p \leqslant .10$ between the Therapeutic Discharge and Transfer sample and between the Transfer sample and the Institutionalization sample). Comparing these figures to the data presented in Table 10-II, there is a clear-cut relationship between the ordering of the levels of loss, perceived control and so forth, and the degree of emotional reaction. Furthermore, an examination of individual differences within each study indicated that statistically significant correlation (averaging about 3.0 across all samples), was found between degree of control the person felt about the upcoming move, feelings about leaving, anticipated loss, anticipated satisfaction, congruence, and subsequent short-term affective reaction (Chiriboga, D., 1972).Little significance was found regarding degree of information and affective reaction. Such findings do suggest that the preparation for relocation, which can be assumed to affect anticipations and expectations, is useful, for this procedure can and does alleviate the human misery inherent in this transition process.

If selection is an elegant and precise tool of limited usefulness in the real world because those usually identified as high risk are the very ones who most need service, and if psychological preparation has great meaning to easing transition but not to reducing the risk factor in any absolute way, what has our research indicated as a practical and viable direction for policy to go? Clearly the maintenance of the elderly in supportive community environments which minimize relocation is the best strategy, but often it is not feasible. Next would be the construction of living arrangements which minimize the alteration of life space. Such a strategy accepts the fact of physical relocation, but takes cognizance of the important distinction between physical relocation and major alterations in lifestyle. This could be accomplished by constructing environments with ranges of resources such that there is minimal disruption in lifestyle as the elderly make the transition from independent status, so change is gradual, rather than abrupt. However, this ideal state may never be approximated in its full complement in the real world.

The area that is most amenable to intervention or manipulation is the institutional environment. The increasing number of gerontological symposia addressed to environment underscores its importace, but also the problems inherent in its development. We know precious little about the critical environmental conditions that affect the well-being of the elderly, and have only achieved a rudimentary beginning in developing an analytical model to examine environments. Institutional categorization systems based on size, administrative arrangements, and definition of population served have proven to be sterile. "Experimental" interventions like those characteristic of mental hospital environmental studies may lead to the same fate that bedeviled such inquiry in psychiatric research. Although providing a major corrective to traditional treatment and alerting an insensitive profession to social psychological dimensions, such research did not yield useable guidelines for constructing facilitative environments. The Hawthorne effect appears to have been greater than the environmental variables that have been introduced. Research effort addressed to the complexities of micro-environments offer the most meaningful data base, but we must recognize that such undertakings are long and arduous, and will not, in the short run, yield useable information for action.

The contribution of environmental characteristics to adaptation can best be illustrated by briefly reviewing findings from the four relocation studies. The best way to look at the contribution of environment as it affects the sequela of relocation is to examine the underlying models used to predict outcome in our four studies. These studies were sequential, beginning with the Transfer study, then Institutionalization, third, Therapeutic Transfer, and fourth, Mass Relocation. Our predictive model was an evolving one, beginning with a perspective which examined the deleterious effects of relocation as a consequence of the characteristics of the aged as a less adaptive, more biologically unstable human being. Environmental change in this perspective was viewed as a generalized stressor, and success or failure in adaptation was examined with regard to the functional capacity of the aged person. Dimensions investigated using this perspective included cognitive abilities, physical capacity and issues of mental health.

A second perspective, still within the psychological domain, again viewed environmental change as a generalized stressor and examined a variety of personality characteristics as a major source of differentiating successful and unsuccessful adaptation. The core idea was that certain personality characteristics or personality functions are instrumental in determining adaptation or nonadaptation, a conception that would fit comfortably with most human stress studied. Within this perspective, the list of personality characteristics studied is long and varies from sample to sample; included are personality viewed from the trait model perspective; the person as an interacting, interpersonal organism; the individual as affective feeling being; and an examination of the self-concept characteristics of the person.

Another alternative appoach for analyzing the source of effects of relocation stems from the assumption that relocation may not be a stressor for all who undergo such an experience and that differences in adaptation/maladaptation may be accounted for by the meaning such an event has to the elderly. Here the focus in our study is on the symbolic meaning of the event—loss, expectations, anticipations and images the aged have prior to and during the relocation.

The fourth perspective for examining a source of effects lies not in the characteristics of the person, but rather in the characteristics of the environment to which the person is relocated. Perhaps what matters most is the quality or characteristics of the new environment into which the person is placed that will explain differences in deteriorative, destructive sequela of relocation as well as the potential enhancement or therapeutic effects.

The last perspective used to analyze the effects of relocation represent an integrated attempt to look at both environment characteristics as well as characteristics of the person. The notion is that relocation is a stressor to the extent that it demands or requires new adaptations for the aged; adaptations which in some sense are burdensome to an organism that may be less adaptive and more biologically unstable. Those aged individuals whose adaptive pattern fits or matches a new environment are less likely to need to make radical adaptations, and hence would be less stressed and fit at low cost to themselves into the new environment; conversely when the fit between a person's adaptive pattern or style noted in the prior environment is ill-matched to the new environment, high stress and frequent failures in adaptation would be observed.

Each of our studies has in some way examined all of these issues, but our last two studies, in which there was sufficient variation in the environments into which the elderly were relocated, provided a means of examining this issue.

Comparison among the predictor models was accomplished by using a multi-variant analysis of variance (Messa 98). This statistical procedure permitted us to evaluate the overall contribution of each of the models as well as specific indices that were significant predictors of outcome. Table 10-III shows the data for the Therapeutic Transfer study, and Table 10-IV for the mass relocation study. For the purpose of this discussion, the most relevant information contained in the tables is the overall probability level which provides a rough measure of the degree of contribution of prediction by each of the areas. It will be noted that the most powerful predictor of outcome for the Therapeutic Transfer study were environmental characteristics, followed by functional capacities and then by several areas of personality functioning. Another means of showing the relative contribution was the use of a linear discriminant analysis. It was found that a twelve-step discriminant analysis correctly identified

TABLE 10-III

THERAPEUTIC TRANSFER OUTCOME PREDICTORS

	Number of Dimensions	Overall 'p'	Significant (p ⩽ .10)
I. Functional Capacity	8	.12	Cognitive (p = .04) Physical Health (p = .03) Mental Health (p = .09)
II. Personality A. Interpersonal Behavior	5	.15	Quantity of Interaction (p = .04)
B. Affects	4	.31	Satisfaction with Hospital Environment (p = .09)
C. Traits	5	.14	Aggressivity (p = .05)
D. Needs	8	.31	N recognition (p = .03)
III. Expectations	8	.47	None
IV. Environments	10	.07	Independence (p = .02) Physical care (p = .05) Warmth (p = .07)

TABLE 10-IV

MASS RELOCATION
COMPARISON OF DETERIORIATED WITH NO CHANGE PREDICTORS

	Number of Dimensions	Overall 'p'	Significant (p ⩽ .10)
I. Functional Capacity	14	.01	Declining Medical Record (p = .002) Verbal Comprehension (p = .001) Verbal Ability (p = .008)
II. Personality A. Behavioral-Social	8	.001	Sociability (p = .0001) Relatedness (p = .03)
B. Anti-Social	6	.38	Hostility (p = .04)
III. Environments	11	.0002	Autonomy (p = .0003) Resources (p = .006) Physical Appeal (p = .02) Tolerance for Deviation (p = .01)

85 percent of the cases in their outcome classification. The initial variable, which accounted for 57 percent of correct identification, was the environmental characteristic, independency fostering; second step amount of interpersonal contact, which brought it up to 61 percent; need recognition, 65 percent; the environmental characteristic, stimulation, 66 percent;

the environmental characteristics, individuation, 67 percent; the environmental characteristic, warmth, 72 percent; the environmental characteristic, health care adequacy, 77 percent; environment-person characteristic congruence on stimulation, 78 percent; need stimulation, 79 percent; person-environmental characteristic congruence recognition, 80 percent; role activity, 82 percent; and the environmental characteristic, achievement, 85 percent. In other words out of the twelve variables that made an independent contribution to discriminant analysis, six of them were environmental characteristics.

The Mass Relocation study contained a broader range of patients and larger numbers within each outcome category. The analysis was conducted in stages for the four classifications of outcome: those who died, those who improved, those who deteriorated, those who showed no change. Those who died could be accounted for almost totally by their physical health status prior to relocation with the addition of other person characteristics, particularly cognitive functioning.

The large sample with sufficient numbers falling in each of four outcome classifications permitted us to assess the specific role of our predictor model *vis-à-vis* possible differences among outcome classifications, unlike in the previous studies where the issue was those who deteriorated versus those who remain unchanged. A look at those who died indicated that physical health issues and cognitive capacities were the most powerful predictors and that environment did not play a role in accounting for outcome. However, when we turned to those who deteriorated and those who improved subsequent to relocation our findings showed that (when contrasted to the unchanged) a number of areas entered into the prediction equation using the statistical model developed in the previous study. Of interest, however, was that both those who deteriorated and those who improved were quite similar in their functioning *prior to relocation* (and distinct from those who died as well as those who remained unchanged). A subsequent analysis of variance between the two outcome groups, deteriorated versus improved, revealed that only three non-environmental variables distinguished them. Those who deteriorated were more sociable, interacted more with staff, and were more highly verbal than those who improved. Table 10-V lists all the significant differences between those who deteriorated and those who improved, according to order of the size of their F ratio. All the variables listed in Table 10-V are significant at a

TABLE 10-V

DETERIORATED VERSUS IMPROVED PATIENTS:
MASS TRANSFER STUDY

Analysis of Variance Rank Ordered According to Size of F Ratio,
Significant Variables Only (p < .01)

F Ratio	Variable
39.90	*Environment*: Autonomy
39.13	Patient Specific *Environment*: Personalization
26.51	Patient Specific *Environment*: Warmth
22.90	Patient Specific *Environment*: Expectations Passivity
22.47	*Environment*: Tolerance for Deviance
22.39	Patient Specific *Environment*: Staff Attitude to Patient
21.37	*Environmental* Discrepancy: Independence
19.36	Patient Specific *Environment*: Succorance
17.05	*Environment*: Personalization
10.98	Sociability "Person" variable
9.43	*Environment*: Community Integration
9.07	*Environment*: Social Integration OR
7.72	Patient Specific *Environment*: Relative Cognitive Condition
7.32	Interaction with Staff "Person" variable
7.13	*Environment*: Succorance
7.08	*Environmental* Discrepancy: Overall
7.08	Verbal Ability "Person" variable

.01 level. It shows that of all the significant variables, only three relatively low down in the order of strength of prediction are person variables, two personality and one cognitive—and in the direction opposite to the general prediction of equation, namely that those in poor condition will do poorly. The results of this study suggest that environment plays a critical role in the sequela of relocation when the function is to understand adaptation for those who manage to survive. Survival is clearly related to the physical condition of the person; however, it is important to hasten to add that whatever evidence we have suggests that it is not simply that these individuals would have died had relocation not taken place—for in contrast to a carefully matched control group in another state hospital, three times as many people died in our study as in the control group.

Facilitative environments were those characterized by relatively high degrees of autonomy fostering, personalization of the patients, and community integration. Critical was that facilitative environments placed the locus of control much more in the hands of the patients, differentiated among them, and permitted them a modicum of privacy. Also, the boundaries between the institution and the larger community were more permeable than nonfacilitative environments. Facilitative environments reduced in an important way the degree of "total institutionalization." Equally important, they tended to be low on care giving and intolerant of deviancy. The findings suggest that, for the population studied, institutions that had relatively high expectational sets for behavior, that treated the elderly as adults with responsibilities, and that were not indulgent or permissive with regard to deviant behavior, presented a facilitative challenge. These findings call to mind some of the psychiatric milieu programs for the elderly and the mentally ill. Making demands in the context of a humanizing, respectful environment appears to be highly facilitative. Tender-loving-care when it implies infantilization seems to be not only nonfacilitative, but potentially destructive. In general, the call heard so frequently to make our institutions for the elderly less total institutions does find support in this research.

It is also important to point out that some environmental characteristics appeared to be not as crucial as might have been expected. For instance, the resource richness of the environment seemed to have little to do with facilitation. From a policy point of view, this may have some important implications—for the environmental changes we are talking about are, in essence, low cost. Resource richness implies much higher expenditures than do the kinds of changes in environment these studies indicate.

Caution must be taken, however, in translating these research findings into policy. The population studied were elderly who had, by and large, grown old in state hospitals, so to what extent these environmental characteristics would be facilitative to community populations moving into institutions is a moot point. Our research efforts have not yielded many environmental findings about community populations moving into institutions. Only a few elderly could be identified who were facilitated by such relocations. Taking individuals out of environments that were sterile and barren, and putting them into environments that were more humanizing and demanding, produced positive results. Yet, relocating individuals from community living into institutions may not follow the same environmental laws.

We have over the years in our studies on relocation impact pursued the hypothesis that stress is dependent on the number of adaptational demands the new environment makes on the elderly. It should be emphasized here, however, that the problem of minimizing life-space alterations is not equivalent to the simple maintenance of the status quo of a person's physical environment. In the aforementioned study, we found that environments that were low in discrepancy (that made few demands) tended to maintain the status quo. Both individuals who improved and who deteriorated were in "discrepant" environments, but environments whose areas of discrepancy were different. For me, the results of our studies raised more questions than they answered. In some of our studies where relatively adequately functioning individuals were forced to make numerous adaptations to entirely new lifestyles, highly discrepant environments were destructive milieus; whereas state hospital patients coming from barren, sterile situations to circumstances that offered both a challenge and a degree of self-control flourished. We have indications that nondestructiveness and perhaps even facilitation could be maximized by person/environment fit—an ideal model that is reflected by some current research, but that is certainly not sufficiently developed for direct action.

In summary, our field does not as yet offer the critical mass of empirical knowledge that would easily lead to policy. The bits and pieces that currently describe the state of our knowledge; the different criteria investigators have used to assess impact ranging from personally reported satisfaction to increased social interaction; and our own work, which has assessed outcome in terms of functioning, do not make building a data base easy. Finally, asking the question what factors can be generated in an environment that make it nondestructive may be a different question than asking what characteristics in an environment make it facilitative. Does the contrast in environments where aged come from sterile, non-stimulating milieus mirror the same environmental conditions as when the aged enter institutions from the high-stimulus environments characteristic of community living? There is no reason either theoretically or empirically to assume that these form a continuum. We must be cautious that when we find environmental conditions that are nondestructive we do not interpret them as necessarily leading to maximally facilitative environments.

REFERENCES

Lazarus, R. S.: *Psychological Stress and the Aging Process.* New York, McGraw-Hill, 1966.

Lieberman, M. A., and Lakin, M.: On becoming an aged institutionalized person. In Williams, R. H., Tibbetts, C., and Donahue, W. (eds.): *Processes of Aging,* Vol. 1: *Social and Psychological Perspective.* New York, Atherton, 1965, pp. 475-503.

Chiriboga, D.: *The prediction of relocation stress among the aged: A comparative study.* Unpublished dissertation, Committee on Human Development, University of Chicago, 1972.

Chapter 11

CONTEXTUAL AND DEVELOPMENTAL ISSUES IN THE EVALUATION OF ADULT LEARNING: TRAINING IN APPLIED GERONTOLOGY AS AN EXAMPLE

Tom Hickey and James W. Hodgson

In keeping with the theme of the book, this chapter will focus on the importance and implications of the environment as they relate to the training of those who provide health and social services to the elderly. The environment, as it will be referred to here, is the context of both providers and recipients, and not necessarily that of the trainer. The title of this paper implicitly refers to at least three current areas of the gerontological research literature—optimum environments for the elderly, adult development, and manpower training needs in gerontology. Nevertheless, the fundamental issue here is really *adult education.* Those who work with the elderly are typically adults; therefore, the way in which gerontological service providers are trained is viewed within the framework of the adult as learner. This chapter will discuss theoretical and methodological issues in adult education, with implications for in-service and in-context training of service providers to the elderly.

ADULT EDUCATION AS A LOGICAL STARTING POINT

Adult education has traditionally been defined according to institutional criteria, frequently limiting itself to remedial and liberal arts programs. This approach has had its parallel in the expectations and perceptions of adults that it is temporary in nature, and a form of compensation for inadequacies in formal schooling. However, a number of more recent writings have indicated the necessity for a change in that approach. Toffler's (1970) portrayal of society's rapidly accelerated intervals between discovery, application, impact, and new discovery, is a good example. Another comes from Dubin and others (1970), who have stressed the existence and dimensions of professional and career obsolescence. A third example (Botwinick, 1970) emerges from geropsychology, where the issues of life-span development are currently becoming a major research concern. It seems clearly outmoded at this time to assume that man will spend the first quarter of his life in preparation, and most of the remainder of it in active productivity. A developmental approach permits frequent and lifelong interaction of the individual with educational content and process—both of which must be modified and adapted to the adult, rather than changing the individual to fit institutional criteria. Adult education classes which operate on a secondary school model are analogous to an equally condescending view of times past, when children were seen as incomplete or defective adults. Neither approach respects either the learner or his contextual and developmental reference.

ADULT EDUCATION AS A LEARNING PROCESS

Despite the previous statements reflecting the need for change, one cannot minimize the role of the adult education movement and its past contributions. One would be very presumptuous to suggest the development of in-context training for gerontological service providers as something completely apart from the adult education system. To underscore the impact adult education has on our society today, one need only review the data. According to Johnstone and Rivera (1965), whose classic survey into numerous areas of adult education participation remains a most authoritative source nearly a decade later, one out of every five adults had recently participated in some form of organized educational activity. In addition, 47 percent of adults had taken some form of continuing education course since leaving school.

The significant influence of such programs has been due in part to their variety, which has attracted people from many different backgrounds. Despite the wide appeal, Johnstone and Rivera also noted certain trends in participation: although men and women seem to be equally represented, the average age was 36.5, or six years younger than the median age of the total sample; and there was a significant loading in favor of the better educated, higher-than-average income, white collar adult. Although the focus of most of these courses had been on the practical and applied skills, rather than on academic content, courses of general information and enlightenment were seen to be gaining wider support. More recent surveys (White, 1973) support the further development of this trend towards a life-centered education, rather than remediation.

Burgess (1971) had earlier reached a similar conclusion. He conducted a highly sophisticated study employing factor analytic techniques with a 70-item rating instrument among large samples of adult participants. Seven ranked factors emerged as reasons for participation: (1) the desire to know; (2) the desire to reach a personal goal; (3) the desire to reach a social goal; (4) the desire to reach a religious goal; (5) the desire to escape; (6) the desire to take part in an activity; and, (7) the desire to comply with formal requirements. While the increasingly complex and impersonal nature of a technological economy require that the adult make a continuing effort to fulfill his occupational and social needs, adult education is increasingly being called upon to meet both kinds of challenges.

The claim is often made that adult education is inherently a democratic enterprise, one which not only serves individual needs but in turn accomplishes societal goals of developing a more highly skilled and satisfied population. The fact that both personal and societal goals operate on many different levels explains much of the imprecision for which the field is sometimes criticized. Obviously, its charge is not as simple as the third-grade teacher's assignment to "education and socialize." The motives of adult education are unquestionably high; and while there have been significant accomplishments in the scope and variety of program offerings, a failure to fully differentiate those characteristics peculiar to the adult learner, or to put them into practice, has continued to limit the success of this field. The child is the captive student, but what of the adult, who ventures into a new situation, and who voluntarily submits himself again to the subordinate student role? How does the learning process itself vary with individuals of different ages—especially when comparing adults with children? What are the implications of such variables as motivation, learning set, and transfer effects?

Motivation is probably the most important determinant of learning in adulthood. Theorists generally agree that decreasing motivation in later life is a major factor in the inhibition of learning, although they disagree on whether the etiology is primarily physiological or psychosocial. One acceptable line of thought would suggest that reduction in drive level due to age-related endocrine changes very likely leads to decreased motivation in the learning situation; while another might contend that both emotional and social factors are paramount, in that society's prejudicial disapproval of strong motivations later in life forces the adult to take an increasingly passive, defensive, and disengaging role—one which would inevitably interfere with learning. It seems quite possible that all of these factors may operate to decrease general motivation with advancing years.

Learning set, or expectancy, is another variable important in a consideration of adult learning. Essentially, every individual comes to any learning situation with certain expectations of what should happen. The more ambiguous the learning situation, the greater the difficulty an adult will have with increasing age. The older learner seems less able to ignore irrelevant stimuli which conflict with his expectations in a situation. As a result, he can less easily focus on relevant stimuli.

The place of transfer effects in adult learning is not as clear. In transfer, one's present reaction to a given situation is influenced by past experience, either for better or worse. Although the negative effects of transfer in adulthood are well-known—e.g. it is certainly more difficult to learn a foreign language later in life—positive effects are often overlooked. Very little attention has been paid to the commonsense notion that the wealth of experiences adults have had would aid them in many learning situations. As Stroud (1963) has concluded, "We simply do not find, in the literature, investigations of learning on the part of an older person that permits him to utilize his experience and store of knowledge built up over a lifetime." Since any kind of environment will provide numerous sources for both positive and negative transfer, it is exceedingly important to assure that an environment which encourages beneficial transfer be established.

Additional factors are commonly proposed to emphasize the differences between adulthood and childhood learning. These include increased concern with accuracy at the expense of speed, important physiological difference and handicaps, and the threatening emotional overtones often felt by adults in a formal learning environment. Another factor is that a classroom of adults is likely to be far more differentiated than a group of children, rendering the educational dynamics far more complex. The adult comes to a learning situation with very different skills, needs, and problems than does his younger counterpart. Such realities emphasize the fact that adult education has its own unique goals and problems. They also point to the crucial role of the specific learning situation in educating the adult.

In suggesting clear differences in adult learning, there is no intent here to perpetuate negative stereotypes of aging. On the one hand, we know that the cognitive processes of adults are slower for each operation, and less efficient in requiring more operations for the same task, and are less capable of handling simultaneous informational stimuli. On the other hand, the social and environmental dynamics of a learning context which too closely resembles a secondary school model, may very well be impeding the full realization of the motivational potential of so many adults returning to the learning situation, as well as inhibiting positive transfer effects from multiple years of varied experiences.

TOWARDS AN EXPERIMENTAL LEARNING THEORY

Although it is apparent that the context or environment plays an important role in adult learning, the learner is still the dominant figure—especially when considering the various motivations for participation in adult education. This would seem to warrant—at least for the moment—taking a look at generic theories of learning from a psychological perspective. For the purposes of this discussion these may be divided into *organismic* and *interactionist* theories.

The two main schools which place their emphasis on the organism alone are behavioral and cognitive theories. To the behaviorists, learning is a process by which a particular stimulus elicits a predictable response. The task of educators, therefore, becomes one of encouraging the development of desired stimulus-response bonds and discouraging others. Only those procedures—or schedules of reinforcement—which have proven to be effective in producing the desired product are acceptable. The emphasis is totally on the amount of knowledge that the student gains as a result; questions of motivation, set, transfer, and student-teacher-environment dynamics are considered secondary or irrelevant.

In cognitive theory, the focus on the organism remains, although with less insistence that only observable behavior is appropriate for analysis. Following the lead of Hull, who originally hypothesized the occurrence of internal mediational processes between stimulus and response, cognitive theorists posit that man organizes the stimuli that are presented to him in various ways and can then act upon them in some reasoned manner. In this framework, the learning process ceases to be the passive exposure to stimuli to which man simply reacts as in the behaviorists' view. The learner takes an active role in organizing the stimuli in some meaningful way.

The roots of both behavioral and cognitive theory are evident in later theories. Mowrer (1960) developed a two-factor theory of learning which synthesized the basic characteristics of each school, so that learning was seen as a combination of both external conditioning and cognitive problem-solving. Gagné (1965) endorsed this general approach, but isolated eight separate learning stages ranging from the simplest form of stimulus-response bonds to problem solving. Of the behaviorists and cognitive theorists, Gagné alone placed the phenomenon of learning in a developmental context, thus implicitly recognizing at least one aspect of the uniqueness of the adult learner. Despite

TABLE 11-I

CLASSIFICATION OF LEARNING THEORIES BY TORBERT'S FOUR LEVELS OF EXPERIENCE

	Environment	Behavior	Cognitive-Emotional-Sensory Structure	Self-Awareness
Behaviorists		X		
Cognitive Theorists			X	
Gestalt Theorists	X		X	
Field Theorists	X		X	
Social Learning Theorists	X	X	X	
Mowrer		X	X	
Gagné		X	X	
Cromwell	X	X	X	
Kobler		X	X	X
Torbert	X	X	X	X

this progressive developmental step, there is no reference to the organism's interaction with the environment. Applying this to the adult education context, his *Conditions of Learning* still presumes a "captive," or at least "predictable," audience. Although there is considerable room for disagreement among advocates of all of these theories, they stand united on the assumption that learning is properly seen as a phenomenon that takes place as a result of some activity on the part of the learner— be it mediated cognitively or through external reinforcement.

A fundamental distinction between these and field theories is the role that the environment plays in learning. The term field theory is used here broadly to include gestalt, phenomenological, and social learning theories. In general, the focus is not solely on the learner, but on the organism-environment interaction. It is not merely what the organism experiences that enables him to learn, but how the environment interacts with his experience to produce new information.

Gestalt psychologists originally postulated the importance of the person-environment equation in learning, asserting that the individual will take an active role in structuring his perceptions of the environment. If the perceptual field is disorganized—that is, if it contains conflicting or overly disturbing cues—he will impose order on it in such a way that it can be acceptable to him. Reality in this scene, becomes relative: what is real is what the individual *perceives* as being real. In Lewin's view (1965), for example, both the individual and the environment are in a constant flux, which explains the emphasis on the concepts of organization and perception in the theory.

The implications of such a theory for adult education are far-reaching. To this way of thinking, in contrast to the organism-centered theorists, learning is a very active process. An individual cannot passively learn at all, because he is constantly coloring every situation with personal perceptions. Consequently, motivation becomes a far more important concept, as it determines the number and kind of situations encountered, and will have some effect on how one perceives them. The organism-centered proponents would dismiss internal motivation as relatively unimportant, only acknowledging the importance of the motivation of others who might control cues and reinforcements. Finally, while the sole determinant of the outcome of learning for behaviorists and cognitivists is the end-result or product, to field theorists, the key to learning is the process of exposure to a new situation and the reworking of one's perceptions until the ambiguities are eliminated.

Social learning theories in many ways can be seen as attempting to synthesize field theories and organism-centered theories. In general, they maintain the focus on the interaction of organism and environment, but rely heavily on concepts from both behavioral and cognitive theorists. The tendency for behavior to occur in any given situation is a function of both the individual's expectation of reinforcement in that situation and of the value of that reinforcement.

Just as Gagné took Mowrer's synthesis of behavioral and cognitive theories and placed it in a developmental frame of reference, Cromwell adapted Rotter's social learning theory into a series of developmental learning theorems. Basically, Cromwell (1963) postulated an internal control mechanism which increases in dominance with age, largely as a function of the progressive interaction of experience and reason over time. Estes (1970) praised this line of thinking, but cautioned that as yet, little empirical research had been conducted to support Cromwell's theorems.

Another theory which may be seen as an attempted compromise or bridge between the organism and interaction schools was proposed by Kobler (1965). At about the same time that Gagné was transforming Mowrer's two factor learning theory into an eight-stage developmental theory, Kobler was adding an *ethical* or *conscience* factor to the two previously proposed. This existential drive for self-integration reflects the humanistic influences which have become increasingly popular; at least for Kobler, is explained adult learning experiences more fully than conditioning and cognitive problem-solving theories. As such, it at least recognized the uniqueness of the adult learner and implied a developmental base, although once again we are left without full appreciation of the role of the environment.

The most intriguing and perhaps significant contribution to date in this progression has come recently from Torbert (1972), who seems to have made the inevitable synthesis of developmental and interaction concepts into a unified theory of learning. Although his philosophical approach requires additional empirical support from other types of learning situations, Torbert's model of *experiential learning* is a useful one here. He maintains that there are four levels of human experience: (1) the world outside; (2) one's own behavior; (3) one's internal cognitive-emotional-sensory structure; and, (4) consciousness, or self-awareness. It should be immediately apparent that all of the previously mentioned theories have attempted in some way to focus upon one or more of these levels, without encompassing all four. Torbert alone has chosen to stress all of them. (Table 11-I) It is consistent with this theory to suggest that experiential learning will take place only to the extent that an individual maintains contact with all four levels, and can experience more than one level at a time.

The full assurance of objectivity in any system emerges from having independent methods of judging and replicating. In Torbert's model, this objectivity derives from the simultaneous experiencing at multiple levels, which serves to check the observations from more than one point of view. Implicitly, the ability to realize experiential learning is closely linked to both emotional and chronological maturity, and is thus developmental in nature.

In summary, this brief review of the major theoretical approaches to learning has not attempted to be either comprehensive or systematic with empirical documentation. That would be outside the emphasis and scope of this book of readings in the sociology of aging. The point to be reiterated here is the need for better theoretical bases for adult education which encompass the learning adult from a developmental point of view, the context of the learning, and the interaction itself. Although Torbert's theory may be questioned by the more rigorous behavioral scientist as having emerged from a narrow empirical base (T-group dynamics), and criticized for its largely descriptive and/or phenomenological approach, nevertheless, its theoretical potential for the area of adult learning is quite significant. Moreover, it is important to note both the empirical strengths of this theory, as well as it applicability to gerontological manpower training.

First of all, in learning about learning (which is the task at hand), there is an obvious circular problem which, an epistemologist might argue, cannot be resolved through one approach alone — either phenomenological or empirical. The interaction of both is evident in Torbert's work, providing as it does an original framework for both phenomenological and empirical theories. Empirical strength is found in the validity of consistent independent measures of T-group behaviors; and reliability in significant correlations with other valid measures. Secondly, the problem of manpower training—especially in gerontology—is a problem generic to adult education. This implies a theoretical problem on the one hand—that limited success will be derived from combining a non-developmental framework for the learning task with the developmental and environmental perspectives of the learner. On the other hand, it becomes a measurement problem when attempting to assess the effectiveness of this dual theoretical framework with unidimensional measures.

THE ISSUE OF EVALUATION

Evaluation is the next issue to be discussed—not only for interpreting programmatic success, but also in order to provide guidelines for program design. Liveright (1968), in his major work on adult education, noted the large-scale inadequacies of educational evaluation. Although he suggested that we seem to be acquiring more sophisticated tools, a number of problems militate against rapid improvement is this area. Not the least of the barriers is the widespread misconception that evaluation is itself a methodological activity which is essentially similar, regardless of what one is attempting to evaluate. Scriven (1967) makes the distinction between *goals* and *roles,* maintaining that the goal of evaluative activities is essentially the same in each setting, whereas the role it will play may vary greatly—i.e. program value for participants, cost-benefits for sponsors, and effectiveness or comparison of techniques, priorities, etc. Although this distinction is an important one—especially when initiating a specific project—it can also turn into an impediment when one assumes grossly that all evaluation is the same. A brief examination of approaches to evaluation may help to clarify this point.

A common classification of evaluation efforts, and one that is useful here, divides them in two ways: intrinsic vs. payoff (Scriven, 1967). The intrinsic method may involve an evaluation of goals, content, teacher attitude, teacher-student relationships, grading procedures, etc. Of particular interest is the *process* of education, and as such this approach may be labeled dynamic. Payoff evaluation, on the other hand, is strictly concerned with examining the effects of the educational experience on the pupil—effects which have been operationally defined. As a result, payoff evaluators rely heavily on standard and classical research designs.

Proponents of the payoff school of evaluation stress the virtues of a rigorous scientific approach, while the intrinsic evaluators would insist that such an approach to evaluation would grossly oversimplify the subtleties of adult education. The need to make a choice or a compromise between these two approaches appears to be indicated. One is reminded here of a similar dilemma reviewed in the previous discussion of learning theory—i.e. is learning best considered an internal or interactional phenomenon. Just as Torbert's synthesis provided a basis for compromise and clarification of this issue for adult learning, perhaps an integration of these two types of evaluation would be useful here.

The commonality between organism-centered learning theories and payoff evaluation is somewhat apparent. Theories of learning which focus on the individual alone place great stress on observable behavior and the measurable products of learning, ignoring the role of the individual's interaction with the environment. Similarly, payoff evaluators are disdainful of attempts to measure the process of learning, thus choosing to ignore concepts which are not easily operationalized. Thus, no efforts are made to measure interactional or process phenomena, which are frequently viewed as irrelevant.

The payoff evaluators and organism-centered theorists may be contrasted sharply with intrinsic evaluators and interaction theorists. The latter are mutually concerned with the *process* of learning. Just as the interaction of the learner and the environment constitutes the central element of learning for field theorists, so are intrinsic evaluators concerned with the dynamics of the learning situation itself, rather than information handling and content mastery on the part of the learner.

The implications previously discussed concerning the relative inadequacies found in applying behavioral and cognitive theories to adult education now become even more important. If such theoretical approaches fail to account for the learning adult from a developmental and contextual view, then similar failures will occur with learning measures which also ignore those developmental components, which have been proven to be of prime importance to the adult learner. The fact that such concepts are appreciably more difficult to accurately quantify would disturb the payoff evaluator and behaviorist alike. However, when such concepts are central to the phenomenon being measured, then such difficulties must be confronted directly, rather than ignored in the research design.

Evaluating adult education programs is unquestionably an

exceedingly complex enterprise, and the inclination to deal only with readily operational concepts as a product of learning is understandable. Qualitatively, the evaluative process is complicated by a number of characteristics of adult education which only add to the difficulty. For example, most programs are both informal and of short duration, making any assessment of change more difficult. It may be of even greater importance that the nature of the goals of any given program will inevitably be multidimensional and are often intangible; and they will probably vary among the students, whose goals in turn will undoubtedly be different from those of the teacher, the program administrators, or society. Moreover, these goals will not be static, and in some cases will be fairly remote, thus complicating the decision of when and how often to attempt to identify them. Finally, there is the critical problem of assigning priorities for goals according to basically qualitative criteria.

Turning to more quantitative concerns, it now appears clear that the classical paradigms favored by payoff evaluators are not well-suited to the complexities of adult education programs. Scriven (1967), for instance, sees a serious problem of construct validity in pure payoff evaluation, questioning whether the complexity of the learning process might not be such that a simple pretest-posttest design can detect changes at a useful level of generality. Campbell and Stanley (1963), on the other hand, stress that while experimental designs may always be desirable in educational evaluation, situations may often arise in which limitations of time or monetary resources, or an inability of the experimenter to gain full experimental control, will necessitate a less stringent, quasi-experimental design. In such cases, they advocate that one of a number of alternatives be used, the most preferable of which are: (1) the time-series experiment, in which a series of measurements is taken on a single sample, and the experiment is introduced at a given time in the series; (2) the equivalent time-samples design, in which one group is given two different treatments, experimental and control, in a recurrent pattern; (3) the nonequivalent control group design, in which two already existing groups (*not* randomized) are pretested and one group receives treatment, after which each receives a posttest; (4) counterbalanced designs, in which all subjects receive all treatments; (5) the separate-sample pretest-posttest design in which a controlled sub-group is pretested while another randomly equivalent sub-group receives treatment and a posttest; (6) the separate-sample pretest-posttest control group design, where a comparable control group can be added to the preceding design; and (7) the multiple time-series design, similar to the simple time-series experiment but with a control group compared.

Although most of these designs may be considered to be subject to internal invalidity (with the notable exception of the separate-sample pretest-posttest design), Campbell and Stanley would argue that, for certain cases, each may be quite satisfactory. In the case of adult education, however, their applicability is less certain. Any design which relies on random sampling, such as designs (4) through (7), assumes a commonality in the population. However, the variation in reasons for participation in adult education are such that one cannot assume with much confidence that he can secure a "typical" sample. Further, the complexity of personal interactions (goals, motives, needs) which occur in adult education classes, and their strong impact on adult learning, assure that any simple design in which there is reliance on a single measure per group, as in all but (5), would be inadequate.

The obvious challenge is to devise an evaluation methodology explicitly for adult education. Such an undertaking is clearly a major one which will undoubtedly require the continued contributions of many people. It is important to note here that thees authors are not attempting to suggest that the reader idenify them with the eminent authorities in the field of educational research or evaluation methodology. It might be useful to clarify again the objective of this chapter.

It was initially assumed that gerontological manpower training is a specific type of adult education activity, with the implication that a developmental and contextual framework becomes even more significant when one considers the training of one group of adults to provide direct services to another group. From a brief review of adult education, the progression was made to learning theory in an effort to discover the differential process of learning for adults, and, therefore, how that fact can be demonstrated empirically for the purpose of better training program design. The limitations of classical learning theories were analogous to the limitations of traditional evaluation approaches. However, Torbert provided a clue in taking both a phenomenological and empirical approach to learning, and in suggesting ways for checking observations against each other simultaneously. This paper has come full circle to its starting point—gerontological manpower development. The focus now becomes one of determining how the design and evaluation of gerontological manpower training programs provides an opportunity for the application of the forementioned recommendations and criteria.

To anticipate any skeptical questioning of whether the following examples justify the breadth of what has been stated—i.e. has a cannon been loaded to fire at a flea—there are two answers. First of all, the preceding is intended to stimulate a wide variety of theory-building efforts. Thus, one of the primary objectives of the chapter has been accomplished with the reader who has already stopped reading in order to return to his own lab and build some new models. Secondly, the bias of the senior author (Hickey and Spinetta, 1974) of this paper is clearly against the design of artificial structures bridging the researcher and the practitioner. In other words, the demonstrated need for new theories and methodologies in adult education and their assessment require in the in-service training context an applied researcher who is willing to develop theory and methodology as well as training programs. This is an important point considering the proliferation of reported findings from an "applied environment" or "naturalistic setting" which frequently represent no more than traditional research with a shift in setting, subjects, or assumptions.

GERONTOLOGICAL MANPOWER DEVELOPMENT— TOWARDS A THEORY AND A METHODOLOGY

The Gerontology Manpower Development Project at The Pennsylvania State University is focused on improving the competency levels of a wide variety of gerontological service providers in Pennsylvania. Operationally, the project is linked both to the historical land-grant university traditions in agriculture, for providing scientific and technical expertise and consultation to its constituency; and linked to its future mission as an educational institution with a high priority assigned to the development of non-campus based instructional programs. In a sense, the social consciousness of the agricultural era has broadened to include the entire fabric, or quality, of life. To gerontologists, the needs of a state university's constituency in the second half of life become analogous to those of the farmer two generations ago. The future mission—non-resident instruction and external degree programs—parallel in time both national and state perceived needs for a wide variety of service providers to older adults. The most effective way to meet such needs would seem to be found in upgrading the competency levels of existing providers in the human services field (or to recruit and retrain them from other labor force surpluses), rather than relying on a small and specialized emerging college graduate and post-baccalaureate trained manpower pool (cf. Hickey, 1973, 1974a, 1974b).

Initially, this approach focused on the *development, evaluation,* and *implementation* of short-term, on-site training. These three processes are inter-related and continue simultaneously. The design of training materials requires, among other things, a detailed description of the population served, program needs, quantity and quality of existing services, and a demographic analysis of projected trainees or participants. Procedural descriptions of this phase are unnecessary in this chapter, yet their importance to program design is not being minimized.

The process of *development* and *evaluation* is outlined here. As will be seen in this description, *implementation* occurs almost at the outset of the design, where the instructor begins to work with the agency. Final implementation takes place in the integration of training pieces into an official program with university endorsements and state incentives. First of all, a topic is selected for development with a specific group of providers (i.e. nursing home personnel, home health volunteers, etc.). The topic is identified from a factor analysis of survey research data from the more generic, "provider" population. This topic is developed into a training module by a core team of at least three people: resource persons from the agency and the university, and the liaison person or instructor (from either setting) who carries the primary responsibilities and burdens for the work. This approach compensates for a frequently noted error in evaluative studies, by including the program goals (agency decision makers) in the research hypothesis formulation, and accounting for the context or environment where the services will be delivered. In this model, the instructor developes the training component at both sites from the outset, and with input from agency and university expertise. This includes content validity checks both with nurses aides and undergraduates, for example. Nothing goes into the module without a basis in both the research literature and the competency needs of a defined group of providers. In its first "final" form, the training module is typically six to ten hours in length, utilizes several presentation media, and has as its objective, either attitude change, information transmission, skill acquisition, or some combination of the three.

In the first formal presentation, a wide variety of descriptive data are collected, and other unobstrusive measures are used to determine what is actually happening. This is the point at which many programs appear in a practitioners' journal ("How we developed our in-service program.") This is also the point at which the typical researcher quickly retreats to more familiar grounds, or at least begins to raise questions regarding controls, randomization, validity, generalizability, etc.

However, this is really the point at which *evaluation* should begin. There are four major variables: intervention, context, participant, and interaction. The intervention is the training material which has been developed and defined by both context and participant, and with an external referent from the academic liaison. This approach differs significantly from the earlier descriptions of adult education programs as remedial, oriented to trainer context, analogous to classroom learning, etc. The context and the participants have already been identified and the original development of the module was accomplished with these in mind, thus encouraging an exchange of ideas and needs of all concerned. In this way, the two principal components of an adult education program—the learner and the learning material—have simultaneous internal and contextual reference points for evaluation.

After this initial cycle and an assessment of its impact, the training module re-enters the development phase for two purposes: content modification (quality, relevancy, updating, etc.); and stratification for multiple levels of trainees—i.e. administrators vs. aides, direct care staff vs. service and support personnel. In general, the latter approach accounts for the differentiated experiential level of adult learners. At the same time, structured measures for a more empirical evaluation during subsequent training with this module are developed. Due to the previous emphasis on the contextual validity of the intervention, these efforts at evaluation may safely be quite specific. For example, if a key concept in a training program dealing with sensory deprivation is time-person-place orientation, then the way in which the material relating to this concept was designed, presented, and learned, will permit the simple counting of trainee behaviors related to reorienting older clients or patients. Also, the module, once stratified to meet different levels of trainee sophistication, presents a number of opportunities for comparative research dealing with process, context, and trainee differences. For example, if younger people in our society are more accustomed than older people to multi-media stimuli, then there should be an age difference in learning the same materials with different processes.

As empirical rigor is introduced into this system, the traditional designs must be modified to account for process variables in the learning situation. Instead of a traditional four-group design, time series observations or the equivalent of a four "plus two" is required (Table 11-II), with all trainees receiving the

TABLE 11-II

FOUR-GROUP DESIGN "PLUS TWO"

O_1	X	O_2		
	X	O_3		
O_4		O_5	X	O_6
		O_7	X	O_8

treatment (since it is preferable not to have "no treatment" controls). Such a design seems best capable of meeting the multiple needs of both the trainee and the evaluator, while still allowing for the exercise of rigor.

CONCLUSION

A subtitle for this final section might be paraphrased from an earlier part: instead of "towards an experiential learning theory," it is now tempting to say, "towards a measurable experiential learning theory." It is rather obvious at this point, however, that the preceding examples from gerontology manpower development cannot be seen as conclusive answers to the many questions raised previously. This is due largely to the tentative nature or infancy stage of many training interventions and measures at this point. Accounting for differentiated experiential levels of adult trainees is still a somewhat open question, even though contextually developed, stratified training provides a realistic learning experience.

In reviewing the dichotomous nature of learning theories and educational evaluation (cognitive/behavioral theories and payoff evaluation vs. interactionist theories and intrinsic evaluation), the approach exemplified in this chapter takes into account both the organism and the environment. The contextual development of the intervention provides a rationale for saying that the person and the environment are not parallel, even though they may be treated independently at various points in the training process. Therefore, a compromise between payoff and intrinsic evaluation becomes possible. Rather than a formal compromise, adult education can be evaluated here with a combination of payoff and intrinsic measures.

Finally, practical examples from the gerontological manpower training process have suggested ways for developing additional reliability in Torbert's four levels of experience. The data gathered from the training environment, for instance, can be measured against data gathered from other levels: *behavior* or the *cognitive, emotional,* and *sensory* structure. Torbert's fourth, or self-awareness level, seems to require additional differentiation in terms of the type of learning which takes place. (cf. Table 11-I) For example, skill acquisition may operate strictly on an overt behavioral level; whereas, attitudinal change may be experiential, and realized through self and group awareness at the end of an entire process. Although this level lacks specific applicability to general adult education (including in-service training), the framework provides a clear potential for differing types of observations, as well as a check on other data. Using the previous example of attitude change, one could say that this approach has the potential for assessing more subtle changes than traditional written inventories; and, of course, they can work together to provide some reliability data. If the premise of this chapter is still accepted—i.e. that developmental and environmental issues must be a paramount consideration in adult education at this stage of the field's development—then the self-referent point implicit in this fourth dimension may become a valuable data source.

REFERENCES

Botwinick, J.: Geropsychology. *Annual Review of Psychology*, 21:239, 1970.

Burgess, P.: Reasons for adult participation in group educational activities. *Adult Education*, 22:3-29, 1971.

Campbell, D. T., and Stanley, J. C.: Experimental and quasi-experimental designs for research on teaching. In N. L. Gage, *Handbook of Research on Teaching*, Chicago, Rand McNally and Co., 1963.

Cromwell, R. L.: A social learning approach to mental retardation. In N. R. Ellis (ed.), *Handbook of Mental Deficiency*, New York, McGraw-Hill, 1963.

Dubin, S. S. (ed.): *Professional Obsolescence*. Springfield, Mass., Heath, 1970.

Estes, W. K.: *Learning Theory and Mental Development*. New York, Academic Press, 1970.

Gagné, R. M.: *Conditions of Learning*. New York, Holt, 1965.

Hickey, T.: Manpower Development in Gerontology: 1972-73. Center for Human Services Development Report, University Park, Pennsylvania, 1974a (in press).

————: In-service training in gerontology: towards the design of an effective educational process. *Gerontologist*, 1974b (in press).

————: Manpower Development in Human Services: 1971-72, Part II—

Geriatrics Project. Center for Human Services Development Report No. 19, University Park, Pennsylvania, 1973.

Hickey, T., and Spinetta, J. J.: Bridging research and application. *Gerontologist,* 1974 (in press).

Hull, C. L.: *Principles of Behavior, An Introduction to Behavior Therapy.*

Johnstone, J. W. C., and Rivera, R. J.: *Volunteers for Learning.* Chicago, Aldine Publishing Co., 1965.

Kobler, F. J.: Contemporary learning theory and human learning. In F. T. Severin (ed.), *Humanistic Viewpoints in Psychology,* New York, McGraw-Hill. 1965.

Lewin, K.: *A Dynamic Theory of Personality: Selected Papers.* New York, McGraw-Hill, 1965.

Liveright, A. A.: *A Study of Adult Education in the United States.* Boston, Center for the Study of Liberal Education for Adults at Boston University, 1968.

Mowrer, O. H.: *Learning Theory and Behavior.* New York, Wiley, 1960.

Scriven, M.: The methodology of evaluation. In R. W. Tuler, R. M Gagne, and M. Scriven (eds.), *Perspectives of Curriculum Evaluation,* Chicago, Rand McNally, 1967.

Stroud, J. B.: Learning in relation to aging. *Continuous Learning,* 2:235-239, 1963.

Toffler, A.: *Future Shock.* New York, Random House, 1970.

Torbert, W. R.: *Learning From Experience.* New York, Columbia University Press, 1972.

White, Thurman J.: Contemporary adult education: implications for higher education. *NUEA Spectator,* 37:25-31, 1973.

CHAPTER 12

SPIRITUAL WELL-BEING IN LATE LIFE

DAVID O. MOBERG

PARADOXICALLY, INTEREST IN the spiritual nature and well-being of humanity seems to be both increasing and decreasing. On the one hand, there are many indications of increasing secularization, materialism, segmentalizing of life, and diminishing concern for institutional religion, the traditional supporter of the spiritual welfare of humanity. On the other hand, a growing awareness of the need to enhance the quality of human life, the importance of sustaining holistic orientations toward people, and the significance of the inner resources of each person contribute to accelerating concern for spiritual well-being.

Growing awareness of the significance of the spiritual dimension of life was symbolized in the 1971 White House Conference on Aging by establishment of a Technical Committee on Spiritual Well-Being to prepare background studies (Moberg, 1971) for a major section dealing with that subject at the WHCA. In many respects this represented a break-through. It drew direct attention to the spiritual dimension of human life without getting caught up in verbal and legal battles about the separation of church and state. It gave tangible recognition to the relevance and importance of governmental concern for the totality of human life and experience, instead of adhering to the "time-honored" perspective of having government deal with everything except the spiritual and the religious as if these were unimportant to the constitutional task of promoting the common welfare of citizens. It overcame the limited perspective that viewed spiritual needs exclusively in the context of religious institutions, and thus it overcame the limitations imposed by those interpretations of the U.S. Constitution which saw the realm of religion as outside the concern of a governmentally sponsored agency.

The recommendations for action that emerged from the WHCA Section on Spiritual Well-Being (1971) constitute an important development in the area of governmental cooperation with religious bodies in their mutual concerns for the needs of people.

Several references in the Post-WHCA Reports (Subcommittee on Aging, 1973) indirectly call attention to the importance of research on spiritual well-being. The need for conceptual or definitional work is indicated by recognition of its broad scope (p. 557) and acknowledgement of its linkage with every other need of man as a whole being (p. 569). It is stated (or hypothesized, to use social science language) that spiritual well-being is enhanced by sustaining a balance of both ministries which are exclusively for the aging and those which are for the elderly together with people of other ages, as well as by the involvement of the aging in the planning and implementation of programs for them (pp. 566-567). It is alleged that friendly visiting and counseling services to assist the elderly in their own homes (p. 568), chaplaincy services in institutions (pp. 561-562), protection of the right to die with dignity (p. 575), and affirming and guarding other basic human rights (pp. 572-573) will contribute to their spiritual well-being. All of these are subject to systematic, scientific testing to determine whether or not the alleged factors do in fact, contribute to spiritual health. Furthermore, such research is highly desirable as a basis for the anticipated national conference on spiritual well-being (pp. 576-577), for testing the effectiveness of various programs of institutional care, and for evaluating government-funded and other services for the aging and elderly (p. 563).

This chapter makes an initial contribution to such research needs by calling attention to the nature of spiritual well-being, spiritual needs in late life, and various topics relevant to scientific and humanistic research on the subject.

WHAT IS SPIRITUAL WELL-BEING?

The range of human experience that has been labelled as "spiritual" includes happiness, aesthetic thrills, empathy and sympathy morale, mental health, optimism, sexual orgasm, a feeling of identity with Nature, gregariousness and other social relationships, ecstatic experiences, feelings of self respect, a sense of human dignity, that which pertains to the unknown future, feelings induced by psychedelic drugs, healthful psychological conditions, the intellect, and many other phenomena. The concept tends to become so broad in its usage that it is meaningless, incapable of differentiating the "spiritual" from anything else. If everything non-material is "spiritual," it is necessary to introduce numerous additional concepts or qualifying adjectives to differentiate between the various domains of the "spiritual," and we are back to the point of non-definition at which we began.

Similarly, to equate "spiritual" with "religious" equally constitutes a conceptual flaw. While it is true that man in many respects is *homo religiosus*, a religious being, to assume that everything "religious" is therefore also "spiritual" is a serious fallacy. Even superficial observation reveals that many aspects of the interests and activities of religious institutions, the clergy, and other religious personnel are outside the realm of the spiritual, dealing largely and sometimes exclusively with various material, organizational, and institutional demands rather than with the directly spiritual needs of people. Similarly, spiritual needs can be, and sometimes are, ignored or overlooked in the activities and "ministries" of religious agencies and institutions.

Dictionary definitions of "Spiritual" are not very satisfying to one who attempts to understand what is meant by that concept. At their best they refer, for example, to the spirit as the seat of the moral or religious nature, to sacred things or matters, and to the soul or spirit as distinguished from physical nature (Urdang and Urdang, 1967, p. 1372).

"The Spiritual" as used in this chapter pertains to the inner resources of people, their ultimate concern around which all other values are focused, their central philosophy of life (whether it is designated as religious or non-religious) which guides their conduct, and all the supernatural and non-material dimensions of human nature. This means that all people are spiritual, even if they have no affiliations with religious institutions, reject the interests and concerns of religious bodies, and practice no personal religious rites or sacred pieties (Moberg, 1971, pp. 1-3).

The spiritual represents the totality of commitment. It incorporates the aggregate of human value orientations. Involving "ultimate concern," it constitutes the meaning-giving substance of culture" (Tillich, 1959; Stough, 1965). It can be likened to the "invisible religion" (Luckmann, 1967) that lies behind religious beliefs and practices, goes beyond them when they are frozen into rigid traditional forms, and is unrecognized by those who seek religion only in churches.

Materialists assume that the spiritual is a figment of the imagination. Actually, their assumption is just as much a metaphysical faith as the contrary assumption that the spiritual is an ontological reality. This "theological predicament" is common to all, not only to those who accept presuppositions that are recognizably "theological." Every ultimate conception of reality, every *Weltanschauung* or basic world view, rests upon postulates and convictions which are not self-evident but are analogous to the conviction of Christians that God has revealed himself and the purpose of man and the universe. The entire structure of reality in a Christian frame of reference rests upon that foundation (McCoy, 1964; see also Friedrichs, 1970). Therefore, "Social reality demands reference to spiritual reality, to the mystery of being" (Morris, 1964, p. 171).

Sturzo (1947, p. 17) saw the supernatural as the essence of the religious life, "the true life" behind everything which is lived outwardly in relationship to others. The supernatural was not juxtaposed to the natural as a separate section of social life which individuals might accept or reject at will. Rather, in studying society concretely in its complex wholeness, Sturzo saw the supernatural as the atmosphere within which society exists. The natural and the supernatural or spiritual order meet in man. Thus, even he who denies the supernatural root and branch of the religious life, seeking purely naturalistic explanations of religion and human behavior, is involved with a "sociology of the supernatural" in a negative sense, while believers are involved in it in a positive sense (Sturzo, 1947).

Behaviorists and other materialists do not find evidence of the spiritual. Believing it to be non-existent, they ignore it and do not try to discover evidence of it. Their self-fulfilling prophecy takes effect; not seeking indications of the spiritual, they find none and therefore assume that it is a non-existent fabrication or fiction. The basic postulates and hidden assumptions with which social and behavioral scientists initially approach their observations greatly influence the results of their work (Friedrichs, 1970).

The spiritual realm of man's nature has special relevance to values, because it lies at the heart of the meaning-giving center of human life. For that reason, social policies for the aging grow, in the final analysis, out of the spiritual realm, which gives rise to the ethical principles that are a basis for the establishment of priorities. The lack of spiritual concern in the public domain of American life is to a considerable extent responsible for the lack of a generally accepted social policy for the aging and elderly. The formation of policy is fundamentally a moral issue (Kent, 1969). Moral issues, in turn, rest upon spiritual issues, which are the crux of the entire problem of public policy recommendations. As William James (1902, p. 516) said, the unseen mystical or supernatural region possesses us in an even more intimate sense than the visible world,

> . . . for we belong in the most intimate sense wherever our ideals belong. . . . When we commune with it, work is actually done upon our finite personality, for we are turned into new men, and consequences in the way of conduct follow in the natural world upon our regenerative change. But that which produces effects within another reality must be termed a reality itself, so I feel as if we had no philosophic excuse for calling the unseen or mystical world unreal.

Those who are blind to the spiritual nature of man remain blind; those who have "the eyes of faith" see evidence of its central importance on every hand.

SPIRITUAL NEEDS IN LATE LIFE

The spiritual in man is invisible and thus not directly susceptible to study by current methodological tools and techniques of the social and behavioral sciences. Nevertheless, many consequences, concomitants, and other indications which reflect it are observable and susceptible to both scientific and humanistic research.

Since the scope of the spiritual is very broad, the observable indications of its presence are likewise numerous and wide-sweeping in scope. The spiritual nature of man influences and is influenced by all his other dimensions and experiences, so it is very difficult to disentangle from them. As I have indicated elsewhere (Moberg, 1967), the spiritual component of life cuts across all the other dimensions of religiosity and human experience. Everything is influenced by it.

Since man is a whole being and can be divided into parts only analytically, it is very difficult to abstract that which is uniquely spiritual even for analytical, academic, or scientific purposes. Nevertheless, some aspects of human concern stand out as much more clearly "spiritual" than others. The Background Paper on Spiritual Well-Being for the 1971 White House Conference on Aging (Moberg, 1971) identified six areas of spiritual need among the aging as deserving special attention:

1. The aging need assistance for coping with the sociocultural sources of spiritual needs and for facing them realistically. Our culture is oriented toward youth, so aging is viewed as involving a series of losses. To cope successfully with these losses and the other problems of old age necessitates increased demands upon strong inner resources. Ageism, discrimination against the aging, is evident in nearly all areas of public life, including even religious institutions. Gerontophobia (Bunzel, 1969, 1972, 1973) is widespread, for people of all ages have a tendency to fear aging and to dislike the aged. Lack of respect for those who are elderly, viewing their knowledge and experience as out of date and irrelevant, is indigenous in contemporary society. Achievement tends to be measured by work; those who are retired are interpreted as no longer worthy of respect. Even religious institutions are oriented toward the future and thus remove a sense of security from many elderly people. As a result of these and other forms of discrimination and prejudice,

society exacts a heavy toll of "spiritual fatigue" (Koeberle, 1969) among the aging. A sense of uselessness and rejection, inner emptiness and boredom, loneliness and fear emerges. The resolution of these needs constitutes a major spiritual task for contemporary society.

2. Anxiety and fears associated with losses that have been suffered and problems anticipated during the declining months and years of life constitute another spiritual need among the aging. "The care of souls" in relationship to these needs has been a traditional role of the clergy. Religious institutions have helped to meet these spiritual needs, providing comfort, love, sympathy, hope, assurance, and other forms of spiritual support.

3. Preparation for death and dying involves many material considerations, but ultimately it is a spiritual task. The interpretations of death that are found in various religious and philosophical groups have a significant impact upon the feelings and experiences associated with anticipated death, to say nothing of the experience of bereavement. The enhancement of spiritual well-being necessitates preparation for life during the remaining days, months, or years, as well as preparation for death itself (Feder, 1965, p. 622).

4. Personality integration is a spiritual need. It is related to every other aspect of well-being, and in turn it influences every other aspect. Major changes in self-concept occur with forced retirement, widowhood, changes in residence, removal from positions of leadership in social organizations, and other social changes commonly associated with the later period of the life cycle. Senility and other psychiatric disorders frequently are associated with the feelings of loneliness, being unwanted, loss of self-respect, sense of uselessness, insecurity, and other problems which result from changes in social roles and status. Satisfactory coping with these problems is a spiritual task.

5. Closely related to problems of personality integration is the blow to personal dignity that often afflicts the aging. Whether social disengagement is voluntary or involuntary, it is frequently associated with injuries to self-concepts. Pushed about by cultural forces that shove them aside like machines outmoded by more recent models, many elderly people are robbed of their self-determination and freedom of choice. Their dignity is diminished in their own eyes, as well as in the eyes of others, by conventional practices of our materialistic culture. The spiritual answer, accentuated most clearly by the Judeo-Christian religion which affirms the dignity of all human beings in its affirmation that man is created in the image of God, can help to restore a sense of personal worth.

6. The need to cultivate and strengthen a satisfactory philos-

ophy of life is a spiritual necessity that cuts across all the others. Personal interpretations of the events of life and answers to such questions as "Who am I?," "Why am I?," and "What is the meaning of my life?" are at the center of this spiritual need. These lead into even deeper questions of the meaning of the universe and thus get to the heart of the problems which conventionally have been answered by man's religions. The competition of diverse religious, ideological, and philosophical perspectives in our pluralistic society accentuates the need to cope personally and directly with the basic questions of the meaning of human existence, for there is no universally accepted resolution for them. Materialistic definitions of the situation become self-fulfilling prophesies of doom for many elderly people. Hope for the immediate and distant future or the loss of it constitutes a central key element. A satisfactory resolution of the problem of one's *Weltanschauung* provides stability in the midst of the confusions resulting from rapid social change and the personal deprivations associated with aging, including the removal of familiar landmarks by which life has been oriented in the past.

These examples make it clear that spiritual needs are interwoven with all of the other social, material, and physical aspects of human life. None of the other needs of mankind can be resolved completely satisfactorily without including attention to spiritual well-being. The spiritual cuts across all of the other dimensions of human life and conduct.

The sacred, which encompasses the spiritual, is the frame of reference or orientation within which all areas of the secular exist. That which is secular—related to the temporal affairs and this-worldly concerns of everyday life—is closely related to the sacred, the all-encompassing realm of the ultimate ground of existence which often evokes attitudes of mystery, awe, and worship and which relates to the ultimate responses to questions about the need for meaning and belonging (Greeley, 1972, pp. 5-18). Sacred and secular are not contradictory concepts nor are they opposite ends of a continuum. Everything that is secular subsists within the realm of the sacred. All that is secular is also a part of the sacred concern of the spiritual, which infuses everything so indirectly, diffusely, and unobtrusively that it is not even recognized by those who are spiritually blind to its reality.

CHANNELS TO SATISFY SPIRITUAL NEEDS

Because spiritual needs are closely related to the sacred, religious institutions have been particularly concerned with spiritual goals and objectives. Most of their basic values can be traced ultimately to a concern with the spiritual domain of life. Above all other social institutions, they have been entrusted with serving spiritual needs. Nevertheless, to delegate the entire burden of meeting spiritual needs exclusively to them would constitute a serious mistake, for large numbers of people are outside their direct domain of activities, and the scope of spiritual needs is so great that no one institution is capable of fully meeting them.

At the same time as we acknowledge the role of non-religious institutions in meeting spiritual needs, however, we should recognize that the majority of contemporary senior citizens in the U.S.A. were socialized during an era in which spiritual ministries were closely identified with organized religions. Whenever they sense that their personal needs are spiritual, they are favorably inclined toward turning for help to churches or synagogues and their ministers, priests, or rabbis to satisfy those needs.

Specific concern for spiritual well-being traditionally has been delegated to religious bodies more than to any other institution. In our highly differentiated society many spiritual needs are met in families, educational and health-related institutions, mental health agencies, the media of mass communications, leisure-time and recreational associations, and non-esclesiastical helping professions, but none of these is oriented directly toward meeting the full range of specifically spiritual needs. With advancing secularization many counseling functions once considered a part of pastoral care have partially shifted to psychiatrists, clinical psychoanalysts, vocational counselors, and other therapists, but it is possible that the clergy still carry a heavier load of this aspect of spiritual care than all the other helping professions together, even though much of their counseling is done informally, without fee, and off the record. The non-ecclesiastical professions and institutions can cooperate with and sustain the contribution of religious bodies to spiritual well-being, and the latter can use the resources of other institutions to strengthen their spiritual ministries, but under present circumstances in our society, the institutionalized channels for meeting such needs focus around organized religion.

SCIENTIFIC ANALYSIS OF SPIRITUAL WELL-BEING

Through empirical scientific research it is impossible either to prove or disprove that man is a spiritual being, at least with present scientific instruments, methods, and techniques. The evidence is beyond the realm of direct empirical observation, residing in the realm of intuition, introspection, insight, and experiential evidence rather than on a strictly sensory level of observation. It is a subject for a *verstehende* research methodology rather than a "positivistic" one.

The conclusion that man is essentially spiritual is supported by centuries of human experience as reflected in the Bible and other sacred writings. The autonomous nature of man, reflected in his will-power and capacity for decision-making, the ability of the human spirit to transcend the matter of the material world through self-consciousness, the contrast between "knowing a person" and knowing facts about him, the perhaps universal desire of people for an all-encompassing object of personal loyalty or ultimate commitment, the contrasts between objective and subjective reality, analogies to the nature of human life as something more than the totality of the identifiable parts of the biological organism, and the "other minds" problem of philosophy all support the conclusion that man is essentially a spiritual being. While these indicators are not directly susceptible to empirical social and behavioral science research, to ignore them is, in effect, to imprison the nature and spirit of man in a three-dimensional universe of space, time, and matter (Moberg, 1967).

Many other subjects studied by behavioral scientists, especially psychologists, are likewise not susceptible to direct empirical research. Human motivation, intelligence, attitudes, authoritarianism, sentiments, the ego, id, and superego, values, pain, and many other topics of the sciences that study mankind are similarly beyond the range of immediate empirical investigation. It is possible, however, to observe indicators which are theoretically associated with them. This makes it possible for behavioral scientists to analyze non-tangible human phenomena under the rubric of "scientific investigation." In like manner, spiritual well-being can be a subject of scientific research as consequences of it and indicators related to it are observed, classified, counted or measured, and analyzed in other ways. Yet it must always be remembered that the total range of what can be studied scientifically is not coterminous with the total scope of "the spiritual." To reduce that which is spiritual to the limited realm of that which can be observed empirically through scientific research procedures would constitute a serious delusory form of reductionistic operationalism.

RESEARCH FINDINGS

A considerable body of research on religion and aging has already been accumulated (Maves, 1960; Moberg, 1965, 1971; Riley and Foner, 1968). Most of it is admittedly piecemeal, incomplete, and not directly focused upon spiritual well-being. Some of the research findings, however, are suggestive of the relationships between spiritual well-being and various other dimensions of life. A few examples of these findings will be summarized in this section.

Careful analysis of the original sources of the studies mentioned here will reveal that most of the research indicators used are very incomplete, generally less than satisfactory within their limited domain and even more so with reference to spiritual well-being, tend to relate primarily to a relatively narrow range of religious affiliations and practices which are institutionally oriented, and can be questioned as to their scientific validity and reliability. Nevertheless, they provide valuable clues which can serve as a stepping-off point for more sophisticated research on spiritual well-being.

One of the studies most directly related to spiritual well-being was that of Wolff (1959), who discovered that religious beliefs and faith in God helped disorganized geriatric patients to overcome grief and to cope with loneliness, unhappiness, and despondency. This suggests that Judeo-Christian religious orientations and self-images have a wholesome impact upon at least one type of believers.

Swenson (1959, 1961; see Jeffers et al. 1961) found that a sense of serenity and a decreased fear of death tend to accompany conservative religious beliefs, possibly because death is viewed as a doorway to immortality. Hinton (1967, pp. 38, 83) similarly found that those who had firm religious faith and attended church weekly or frequently were the most free of anxiety, only a fifth being apprehensive when dying. The next most confident group, only a quarter being anxious, frankly stated that they had practically no faith. The "tepid believers" who professed faith but made little outward observance of it were significantly more anxious when dying. It thus appears that those who had reached a personally satisfactory conclusion about matters of faith and a future life had a higher level of serenity (an indicator of spiritual well-being) as they approached their death than those who had not satisfactorily resolved the questions of faith and action associated with death and dying.

It is possible that variations in social integration have a bearing upon observed differences in attitudes toward death among the religiously faithful in contrast to non-religious people (Treanton, 1961). Those who are religious are more likely to have a reference group that gives them social support and security at the time of death. The greatest fear of all who are dying apparently is social isolation, the desertion by friends, relatives, and other visitors which Hinton (1967, pp. 86-87) has called "the bereavement of the dying" (see Strauss, 1969; Swenson, 1961). If this is the case, then the compounding of social relationships with spiritual perspectives and experiences becomes all the more complex.

At the Menorah Home and Hospital and its Geriatric Guidance Clinic in Brooklyn, psychiatric probes of the "inner space of man" have been very helpful in improving the condition of many people past the age of sixty. This inner space includes the mind, heart, soul, spirit, and inner life, for it is "a synthesis of multiple systems" with a focus upon the psyche, not the soma. Treating these emotional and mental problems, which are major components of the spiritual, has been found to have an impact upon the body as well (Loomer, 1969).

Gubrium's (1973) research on aged persons interviewed in Detroit found that persons who said they had no fears fell into three major categories. They were prepared for death, felt healthy and/or solvent, or were God-fearing. Some of them also resided in relatively protective church-related environments, multi-unit residences which specifically served the needs of the elderly. At least two of the factors he identified—being prepared for death and being God-fearing—are clearly in the category of spiritual variables.

Numerous studies (many which are summarized in Moberg, 1965) have shown that there is a relationship between various forms of religiosity and personal adjustment, happiness, morale, and feelings of life satisfaction. Experimental designs to control other factors linked with personal adjustment while studying church membership have revealed that it is not a primary variable but only a derivative of religious beliefs and participation in church actiivties which are correlated with membership (Moberg, 1953; Moberg and Taves, 1965).

Purpose in life is closely associated also with religion, at least for retired professors (Acuff and Allen, 1970, p. 127). It may be an intervening variable helping to account for the association of religious orientations and behavior with good morale and happiness in the later years of life. Family background, especially being raised in a psychologically secure family, seems to be correlated with religious orthodoxy, which may be another intervening variable that helps to explain the association of religious beliefs and behavior with a sense of well-being in the later years (Robb, 1968, p. 103).

Although old age is viewed by most elderly persons as the least happy period of life, with the one exception of finding it the most satisfactory period for religious activity (Bromley, 1966, p. 87), it is possible that good personal and social adjustment (including life satisfaction, morale, happiness, and wholesome adaptations to the total sociocultural milieu) is more a cause of conventional religious beliefs and activities than a result of them. At any rate, there is a correlation between the two.

This is not to deny the fact that some problems of the elderly are caused or accentuated by circumstances in their religious organizations. Many are offended when, after a lifetime of energies expended and financial contributions given to their church congregations, old patterns of activities and programs are discarded by their church or synagogue in favor of new ones that are presumed to be "more in keeping with the times." At a period in life in which their greatest personal need is comfort many of the elderly instead have been given a challenge to use their energies to change the world. Having lost much of their physical strength, denied the opportunity to exercise whatever social power they may still retain, and feeling that they are pushed out of the very institution outside the family which they believe ought to give them the greatest help in their declining years, many of the elderly are disillusioned with new developments in their churches (Gray and Moberg, 1962, pp. 96-117).

Aging church members also may feel that their limited financial resources prohibit them from dressing well enough to attend church or from making financial contributions. Physical limitations or transportation costs may make it difficult to attend religious services. They tend to feel that their opinions are ignored, even if they are members of a democratically governed religious body. Feeling that they are pushed aside by younger members, no longer respected and wanted for their wisdom and experience, the elderly often find the church a place of disillusionment and discouragement (Gray and Moberg, 1962, pp. 96-117).

Ministries by the clergy may create psychological and spiritual harm to the aged who belong to religious bodies in which the visit of a pastor or rabbi is expected shortly before death. His arrival for a sickbed, convalescent, or hospital visit, even if without any intent to administer last rites, may introduce an undue degree of the fear of dying and cause a psychosomatic reaction which implements the self-fulfilling prophecy. In such groups ministries by lay people, such as those supported through Project Compassion of the Missouri Synod Lutherans, may do more to promote spiritual well-being than those of the clergy.

In regard to the amount of religious participation, research has demonstrated that ritualistic behavior of an external or objective kind outside the home tends to diminish during later maturity, while religious attitudes, beliefs, and feelings of a personal, internalized kind apparently increase among those who acknowledge having a religion. Even while institutionally oriented religious participation decreases, the religious beliefs, feelings, and personalized ritualistic practices like prayer and Bible reading become more intense and devout for the religious person. Because the various dimensions and aspects of religiosity are not completely correlated with each other, it is dangerous to conclude that a decline in any one dimension, such as participation in organized religious services, is necessarily an indicator of a decrease in faith. The total religiosity of a person is not necessarily reflected accurately on the basis of any single indicator (Moberg, 1965).

INDICATORS OF SPIRITUAL WELL-BEING

Although spiritual well-being cannot be studied directly, it is allegedly related to or associated with observable phenomena which can be identified through various forms of empirical investigation. These include the following:

1. *A satisfying philosophy of life.* Basically a faith commitment, this has to do with life and with death. It can be determined through questionnaires, interviewing procedures, personal documents, and other information sources whether or not a person believes that he has attained satisfaction in this realm.

2. *Satisfactory relationships with other people.* The extent to which a person experiences life satisfactions through the exercise of creative energies on behalf of others is one indicator of this. Creative outlets for serving others are available in volunteer services, assistance given in times of special need, visiting, organizational service in the church and other community associations, and general helpfulness. These outlets are available even to persons who are shut in by illness or physical disability, for they can provide the therapeutic ministry of listening to those who visit or telephone them. They can engage in intercessory prayers for others. They can write greetings and in

various other ways demonstrate helpfulness to people around them. The spiritually healthy will be considerate of the needs of others, not selfishly oriented toward grasping every benefit for themselves and giving nothing in return. They will share their faith and their life experiences, but they will not do so by compulsive mechanisms forcing attention on others when they are not welcomed.

3. *Constructive and wholesome self-concepts.* A creative and constructive orientation toward the world is likely to emanate from a creative and constructive orientation toward oneself. Persons with spiritual health will have positive, rather than denigrating and degrading, conceptions of themselves.

4. *Preparedness to die as well as to live.* The confidence of faith enables those who have spiritual well-being to face the certainty of their own death with equanimity and assurance.

5. *A realistic orientation toward losses and deprivations.* In the midst of social disengagement, physical decline, and material privation, the spiritually healthy will view their lives positively rather than negatively. Enriching experiences they have had in the past, increased freedom during retirement to do what they wish (within realistic bounds of opportunities and resources available), the need for continuing personal growth and new experiences, and an orientation toward aging as an achievement or an opportunity to grasp rather than as a negative experience will prevail.

6. *Ethical and moral conduct.* The person with spiritual well-being will have an inner-directed orientation which leads him to uphold righteous conduct and justice even when it would be more to his material or social benefit to indulge in technically legitimate forms of selfish conduct. Similarly, he will not seek out legal ways of being dishonest or harmful to his fellowmen in order to promote his own selfish gain. Menninger's (1974) insistence that moral or spiritual health and mental health are identical necessitates giving attention to the role of sin in human affairs.

Research on the normative values of religious bodies can reveal the alleged relative importance of each of these indicators (and others) to spiritual health. Eventually a scale to measure the degree of spiritual well-being of individual persons, and hence of groups, could be produced. Then a subsequent stage of the research process could analyze relationships between spiritual health and other variables in order to test hypotheses derived from relevant social and behavioral science theories and to provide a rational basis for developing programs of service and care for the aging which will produce and sustain spiritual health.

CRITERIA OF SPIRITUAL WELL-BEING

The identification of various forms and degrees of self satisfaction in regard to each of the above indicators may be as far as we can go in the context of empirical social and behavioral science research until a considerable amount of additional work has been completed. Each major religious orientation is likely to have its own criteria of what constitutes a wholesome pattern of spiritual well-being. That which is considered satisfactory by certain groups may be considered heretical and based upon false premises by others. In our pluralistic society, it is probable that we cannot arrive at any overarching set of objective criteria of spiritual well-being that would be acceptable to members of all belief systems.

Research on the largely implicit criteria of spiritual well-being that are found among the religious bodies nevertheless would constitute a valuable resource in and of itself. It would constitute a valuable resource in and of itself. It would help to answer the questions of whether any of the criteria of spiritual health and illness are universally acceptable. It would differentiate between the perspectives of Orthodox Jews in contradistinction to Conservative and Reform Jews, theologically liberal Protestants in contrast to fundamentalists and evangelicals, Eastern Orthodox Christians in relation to Roman Catholics, Protestant Pentecostalists in comparison to Catholic charismatics, and liberal Catholics in contrast to conservative Catholics, to mention but a few anticipated variations.

CONSEQUENCES OF SPIRITUAL WELL-BEING

Having a clear definition of what is considered as constituting spiritual well-being could help to provide a foundation for improved services to people who are institutionalized. For example, patients in nursing homes typically lack formal opportunities to fulfill their needs for spiritual care. When this happens, the constitutional right of citizens to religious liberty is infringed upon by the unavoidable circumstances in which they find themselves. Like others in total institutions (prisons, armed forces located in restrictive circumstances, patients in mental hospitals, etc.), they may be incapable of attending religious services outside the institution. If chaplaincy services or equivalent visits by clergymen are not provided, the residents' needs for spiritual care may be completely ignored.

Since spiritual well-being influences every other aspect of patient care, serving the spiritual needs should contribute to physical and mental health as well as the spiritual health of patients. This suggests the importance of developing chaplaincy services and coordinating these chaplaincies with other professional care. It implies that access to printed and audiovisual mass media provided by religious groups, protection of the rights of patients against infringements upon their religious liberty which could result if compulsion were used to force exposure to unwanted religious activities, and other positive and preventive activities should be introduced into total-care institutions for the aging. But their impact upon spiritual well-being can be gauged accurately only after valid and reliable measures of the degree of spiritual well-being have been developed.

Research should be conducted to test the commonly made statement of persons in the health professions that their patients are in better physical and psychological health when there is an adequate program of spiritual ministries in a hospital or nursing care facility than when that dimension of life is ignored.

Obviously, research on spiritual well-being is closely related to research on mental health and the quality of life. To ignore it in studies of "comprehensive programs of mental health" is a serious mistake.

In the context of Christian values, the person who has spiritual well-being is characterized by the "fruit of the Spirit" (Galatians 5:22-23) in contrast to the "works of the flesh" (Galatians 5:19-21), which are characteristic of persons who lack spiritual well-being. Although all of these fruits have outward indicators, they pertain basically to inner virtues which are not directly observable, so measurement of the degree to which they are present or absent is not an easy task and demands the use of additional indicators. Walker (1973) has stated that

> Modern technology has levelled our lives to a thin, horizontal plane of materialism and functionalism, and many appear to be suffering from . . . "acedia," or spiritual torpor. It was one of the seven deadly sins.
> . . . Something is missing, something that neither science or technology, computers nor affluence can provide. It is the vertical dimension of life which is the bequest of the Gospel.

"Spiritual torpor" indeed may be characteristic of a large proportion of our current population. Such acedia or slothfulness undoubtedly contributes to a lack of spiritual well-being on the part of those who experience it. How to identify its presence, measure the relative degree to which it prevails, and determine its impact is a topic that deserves development in connection with research on spiritual well-being.

One of the most beneficial approaches to research on this subject may be to identify and study persons who are noted for their attainment of outstanding levels of spiritual well-being. Case studies of them and descriptions of their characteristics may help considerably to sharpen the subject for further research on other people.

If, in addition, a comparison group of persons who lack spiritual well-being could be identified and studied, the contrasts between them and those with spiritual health would help to identify the leading observable elements and indicators of spiritual health and illness. Such work could study the differential consequences of "healthy" religion and problems of "the sick soul" as well (James, 1902).

The implications for action that would grow out of such research are so obvious as to need no more than brief mention.

Once the components of spiritual well-being and ill-being have been identified, goals for action in effect will have been developed. It then will be possible to determine the extent to which spiritual well-being is associated with various kinds of educational, religious, psychological, health, and other care programs for people in institutions as well as for those living independently.

It is highly likely that most types of religiously sponsored activities generally contribute more to spiritual well-being than ill-being for most people. Yet "it is wise to remember that activities which contribute to the spiritual well-being and functional adjustment of most people may be detrimental to the adjustment of others" (Moberg, 1972, p. 57). What helps one kind of person may harm another; individual differences must be recognized in any and all activities and programs designed to meet spiritual needs. Similarly, it is possible that giving direct attention only to certain components of spiritual well-being has such dysfunctional consequences that the goals would be attained better by leaving them alone than by giving them explicit attention. Hence implications for religious institutions and their personnel, particularly the clergy and religious educators, may emerge out of such research.

Spiritual well-being is not, we hypothesize, highly correlated with material well-being. Many people who live in wealth and material comfort have a deep sense of boredom, ennui, and despair. Many, on the contrary, who live in dire poverty have a sense of gratitude to God for his goodness and an optimistic outlook upon their ultimate future which gives them joy in the midst of deprivation and provides them with happiness even in their experiences of suffering. A corrolary of this is that efforts to improve material well-being will not, in and of themselves, improve spiritual well-being.

The abuse of this fact by persons of wealth and power who manipulate religious institutions and personnel to make the laboring classes content with their deprivations has contributed to the label of religion as "the opiate of the people." Everything good can be manipulated by self-centered persons of power and influence to produce undesirable results among the masses, but such abuse should not blind us to the relevance and significance of spiritual concepts when seen in their proper perspective. Such abuses, in fact, can be taken as an indication that the persons who are perpetrating them lack spiritual well-being.

It is probable that when good spiritual health is present in the later years, it results from spiritual health developed earlier in life and represents continuation of a long-term trend. Nevertheless, research to compare the spiritual well-being of persons who have had an unusual spiritual experience, such as a religious conversion, during the later years with those who made basic spiritual life-commitments earlier in life would help to reveal the extent to which and conditions under which spiritual ill-health could be turned to spiritual well-being during senescence.

In the context of Christian values, spiritual growth is never entirely complete in this life. Even St. Paul, the Apostle, affirmed that he had not already attained spiritual perfection (Philippians 3:12-14), and he held before Christian believers the goal of continuing to grow in spiritual maturity toward "the measure of the stature of the fullness of Christ" (Ephesians 4:13). This means that the old joke about grandma as a person who is "preparing for final examinations by reading the Bible" is not simply a laughing matter! Even the most religious among the elderly can develop still more spiritually by cultivating their spiritual well-being. Late life can be a period of significant spiritual growth; for many it represents a major developmental stage of the spiritual life cycle.

As Beard (1969, p. 4) observed, many activities of the younger years of life are withdrawn from the elderly or cease to be satisfying to them, but there is no age limit to religious faith and practice. There may be disengagement from nearly everything else in the late years of life, but those who reach them with spiritual health find that spiritual well-being is not dependent upon physical and material circumstances. To them the late years of life can be the best years. Robert Browning's Rabbi Ben Ezra described them as "the last of life for which the first was made."

REFERENCES

Acuff, Gene, and Allen, Donald: Hiatus in meaning: disengagement for retired professors. *Journal of Gerontology,* 25:126-128, 1970.

Beard, Belle Boone: Religion at 100. *Modern Maturity,* 12:1-4, No. 3, 1969.

Bromley, D. B.: *The Psychology of Human Aging.* Baltimore, Penguin Books, 1966.

Bunzel, Joseph H.: Gerontophobia—some remarks on a social policy for the elderly. *The Humanist,* 31:17-18, No. 4, 1969.

Bunzel, Joseph H.: Gerontophobia pervades U.S. life, sociologist says. *Geriatrics,* 27:31, 45, 1972.

Bunzel, Joseph H.: Recognition, relevance and reactivation of gerontophobia: theoretical essay. *Journal of the American Geriatrics Society,* 21:77-80, No. 2, 1973.

Feder, Samuel L.: Attitudes of patients with advanced malignancy. In Group for the Advancement of Psychiatry, *Death and Dying: Attitudes of Patient and Doctor,* V, Symposium No. 11, New York: 1965.

Friedrichs, Robert: *A Sociology of Sociology.* New York: Free Press, 1970.

Gray, Robert M., and Moberg, David O.: *The Church and the Older Person.* Grand Rapids, Michigan: Wm. B. Eerdmans Publishing Co., 1962.

Greeley, Andrew M.: *The Denominational Society: A Sociological Approach to Religion in America.* Glenview, Illinois, Scott, Foresman and Co., 1972.

Gubrium, Jaber F.: Apprehensions of coping incompetence and responses to fear in old age. *International Journal of Aging and Human Development,* 4:111-125. No. 2, 1973.

Hinton, John: *Dying.* Baltimore, Maryland, Penguin Books, 1967.

James, William: *The Varieties of Religious Experience.* New York: Longmans, Green and Co., 1902.

Jeffers, Frances C., Nichols, Claude R., and Eisdorfer, Carl: Attitudes of older persons toward death: a preliminary study. *Journal of Gerontology,* 16:53-56, 1961.

Kent, Donald P.: Aging Without Plan. Paper presented at Conference on Aging, Philadelphia Geriatric Center, October 13, 1969.

Koeberle, A.: Seelische anfechtungen in alter als aufgabe der seelsorge. *Zeitschrift fuer Gerontologie,* 11:58-60, No. 1, 1969.

Loomer, Harry P.: A philosophy for geriatric research. *Journal of the American Geriatrics Society,* 17:406-407, No. 4, 1969.

Luckmann, Thomas: *The Invisible Religion.* New York: Macmillan Co., 1967.

Maves, Paul B.: Aging, religion and the church. In Tibbitts, Clark (Ed.), *Handbook of Social Gerontology,* Chicago: University of Chicago Press, pp. 698-749, 1960.

McCoy, Charles S.: *The Meaning of Theological Reflection.* New York: Faculty Christian Fellowship. (Faith-Learning Studies, No. 1), 1964.

Menninger, Karl: Whatever became of sin? *The Rotarian,* 124:16-19, 49, No. 1, January 1974.

Moberg, David O.: Church membership and personal adjustment in old age. *Journal of Gerontology,* 8:207-211, 1953.

Moberg, David O.: Religiosity in old age. *Gerontologist,* 5:78-87, No. 2, June 1965.

Moberg, David O.: The encounter of scientific and religious values pertinent to man's spiritual nature. *Sociological Analysis,* 25:22-33, No. 1, Spring 1967.

Moberg, David O.: *Spiritual Well-Being: Background and Issues.* Washington, D.C., White House Conference on Aging, 1971.

Moberg, David O.: Religion and the aging family. *The Family Coordinator,* 21:47-60, 1972.

Moberg, David O., and Taves, Marvin J.: Church participation and adjustment in old age. In Arnold M. Rose and Warren A. Peterson (Eds.), *Older People and Their Social World,* Philadelphia: F. A. Davis Co., 1965, pp. 113-124.

Morris, Rudolph: The concept of the spiritual and the dilemma of sociology. *Sociological Analysis,* 25:167-173, No. 3, 1964.

Riley, Matilda White, and Foner, Anne: *Aging and Society, Volume One: An Inventory of Research Findings.* New York: Russell Sage Foundation, 1968.

Robb, Thomas Bradley: *The Bonus Years: Foundations for Ministry with Older Persons.* Valley Forge, Pa.: Judson Press, 1968.

Stough. Ada Barnett: *Brighter Vistas: Four Church Programs for Older Adults.* Washington, D.C.: Administration on Aging, 1965.

Strauss, Anselm: When elderly Americans die. In *Proceedings of the Eighth International Congress of Gerontology.* Bethesda, Md.: The Congress, 1969, pp. 267-270.

Sturzo, Luigi: *The True Life: Sociology of the Supernatural.* Trans. by Barbara Barclay Carter. London: Geoffrey Bles, 1947.

Subcommittee on Aging: *Post-White House Conference on Aging Reports,* Washington, D.C.: U.S. Government Printing Office, Joint Committee Print, 93d Congress, 1st Session, Committee on Labor and Public Welfare and the Special Committee on Aging, U.S. Senate, 1973.

Swenson, Wendell M.: Attitudes toward death among the aged. *Minnesota Medicine,* 42:399-402. 1959.

Swenson, Wendell M.: Attitudes toward death in an aged population. *Journal of Gerontology,* 16:49-52, No. 1, 1961.

Tillich, Paul: *Theology of Culture.* New York: Oxford University Press, 1959.

Treanton, Jean-René: Comments, Symposium on attitudes toward death in older persons. *Journal of Gerontology,* 16:63, 1961.

Urdang, Jess, and Urdang, Laurence (Eds.): *The Random House Dictionary of the English Language,* New York: Random House, 1967.

Walker, Harold Blake: Living faith. *Chicago Tribune,* Section 3, p. 17, November 8, 1973.

White House Conference on Aging: *Section Recommendations on Spiritual Well-Being.* Washington, D.C., White House Conference on Aging, 1971.

Wolff, Kurt: Group psychotherapy with geriatric patients in a state hospital setting: results of a three year study. *Group Psychotherapy,* 12:218-222, 1959.

INDEX

A

Acuff, G., 268
Adams, B. N., 152, 156
Adams, D., 18
Aged Baganda
  generational relations, 159-164
  status, 157-159
Aged Japanese-Americans
  acceptance of death, 191-193
  adjustment to aging, 179-193
  authority and autonomy, 184-186
  companionship, 179-184
  home culture, 168-173
  productivity, 186-191
Age groups
  age structure (U.S.A., 1960), 40-46
  area structure (U.S.A., 1960), 46-54
Albrecht, R., 137
Alexander, N., 26
Allen, D., 268
Anderson, B., 191
Armer, M., 126
Arth, M., 149, 156

B

Barker, M., 21
Barker, R. G., 204
Barndt, D., 126
Basowitz, S., 208
Beard, B. B., 276
Bell, W., 41
Bendix, R., 125, 128, 139
Benedict, R., 173, 184
Bennett, R., 18
Berger, P., 61
Berkowitz, L., 184
Blau, Z., 19, 26
Botwinick, J., 236
Boyle, R. P., 6

Bromley, D. B., 268
Bultena, G., 18, 19, 20, 26, 29, 111, 117, 118, 203
Bunzel, J. H., 261
Burgess, E., 237

C

Camilleri, S., 41
Campbell, D. T., 247, 248
Campbell, E., 26
Caudill, W., 110, 183, 186
Chevan, A., 33, 53
Chiriboga, D., 225
Cicourel, A., 95
Clark, M., 134, 167, 191
Cogswell, B. E., 136
Coleman, J. S., 133
Collins, M. E., 9
Coombs, J. W., 148
Coughenour, C. M., 126, 128
Cowgill, D. O., 123, 124, 132, 134, 136, 143, 148
Cromwell, R. L., 242
Cumming, E., 26, 193, 202, 208
Cutler, S., 143

D

Davis, K., 148
deBriey, P., 134
Deutsch, M., 9
DeVos, G., 179
Disengagement, 193-195
Doi, T., 186
Dore, R. P., 125, 128
Doxiadis, C. A., 11
Dubin, S. S., 236
Duncan, O. D., 35, 53
Dunham, H. W., 148

E

Ehrlich, E., 125
Eisenstadt, S., 20, 28, 125, 126, 127,
    128, 131, 139
Environment
    age-composition, 18-20, 203-207
    dwelling units, 12-13
    ecology of age groups (U.S.A.),
        32-57
    formal communities, 61-120
    and life satisfaction, 21, 23-25
    matching, 201-213
    neighborhoods, 10-12
    and normative meanings, 10-13,
        136-140
    nursing home, 61-98
    pre-industrial, 123-144, 150-165
    resources in, 14
    retirement residence, 21, 23-28,
        99-119
    and self, 8-10, 13-15
    spiritual, 256-276
    total institutions, 203
Environmental policy
    matching, 201-213
    relocation, 215-234
    spiritual, 264-265
    training, 249-253
Epstein, A., 148
Erikson, E., 179, 188
Estes, W. K., 243
Etzioni, A., 126

F

Fallers, L., 155, 157
Fallers, M. C., 156
Festinger, L., 9, 13
Foner, A., 32, 33, 130, 266
Formal communities
    nursing home, 61-98
    retirement residence, 99-120
    total institutions, 203
Frank, L. K., 148
Friedman, E. P., 107, 112

Friedrichs, R., 259, 260
Friendship, 20, 22, 25-28
    and morale, 25-28

G

Gagné, R. M., 240, 242
Generational relations, 134-136,
    159-164
Gerth, H., 62
Giallombardo, R., 103
Gibbs, J., 155, 156
Glaser, B., 92
Goffman, E., 102, 201, 203, 204
Gouldner, A., 87
Gray, R. M., 269
Greeley, A. M., 263
Gross, L., 87
Gubrium, J. F., 13, 29, 268
Gutman, D., 186

H

Hamovitch, M., 20
Harlan, W. H., 148, 149
Harmon, H. H., 39
Havighurst, R. J., 137, 194, 202
Haynes, M. S., 149
Heise, D. R., 6
Henry, W., 26, 193, 202, 208
Hickey, T., 249, 250
Hinton, J., 267
Hoestetler, J. A., 103
Holmes, L., 123, 124, 132, 134, 143,
    148
Hull, C. L., 240
Hunt, J., 201
Hunter, A., 41
Huntington, G. E., 103

I

Ichheiser, G., 70
Inkeles, A., 126

J

James, W., 260, 274
Janossy, F., 125
Jeffers, F. C., 267
Johnstone, J. W. C., 236
Jung, C. G., 179, 189

K

Kahana, B., 208
Kahana, E., 201, 208
Kastenbaum, R., 208
Kent, D. P., 260
Kiefer, C., 195
Kitano, H. H. L., 181
Kleemeier, R. W., 110, 201, 203, 204,
    205
Kobler, F. J., 243
Koeberle, A., 262
Koons, P. B., 46
Korchin, S. J., 207, 208
Koyama, T., 170

L

Labovitz, S., 6
Lakin, M., 224
Laumann, E., 19
Lawton, M. P., 201, 205, 212
Lazarsfeld, P., 19
Lazurus, R. S., 222
Lerner, D., 125, 134
LeVine, E., 149
Levy, M. J., 125, 127, 128, 131
Lewin, K., 204, 242
Lieberman, M., 224
Lipset, S. M., 133, 134, 137
Litwak, E., 133
Liveright, A. A., 245
Livson, F., 202
Loomer, H. P., 268
Lowenthal, M. F., 189
Luckmann, T., 61, 259

M

Maddox, G., 33
Mair, L., 152
Manton, K., 142, 143
Matching environments and needs,
    201-213
Maves, P. B., 266
McCoy, C. S., 259
McKool, M., 148
Menninger, K., 271
Merton, R. K., 19
Messer, M., 9, 10, 19, 28
Meyerhoff, H., 193
Mills, C. W., 62
Moberg, D. O., 256, 259, 261, 265, 268,
    270, 275
Modernization
    and aging, 129-140
    concept of, 124-128
    economic change and aging, 130-132
    education and aging, 134-136
    and generational relations, 134-136
    urbanization and aging, 132-134
Moore, W. E., 136, 148
Morale, 13, 21-22
    and aged Japanese-Americans,
        179-193
    and friendship ties, 25-28
    Life Satisfaction Scale, 21-22
Morioka, K., 171
Morris, R., 259
Mowrer, O. H., 240, 242, 243
Murray, H., 179, 204
Myrdal, G., 139

N

Nahemow, N., 156
Nettl, J. P., 125, 127, 128
Neugarten, B., 18, 194, 202, 207, 208
Nursing home, 61-98
    definitions of patient care, 68-88
    practical rule-breaking in, 90-92
    social structure, 62-68
    staff/patient accommodation in,
        89-97

O

O'Rourke, J., 33, 53

P

Palmore, E., 140, 142, 143
Parsons, T., 127, 139
Peck, R. F., 208
Pergeaux, Y., 100
Petersen, P. G., 202
Peterson, W. E., 32
Pincus, A., 204, 205
Plath, D., 172, 187, 192
Pollack, K., 208
Pre-industrial societies
    aging in, 123-144
    Baganda, 150-165
    grandparenthood in, 150-165
    Ibo, 149
    Village India, 148
Press, I., 148

R

Radcliffe-Brown, A. R., 152
Reichard, S., 202, 207
Reiss, A. J., 35, 53
Relocating elders, 215-234
Retirement residence, 21, 23-38, 99-119
    and age, 105-109
    and health, 109-110
    and outside contacts, 110-111
    and political identification, 113-115
    and previous roles, 111-112
    and seniority, 112-113
    social organization in (hypotheses),
        102-103
Richards, A., 154, 155
Riesman, D., 137
Riley, M., 5, 32, 33, 130, 266
Rivera, R. J., 236
Robb, T. B., 268
Rose, A., 19, 28, 32, 56, 109, 138

Rosow, I., 9, 18, 19, 22, 26, 125, 132,
    202
Ross, J-K., 103, 105, 113
Ross, M. H., 105

S

Scheff, T., 97
Schnaiberg, A., 126
Schnore, L., 53
Schooler, K. K., 9, 10
Scriven, M., 245, 247
Shanas, E., 133, 158
Sheldon, H. D., 32
Simmons, L., 147, 148
Smelser, N., 133, 134, 137
Smith, D. H., 126
Smith, T. L., 148
Sociology of aging, 5
    multivariate analysis in, 5-8
    theory building, 6, 123-144
Sparks, D., 167
Spinetta, J. J., 249
Spiritual well-being, 256-276
    consequences of, 273-276
    definition of, 258-260
    indicators of, 270-272
    research findings on, 266-270
    scientific analysis of, 265-266
    spiritual needs in late life, 261-263
Stanley, J. C., 247, 248
Status of the aged
    among Baganda, 157-159
    and modernization, 123-144
Stephenson, J. B., 126
Stern, B., 204
Stough, A. B., 259
Strauss, A., 92, 267
Streib, G., 56, 133
Stroud, J. B., 239
Sturzo, L., 259, 260
Subculture of aging, 138-140
    and youth culture, 136-140
Sudnow, D., 95
Sussman, M. B., 133
Swenson, W. M., 267

T

Taves, M. J., 268
Theil, H., 6
Tillich, P., 259
Thompson, W. E., 133
Tobin, S. S., 194, 202
Toffler, A., 236
Torbert, W. R., 243, 244, 246, 249
Training in applied gerontology,
    235-254
  adult education, 235-239
  evaluation, 245-249
  and learning theory, 239-244
  manpower development, 249-253
Treanton, J-R., 267

U

Urdang, J., 258
Urdang, L., 258

V

Van Arsdol, M., 41
Van de Geer, J. P., 7

W

Waisanen, F., 126
Walker, H. B., 274
Weber, M., 138
Weiner, M., 126, 140
White, T. J., 237
Whittington, F., 140
Williams, R. M., 133
Wolff, K., 266
Wood, V., 20, 22, 29, 117, 118

Z

Zeisel, H., 7